Organizational Behaviour

Organizational Behaviour

NINA SINGH

MBA., M.Phil., M.A. (Eco.)

Lecturer,

Department of Management

Drona College of Managment and Information Technology,

Dehradun

AN ISO 9001:2008 CERTIFIED COMPANY

Vayu Education of India

2/25, Ansari Road, Darya Ganj, New Delhi-110 002

Organizational Behaviour

ISBN: 978-93-80712-52-9

First Edition: 2010
Reprint: 2014, 2021

Price: ₹ 200/-

Printed & bound in India

Published by:
AN ISO 9001:2008 CERTIFIED COMPANY
VAYU EDUCATION OF INDIA
2/25, Ansari Road, Darya Ganj, New Delhi-110 002
Ph.: 91-11-43526600, 41564445
Fax: 91-11-41564440
E-mail: vei@veiindia.com, vayueducation1@gmail.com
Web: www.veiindia.com

Preface

Organisational behavior deals not merely with business organizations but with all kinds of organizations. It is wholly distinct discipline in its own right, though it draws heavily upon a host of other disciplines all of which may claim some synonymity with it. This book is designed for the management students who are primarily interested in behavioural science as a systematic interpretation of human behavior at work and are interested in its application to current problems in organizational settings. The fundamental guiding force has been the assumption that a theoretically sound organizational behavior is useful in developing sound human relations.

In order to make this book more interesting, we have utilized the concept of formulating the plan to divide the book contents into small paragraphs. Attempts have been made to stress empirically derived knowledge about the behavior and to relate this knowledge to the practical problems of organizational behavior.

– Nina Singh

Acknowledgement

It is not possible to write a textbook without the help of others. A large number of individuals have helped in this evdeavour. I am thankful for their contribution.

A number of problems and illustrations in this book are based on the public examinations of a number of professional bodies. I express my gratitude to them. I owe my sincere gratitude to my parents for making me capable of writing this book.

Though it is difficult to thanks to all of them individually, it is my pleasure to express grateful thanks to Dr. Rajiv Kumar Jain, (Managing Director), Prof. Sanjeev Kumar Sharma (Chairperson) of Vayu Education of India, Darya Ganj, New Delhi. 110002 and also thanks to Mr. Vijay Kumar Saini (Production Manager), Mr. Jitender Kumar Sharma (Sr. Sales Executive) and other production team member of Vayu Education of India, published our book within a quite short duration in order to deliver a good quality book for the students who will really be benefited when they go through this book.

– Nina Singh

Reviewing Committee

Name	Designation
1. Prof. Sanjeev Kumar Sharma *Professor and Head* of Computer Science and Engg. J.P.E.I.T. Meerut	**Chairman**
2. Mr. Ashok Kumar *Asstt. Prof.* in Computer Science and Engg. GRD Institute of Technology, Dehradun	**Member**
3. Sanjay Kumar *Sr. Lecturer,* Computer Science and Engg. Roorkee Institute of Technology, Roorkee	**Member**
4. Mr. Harish Sharma *Lecturer* MCA Department, SGRRI, Dehradun	**Member**
5. Anuj Pundir *System Analyst* HCL Noida	**Member**
6. Manoj Kumar Saini *System Analyst* B.dot Software Solution, Noida	**Member**
7. Amit Gupta *Assistant Professor* JPIET, Meerut.	**Member**
8. Abhinay Agarwal *Head,* Mechanical Engineering Deptt. JPIET, Meerut.	**Member**

According to Prescribed Syllabus
for
B.B.A. IInd, Third Semester
of
H.N.B. Garhwal University (Uttrakhand)

Syllabus

302–Organizational Behavior

Objective

The objective is to develop an understanding of an individual personality motivational as well their impact on organization. It also aims to develop skills in team building Leadership, managerial effectiveness and conflict resolutions.

Course Contents

(i) Organization and Its Analysis, Nature of Organization. Nature, Scope and Significance of Organizational Behaviour, Relevance O.B. in To-days Business Environment.

(ii) Individual Dimensions of Organizational Behaviour: Nature of Human Behaviour, Perception, Learning and Behaviour Modification, Personality, Attitudes, Motivation, Socio-cultural Factors and Behaviour Dynamics of Groups

(iii) Interactive Dimension of Organizational Behaviour: Interpersonal Behaviour, Group Dynamics and Behaviour, Power Authority, and Politics, Leadership, Communication, Organizational Conflicts, Organizational Climate.

(iv) Structural dimensions of Organizational Behaviour: Organization Theory, Determinants of Organization Sturcture. Designing of Organization Structure. Forms of Organization Structure, Bureaueratic Organization.

(v) Organizational Effectiveness and changes: Organizational effectiveness. Organizational change and Development. Major Forces of change, Types of change, Reaction to Change. Developing Support for change.

Suggested Readings

(1) Nina Singh - Organisational Behaviour

(2) Korman, Abhrahim K - Organizational Behaviour

(3) Singh and Chhabra - Organization Theory and Behaviour

(4) Khanka S S - Organizational Behaviour

(5) Maslow A H - Motivation and Personality

(6) Stephen P Robbins - Organizational Behaviour

Contents

CHAPTER 1

Organisational Behaviour

1.0 INTRODUCTION

Organisational behaviour is not a discipline in the usual sense of the term, but is rather an electric field of study involving the integration of the behavioural sciences e.g., psychology, sociology, anthropology, etc. into the study of the people's behaviour within organisations. Organisational behaviour can be defined as follows:

Organisational behaviour (OB) is the study and application of knowledge about human behaviour related to other elements of the organisation such as structure, technology, and social system,.

Thus OB is primarily concerned with that aspect of human behaviour which is relevant for organizational performance. Therefore, it studies human behaviour at individual level, group level and organizational behaviour.

1.1 OBJECTIVES

The purpose of this lesson is to note the origins and bases of modern organizational thinking. After studying this lesson you will be able to:

(i) understand meaning and nature of organisational behaviour.

(ii) describe the challenges and opportunities of organisational behaviour.

(iii) discuss the emerging thoughts in organisational behaviour.

(iv) describe interdisciplinary influences on organisational behaviour.

HISTORY AND EVOLUTION OF ORGANISATIONAL BEHAVIOUR

Historical Perspective of Organisational Behaviour

In 1776, Adam Smith advocated a new form of organisational structure based on the division of labour. One hundred years later, German Sociologist Max Weber introduced the concept about rational organisations and initiated the concept of charismatic leadership.

Though the origin to the study of Organisational Behaviour can trace its roots back to Max Weber and earlier organisational studies, it is generally considered to have begun as an academic discipline with the advent of scientific management in the 1890's, with Taylorism representing the peak of the movement. Thus, it was Fredrick Winslow Taylor who introduced the systematic use of goal setting and rewards to motivate employees that could be considered as the starting of the academic discipline of Organisational Behaviour. Proponents of scientific management held that rationalising the organisation with precise sets of instructions and time-motion studies would lead to increased productivity. Studies of different compensation systems were also carried out to motivate workers.

In 1920's Elton Mayo an Australian born Harvard Professor and his colleagues conducted productivity studies at Western Electric's Hawthorne Plant. With this epoch making study the focus of organisational studies shifted to analysis of how human factors and psychology affected organisations. This shift of focus in the study of organisations was called the Hawthorne Effect.

The Human Relations Movement focused on teams, motivation, and the actualisation of goals of individuals within organisations. Studies conducted by prominent scholars like Chester Barnard, Henri Fayol, Mary Parker Follett, Frederick Herzberg, Abraham Maslow, David McCellan and Victor Vroom contributed to the growth of Organisational Behaviour as a discipline.

In the 1960's and 1970's, the field was strongly influenced by social psychology and the emphasis in academic study was quantitative research. An explosion of theorising, bounded rationality, informal organisation, contingency theory, resource dependence, institution theory and population ecology theories have contributed to the study of organisational behaviour.

Various Historical Concepts

1. ***Industrial Revolution:*** It has only been since the Industrial Revolution of the nineteenth century that relatively large number of individuals have been required to work together in manager-subordinate relationships. Prior to this many of the large organisations that did exist, were military ones in which the authority of the leader was supreme and practically unquestioned, since membership was not voluntary.

Behavioural problems were relatively easy to deal with under these conditions. It is certainly no accident that much of our current knowledge about human behavior has been derived from organisations in which influencing behaviour consists of more than just giving orders.

Famous industrialist like William C Durant, Henry Ford, Andrew Carnegie, and John D Rockfeller were men of brilliant managerial qualities. They possessed the managerial qualities necessary for the initial stages if industrialization. However, when the industrial revolution began to mature and become stabilized, this approach was no longer appropriate.

2. ***Scientific Management:*** The great industrialist was primarily concerned with overall managerial organisation in order for their companies to survive and prosper. The scientific management movement around the turn of the century took a narrower, operations perspective. Yet, the two approaches were certainly not contradictory. The managers in both cases applied the scientific method to their problems and they thought that effective management at all levels was the key to organisational success.

Fredrick W Taylor (1856 - 1915) is the recognized father of scientific management. Taylor started scientific management in his time-and-motion studies at the Midvale Steel Company in the early 1900's. As an industrial engineer, he was concerned with inefficiencies in manual labour jobs and believed that by scientifically studying the specific motions that made up the total job, a more rational, objective and effective method of performing the job could be determined. In his early years as a foreman in the steel industry, he saw different workers doing the same job in different ways. It was his opinion that each man could not be doing his job in the optimal way, and he set out to find the "one best way" to perform the job efficiently. His argument proved to be correct and in some instances "taylorism" resulted in productivity increases of 400 percent. In almost all cases, his methods improved productivity over existing levels.

Taylor had actually shop and engineering experience and therefore was intimately involved with tools, products and various machining and manufacturing operations. His well-known metal-cutting experiments demonstrated the scientific management approach. Over a period of twenty-six years, Taylor tested every conceivable variation in speed, feed, depth of cut, and kind of cutting tool. The outcome of this experimentation was highspeed steel, considered one of the most significant contributions to the development of large-scale production.

Coupled with Taylor's logical, rational, engineering-like approach to management was a simple theory of human behaviour: people are primarily motivated by economic rewards and well take direction if offered the opportunity to better their economic positions. Put simply, Taylor's theory stated that:

- Physical work could be scientifically studied to determine the optimal method of performing a job. Workers could thereafter be made more efficient by being given prescriptions for how they were to do their jobs.
- Workers would be willing to adhere to these prescriptions if paid on "differential piecework" basis.

In addition to advocating the use of scientific means to develop the best way to do a task, Taylor argued that several other principles were important.

1. Workers with appropriate abilities had to be selected and trained in the appropriate task method.
2. Supervisors needed to build cooperation among the workers to ensure that they followed the designated method of work. Building such cooperation included soliciting workers' suggestions and being willing to discuss ideas for improved work methods.
3. There needed to be a clear division of work responsibilities. Previously, the workers planned how to approach a task, and then they executed it. Under the Taylor scheme, it was management's job to do the task planning, using scientific methods.

Taylor's four principles of scientific management are summarized here:

- Scientifically study each part of a task and develop the best method for performing the task.
- Carefully select workers and train them to perform the task by using the scientifically developed method.
- Cooperate fully with workers to ensure that they use the proper method.
- Divide work and responsibility so that management is responsible for planning work methods using scientific principles and workers are responsible for executing the work accordingly.

Many have criticized Taylor's work for dehumanizing the work place and treating workers like machines, but his overall contribution to management was significant. Although others were studying similar methods at the same general time, Taylor was one of the first to take the theory and practice of management out of the realm of intuitive judgment and into the realm of scientific inquiry and reasoning. Taylor's ideas on time study, standardization of work practices, goal setting, money as a motivator, scientific selection of workers and rest pauses have all proved to be successful techniques of management today.

Taylor was by no means the only noteworthy scientific manager. Others in the movement, such as Frank and Lillian Gilberth and Henry L Gantt made especially significant contributions.

The Gilbreths: Other major advocates of scientific management were the husband and wife team of Frank Gilbreth (1868 - 1924) and Lillian Moller Gilberth (1878 - 1972). As Frank become involved in training young bricklayers, he noticed the inefficiencies that were handed down from experienced workers. To remedy the situation he proposed using motion studies to streamline the bricklaying process. Frank also designed special scaffolding for different types of jobs and devised precise directions for mortar consistency.

On the basis of these and other ideas, Frank was able to reduce the motions involved in bricklaying from 18 ½ to 4. Using his approach, workers increased the number of bricks laid per day from 1000 to 2700 with no increase in physical exertion.

Frank married Lillian Moller, who began working with him on projects while she completed her doctorate in psychology. The two continued their studies aimed at eliminating unnecessary motions and expanded their interests to exploring ways of reducing task fatigue. Part of their work involved the isolation of 17 basic motions, each called a therblig ("Gilbreth" spelled backward, with the "t" and "h" reversed). Therbligs included such motions as select, position, and hold - motions that were used to study tasks in a number of industries. The Gilbreths used the therblig concept to study tasks in a number of industries. The Gilbreths used the therblig concept to study jobs and also pioneered the use of motion picture technology in studying jobs.

Lillian's doctoral thesis was published as a book, The Psychology of Management, making it one of the early works applying the findings of psychology to the workplace. At the insistence of the publisher, the author was lilted as L.M. Gilbreth to disguise the fact that the book was written by a woman.

Lillian helped define scientific management by arguing that scientific studies of management must focus on both analysis and synthesis. With analysis, a task is broken down into its essential parts or elements. With synthesis, the task is reconstituted to include only those elements necessary for efficient work. She also had a particular interest in the human implications of scientific management, arguing that the purpose of scientific management is to help people reach their maximum potential by developing their skills and abilities. Lillian Gilbreth ranks as the first woman to gain prominence as a major contributor to the development of management as a science.

Henry L Gantt (1861-1919): One of Taylor's closest associates, Henry Gantt latter become an independent consultant and made several contributions of his own. The most well-known is the Gantt Chart, a graphic aid to planning, scheduling and control that is still in use today. He also devised a unique pay incentive system that not only paid workers extra for reaching standard in the allotted time but also awarded bonuses to supervisors when workers reached standard. He wanted to encourage supervisors to coach workers who were having difficulties. The scientific managers like Taylor, Frank and Lillian Gilberth and Henry Gantt were not the first or only group that recognized the importance of the operating functions. A hundred years earlier, Adam Smith had carefully pointed out the advantages of division of labour and in 1832, Charles Babbage, a British mathematician with some astounding managerial insights, discussed transference of skill in his book Economy of Machinery and Manufacture.

3. ***The Human Relations Movement:*** The second major step on the way to current organisational behaviour theory was the Human Relations Movement that began in the 1930's and continued in various forms until the 1950's. The practice of management, which places heavy emphasis on employee cooperation and morale, might be classified as human relations. Raymond Mills states that the human relation approach was simply to *"treat people as human beings (instead of machines in the productive process), acknowledge their needs to belong and to feel important by listening to and heeding their complaints where possible and by involving them in certain decisions concerning working conditions and other matters, then morale would surely improve and workers would cooperate with management in achieving good production".*

The Human Relations Movement, popularized by Elton Mayo and his famous Hawthorne studies conducted at the Hawthorne Plant of the Western Electric Company, in many ways it remained the foundation of much of our management thinking today. Before the Hawthorne studies officially started, Elton Mayo headed a research team, which was investigating the causes of very high turnover in the mule-spinning department of a Philadelphia textile mill in 1923 and 1924. After interviewing and consulting the workers, the team set up a series of rest pauses, which resulted in greatly reduced turnover and more positive worker attitudes and morale.

1.2 CONCEPT OF ORGANISATIONAL BEHAVIOUR

What is Organizational Behavior?

Organizational Behavior is a field of study that investigates the impact that individuals, groups and structure have on behavior within organizations, for the purpose of applying such knowledge toward improving an organization's effectiveness.

An organization is a collection of people who work together to achieve a wide variety of goals, both goals of the various individuals in the organization and goals of the organization as a whole. Organizations exist to provide goods and services that people want. These goods and services are the products of the behaviors of workers.

Organizational behavior is the study of the many factors that have an impact on how individuals and groups respond to and act in organizations and how organizations manage their environments.

Although many people assume that understanding human behavior in organizations is intuitive, many commonly held beliefs about behavior in organizations, such as the idea that a "happy worker is a productive worker," are either entirely false or true only in specific situations. The study of organizational behavior provides a set of tools—concepts and theories—that help people understand, analyze, and describe what goes on in organizations and why. How do the characteristics of individuals, groups, work situations, and the organization itself affect how members feel about their organization?

The ability to use the tools of organizational behavior to understand behavior in organizations is one reason for studying this subject. A second reason is to learn how to apply these concepts, theories, and techniques to improve behavior in organizations so that individuals, groups, and organizations can achieve their goals.

Managers are challenged to find new ways to motivate and coordinate employees to ensure that their goals are aligned with organizational goals.

The term 'Organisational Behaviour' is a combination of two separate words: organisational and behaviour. The word 'organisational' means 'relating to organisation'.

What is Organization?

A consciously coordinated social unit composed of two or more people, those functions on a relatively continuous basis to achieve a common goal or set of goals. Organizational structure is used manage individuals and inter-group relations effectively, particularly between different functions and divisions.

It describes how managers group people and resources, integrate people and groups to stimulate them to work together, and how organizational values and norms influence inter-group relationships and organizational effectiveness.

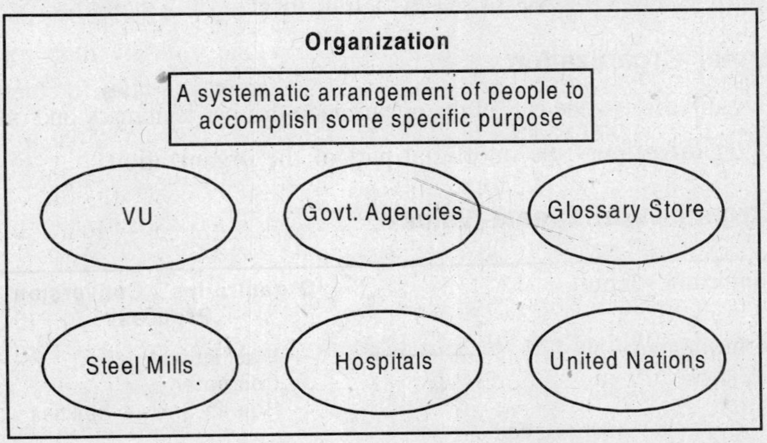

Managers try to: encourage employees to work hard, develop supportive work attitudes, and allow people and groups to cooperate and work together effectively. An organization's structure and culture affect the way people and groups behave. Organizational structure is the formal system of task and reporting relationships that controls, coordinates, and motivates employees so they cooperate and work together to achieve organizational goals.

Organizations are :

- Social entities
- Goal oriented
- Deliberately structured

According to *Mooney and Reiley*, "Organisation is the form of every human association for the attainment of a common purpose".

According to *Theo Haimann*, "Organisation is a process of defining and grouping the activities of an enterprise and establishing the authority relationship among them."

COMPONENTS OF AN ORGANIZATION

The environment influences organizational design. When uncertainty exists, the ability to respond quickly and creatively is important; when the environment is stable, an organization improves performance by making attitudes and behaviors predictable. Creativity and predictability are fostered by certain structures and cultures.

- **Task** - an organization's mission, purpose, or goal for existing
- **People** - the human resources of the organization
- **Structure** - the manner in which an organization's work is designed at the micro level; how departments, divisions, & the overall organization are designed at the macro level
- **Technology** - the intellectual and mechanical processes used by an organization to transform inputs into products or services that meet

Formal vs. Informal Organization

- **Formal Organization** - the part of the organization that has legitimacy and official recognition
- **Informal Organization** - the unofficial part of the organization.

How does an Organization Create Value?

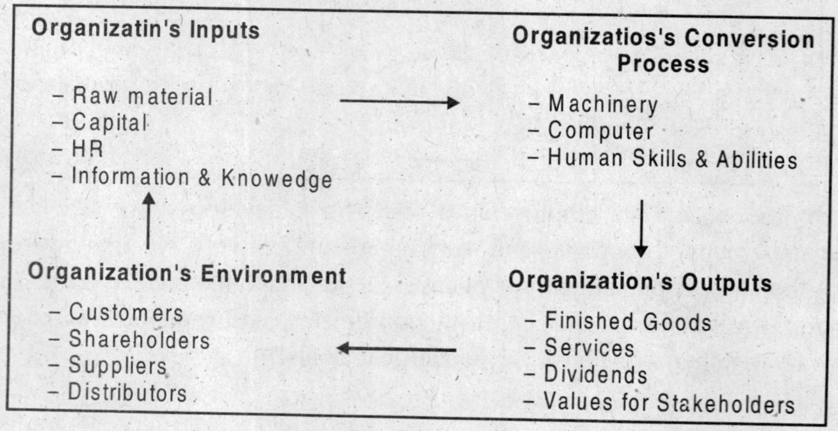

UNDERSTANDING THE HUMAN BEHAVIOR

Overview

- Organizational behavior is not a designated function or area. Rather, it is a perspective or set of tools that all managers can use to carry out their jobs more effectively.
- The ability to use the tools of organizational behavior to understand behavior in organizations is one reason for studying this topic. A second reason is to learn how to apply these concepts, theories, and techniques to improve behavior in organizations so that individuals, groups, and organizations can achieve their goals. Managers are challenged to find new ways to motivate and coordinate employees to ensure that their goals are aligned with organizational goals.
- A manager supervises one or more subordinates. Managers include CEOs, who head top management teams of high-ranking executives responsible for planning strategy to achieve top-level managers might be responsible for thousands of workers. But managers are also found throughout the lower levels of organizations and often are in charge of just a few subordinates. All managers face the challenge of helping the organization achieve its goals. Knowledge of organizational behavior increases effectiveness by providing managers with a set of tools. Managers can raise a worker's self-esteem and increase worker productivity by changing the reward system or the job design.

UNDERSTANDING THE BASICS OF HUMAN BEHAVIOR

An organization's human resource policies and practices represent important forces for shaping employee behavior and attitudes. In this chapter, we specifically discussed the influence of selection practices, training and development programs, performance evaluation systems, and the existence of a union. Human resource policies and practice influence organizational effectiveness. Human resource management includes: employee selection, training performance management, and union-management relations and how they influence organizations effectiveness.

Biographical Characteristics

1. Finding and analyzing the variables that have an impact on employee productivity, absence, turnover, and satisfaction is often complicated.
2. Many of the concepts—motivation, or power, politics or organizational culture—are hard to assess.

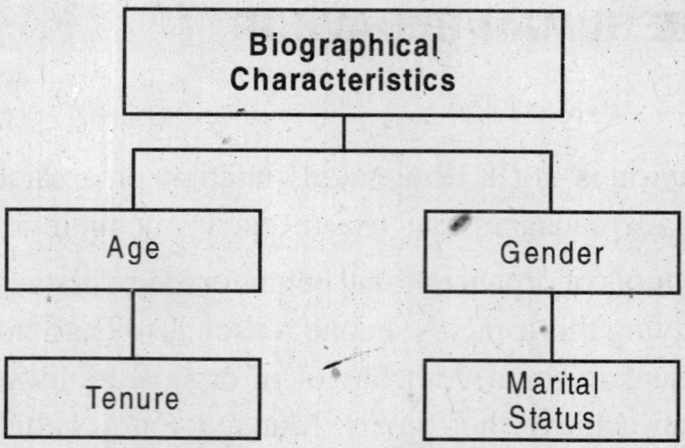

3. Other factors are more easily definable and readily available—data that can be obtained from an employee's personnel file and would include characteristics such as:
   - Age
   - Gender
   - Marital status
   - Length of service, etc.

A. Age

1. The relationship between age and job performance is increasing in importance.
   - First, there is a widespread belief that job performance declines with increasing age.
   - Second, the workforce is aging; workers over 55 are the fastest growing sector of the workforce.
2. Employers' perceptions are mixed.
   - They see a number of positive qualities that older workers bring to their jobs, specifically experience, judgment, a strong work ethic, and commitment to quality.
   - Older workers are also perceived as lacking flexibility and as being resistant to new technology.
   - Some believe that the older you get, the less likely you are to quit your job. That conclusion is based on studies of the age-turnover relationship.
3. It is tempting to assume that age is also inversely related to absenteeism.
   - Most studies do show an inverse relationship, but close examination finds that the ageabsence relationship is partially a function of whether the absence is avoidable or unavoidable.
   - In general, older employees have lower rates of avoidable absence. However, they have higher rates of unavoidable absence, probably due to their poorer health associated with aging and longer recovery periods when injured.

4. There is a widespread belief that productivity declines with age and that individual skills decay over time.
    - Reviews of the research find that age and job performance are unrelated.
    - This seems to be true for almost all types of jobs, professional and nonprofessional.
5. The relationship between age and job satisfaction is mixed.
    - Most studies indicate a positive association between age and satisfaction, at least up to age 60.
    - Other studies, however, have found a U-shaped relationship. When professional and nonprofessional employees are separated, satisfaction tends to continually increase among professionals as they age, whereas it falls among nonprofessionals during middle age and then rises again in the later years.

B. Gender

1. There are few, if any, important differences between men and women that will affect their job performance, including the areas of:
    - Problem-solving
    - Analytical skills
    - Competitive drive
    - Motivation
    - Sociability
    - Learning ability
2. Women are more willing to conform to authority, and men are more aggressive and more likely than women to have expectations of success, but those differences are minor.
3. There is no evidence indicating that an employee's gender affects job satisfaction.
4. There is a difference between men and women in terms of preference for work schedules.
    - Mothers of preschool children are more likely to prefer part-time work, flexible work schedules, and telecommuting in order to accommodate their family responsibilities.
5. Absence and turnover rates
    - Women's quit rates are similar to men's.
    - The research on absence consistently indicates that women have higher rates of absenteeism.
    - The logical explanation: cultural expectation that has historically placed home and family responsibilities on the woman.

C. Marital Status

1. There are not enough studies to draw any conclusions about the effect of marital status on job productivity.
2. Research consistently indicates that married employees have fewer absences, undergo fewer turnovers, and are more satisfied with their jobs than are their unmarried coworkers.
3. More research needs to be done on the other statuses besides single or married, such as divorce, domestic partnering, etc..

D. Tenure

1. The issue of the impact of job seniority on job performance has been subject to misconceptions and speculations.
2. Extensive reviews of the seniority-productivity relationship have been conducted:
    - There is a positive relationship between tenure and job productivity.
    - There is a negative relationship between tenure to absence.
    - Tenure is also a potent variable in explaining turnover.
    - Tenure has consistently been found to be negatively related to turnover and has been suggested as one of the single best predictors of turnover.
    - The evidence indicates that tenure and satisfaction are positively related.

Individual differences can be divided into personality and ability differences. Understanding the nature, determinants, and consequences of individual differences is essential for managing organizational behavior.

An appreciation of the nature of individual differences is necessary to understand why people behave in certain ways in an organization.

1. Organizational outcomes predicted by personality include job satisfaction, work stress, and leadership effectiveness. Personality is not a useful predictor of organizational outcomes when there are strong situational constraints. Because personality tends to be stable over time, managers should not expect to change personality in the short run. Managers should accept workers' personalities as they are and develop effective ways to deal with people.
2. Feelings, thoughts, attitudes, and behaviors in an organization are determined by the interaction of personality and situation.
3. The Big Five personality traits are extraversion (positive affectivity), neuroticism (negative affectivity), agreeableness, conscientiousness, and openness to experience. Other personality traits particularly relevant to organizational behavior include locus of control, self-monitoring, self-esteem, Type A and Type B personality, and the needs for achievement, affiliation, and power.

4. In addition to possessing different personalities, workers also differ in their abilities, or capabilities. The two major types of ability are cognitive and physical ability.
5. Types of cognitive ability can be arranged in a hierarchy with general intelligence at the top. Specific types of cognitive include: verbal, numerical, reasoning, deductive, ability to see relationships, memory, spatial, and perceptual.
6. There are two types of physical ability: motor skills (the ability to manipulate objects) and physical skills (a person's fitness and strength).
7. Both nature and nurture contribute to determining physical and cognitive ability. A third, recently identified, ability is emotional intelligence.
8. In organizations, ability can be managed by selecting individuals who have the abilities needed to accomplish tasks, placing workers in jobs that capitalize on their abilities, and training workers to enhance their ability levels.

Thus, **Organisational Behaviour** can be defined as the study of human behaviour in organizations and application of knowledge to make it more purposive, responsible, responsive and co-operative. Organisational behaviour tries to understand the behaviour, attitudes and performance of people in organisations.

Almost in every type of organisation such as business enterprise, schools, government etc., interaction of people over organisation exists. How people behave in a formal organisation in given circumstances is the subject matter of organisational behaviour.

Few important definitions of organisational behaviour are as follows:

1. According to **Keith Davis**, "Organisational Behaviour is the study and application of knowledge about human behaviour in organizations as it relates to other systems or elements, such as, structure, technology and external social system."
2. According to **Sherman Krupp**, "Organisational behaviour deals with micro aspect of the organisation, that is, individual and group behaviour in the organisation."
3. **Joe Kelly** defines OB as follows : "Organisational behaviour is a systematic study of the nature of organisations, how they begin, grow, develop and their effect on individual members, constituent groups, other organisation and larger institutions."

From the analysis of the foregoing definitions the following four elements of organisational behaviour emerge :

1. **People:** The people constitute the internal social system of the organisation. All organisations are made up of people which may consist of individuals or groups. Groups may be formal or informal, large or small, inter-related or complex, effective or non-effective.
2. **Structure:** Structure defines the role and relationship of people in an organisation. Different people in an organisation are given different roles and they have certain relationship with others. It leads to division of labour so that people can perform their duties or work to accomplish the organisational goal. Work is complex and different duties are to be performed

by different people. Some may be accountant, others may be mangers, clerks, peons or workers. All are so related to each other to accomplish the goal in a co-ordinated manner.

3. **Technology:** Technology imparts the physical and economic conditions within which people work, with their bare hands people can do nothing so they are given assistance of buildings, machines, tools, process and resources. The nature of technology depends very much on the nature of the organisation and influence the work or working conditions. Thus, technology brings effectiveness and at the same time restricts people in various ways.
4. **Social System:** Social system provides external environment within which the organisation operates. A single organisation cannot exist also. It is a part of the whole. On e organisation cannot give everything and therefore there are many other organisation. All these organisation influence each other. It influences the attitudes of people, their working conditions and above all provides competition for resources and power.

1.3 NATURE OF ORGANISATIONAL BEHAVIOUR

1. **Social Science:** The main subject matter of OB is people and their behaviour and therefore OB is social science. OB integrates behavioural science like psychology, sociology, anthropology etc for the study of human behaviour in and around organisations.
2. **Science as well as Art:** OB is both a science as well as an art. The knowledge about human behaviour proves it a science while application of this knowledge and skill leads toward being an art.
3. **An Inexact Science:** OB is an inexact science. It cannot provide specific answers to specific organisational problems. The exact prediction of the behaviour of people in organisations is also not possible. "It is possible to predict relationships between variables on a broad scale but it is difficult to apply predictive models on an individual basis."
4. **Action and Goal-oriented discipline:** OB is an action-oriented and goal-directed discipline. The major goal of OB is to explain and predict human behaviour in organisational context so that it may be moulded to result-yielding situations. It provides a rational thinking, not an emotional feeling about people and their behaviour.
5. **Integrating approach:** OB is of integrating character. It seeks to balance human and technical values at work. It tries to develop a new socio-technical system where human dignity may be preserved with growth and development.
6. **OB exists at multiple levels:** OB has a three-tier system. It deals with the individual behaviour, group behaviour and organisational behaviour as a whole. All these three levels interact with each other and OB tries to assimilate them to the good results.
7. **A Dynamic discipline:** OB is very dynamic discipline. Its main focus is on human behaviour but does not ignore technical component of the organisations at all. It fully appreciates and recognizes the constraints of the working environment and its changes and takes due note of their implications—behavioural as well as operational.

8. **Humanistic and Optimistic:** The main focus of OB is on people from humanistic point of view. It is based on the assumption that needs and motivation of people are of high concern. There is an acceptance of the value of the individual as a thinking, feeling organism, and without these considerations the organisations may not be fully operational as a social entity. There is optimism about the innate potential of man to be independent, creative, productive, and capable of contributing positively to the objectives of the organisation.

1.4 DISCIPLINES CONTRIBUTING TO OB

As discussed earlier, OB is not a discipline in itself but it uses knowledge developed in the relevant disciplines. OB basically draws concepts and principles from behavioural sciences and the core disciplines of behavioural sciences are psychology, sociology, and anthropology. Since these disciplines themselves are part of social sciences, it can be said that OB draws something from social sciences like economics, history, and political science. However, OB does not draw the whole knowledge of these disciplines but only the relevant knowledge which helps in predicting and directing human behaviour in the organisation. The contributions of core disciplines of behavioural science to organisational behaviour are as follows:

Psychology

The term psychology comes from the Greek word 'psyche' meaning soul or spirit. Modern psychology is almost universally defined as the science of behaviour which is nearly identical with behavioural science, in general. Though there are two other disciplines which make behavioural science, psychology is more closely identified with overall behavioural science.

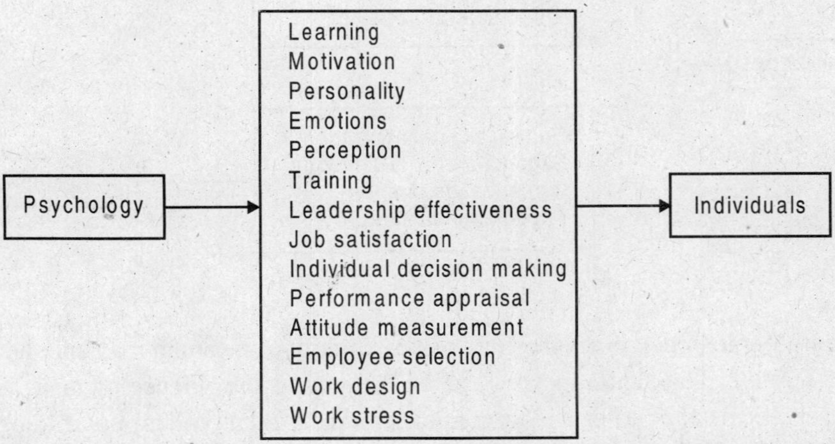

Psychology is a science of behaviour, the term behaviour being interpreted literally, for it comprehends not only objective and subjective form of human behaviour but also the behaviour of the animals. Psychology studies behaviour in various conditions – normal, abnormal, social, industrial, legal; childhood, adolescence, old age, etc. It also studies processes of human behaviour, such as learning, thinking, memory, sensation, perception, emotion, feeling, and personality. Its contributions to behavioural science, as applied to managerial practices, are in the field of learning, perception, motivation, individual and group decision-making, pattern of influence, and change in organisations, group process, vocational choice and satisfaction, communication, and personnel selection and training. In fact, there is a separate branch of industrial psychology which deals with the application of psychological facts and principles to the problems concerning human relations in organisations. Human relations is the integration of human factor into work situation which motivates it to work together effectively providing it social, psychological and economic satisfaction. From this point of view, the contribution of psychology is quite significant.

Sociology

Sociology can be described as an academic discipline that utilises the scientific method in accumulating knowledge about man's social behaviour. It studies the patterned, shared human behaviour; the way in which people Act toward one another. It specifically studies social groups, social behaviour, society, Customs, institutions, social class, status, social mobility and prestige. It has also developed sub-fields of political sociology, industrial sociology, sociology of law, family sociology, educational sociology, and sociology of religion. To the managerial practice, its contribution is mainly in the field of bureaucracy, role structures, social system theory, group dynamics, effect of industrialisation on the social behaviour, etc.

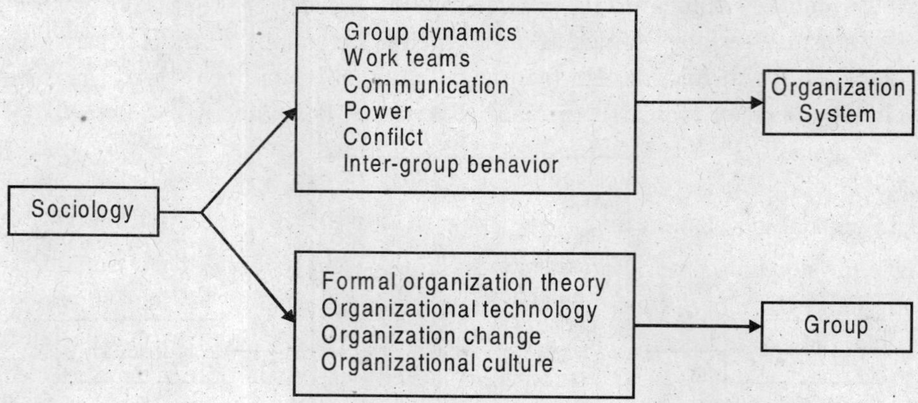

Anthropology

The term anthropology combines the Greek stem 'anthropo' meaning man and the noun ending 'logy' meaning science. Thus anthropology can be defined as the science of man. It particularly studies civilisation, forms of cultures and their impact on individuals and groups, biological features of man and evolutionary pattern, speech and relationship among languages. Anthropology contributes in understanding the cultural effects on organisational behaviour, effects of value systems, norms, sentiments, cohesion, and interaction.

Besides these three basic behavioural disciplines, economics contributes in understanding the decision process, methods of allocating scarce resources in the organisations, and the impact of economic policy on organisations. Political science provides clue to conflicts in organisations, power and authority structure, and overall administrative process. From historical approach, case studies have emerged which have helped in clarifying the roles of decision-makers.

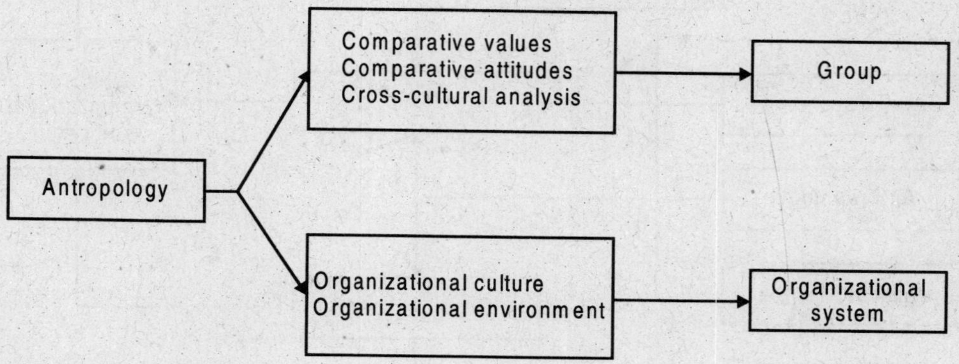

Social Psychology

An area within psychology that blends concepts from psychology and sociology and that focuses on the influence of people on one another.

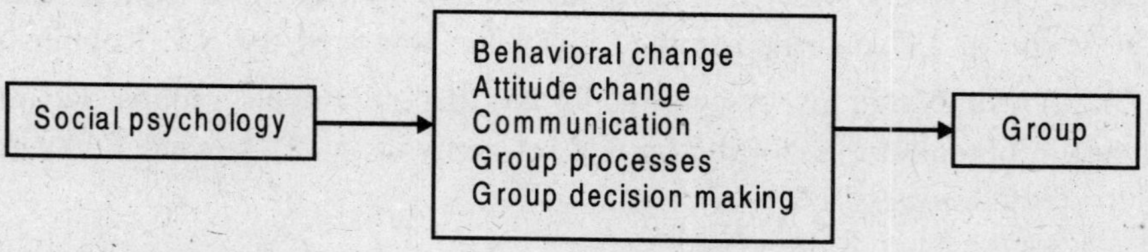

Political Science

The study of the behavior of individuals and groups within a political environment

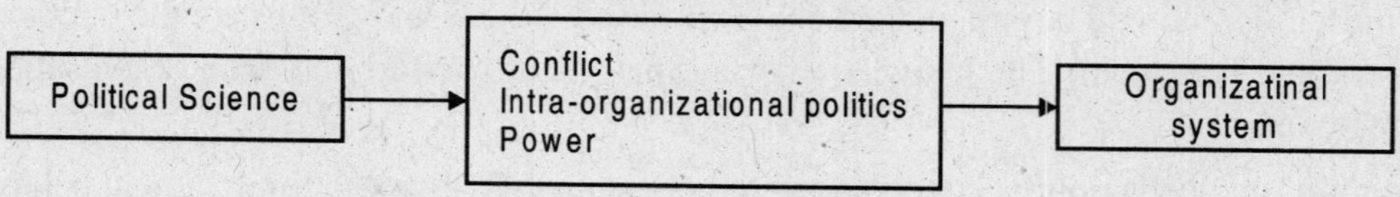

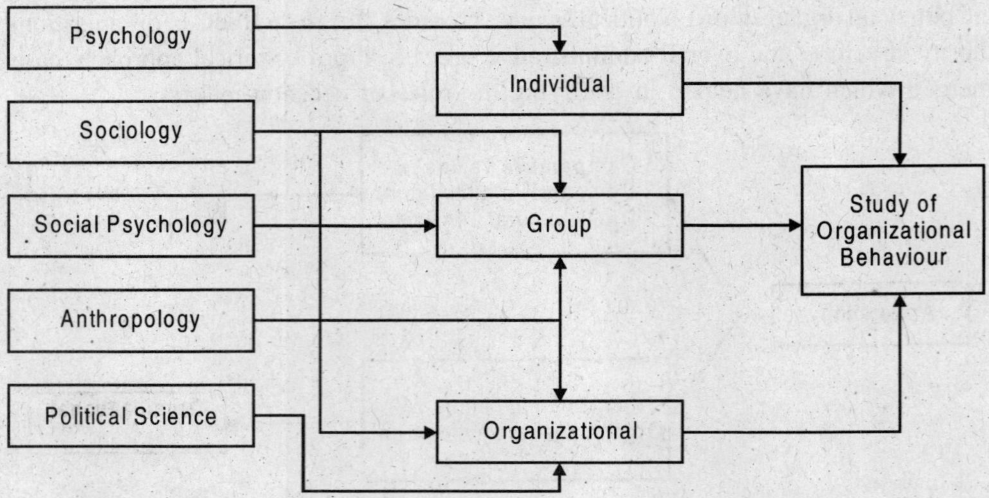

1.5 SCOPE OF ORGANISATIONAL BEHAVIOUR

The scope of OB is very wide. It is a social science as it is the scientific study of human behaviour. The scope of OB may be summed up in the words of the S.P. Robbins as follows :

"OB is a field of study that investigates the impact that individuals, groups, and structure have on behaviour within organisations, for the purpose of applying such knowledge toward improving an organisation's effectiveness".

Organisational behaviour is a field of study. It is relatively a new discipline which has a distinct area of expertise with a well-defined body of knowledge. OB studies three determinants of behaviour in organisations : individuals, groups and structure. The behaviour of individuals and groups and the impact of structural design on the behaviour of individuals and groups are the major concern of organisational behaviour. The knowledge of all these is applied to make the organisation work more effectively.

Organisational behaviour is concerned with understanding and describing human behaviour in an organisational setting. It seeks to shed light on the complex human factor in organisations by identifying causes and effects of human behaviour. It is called a social science because its main concern is people and their behaviour. It is the field of study that integrates behavioural sciences like psychology, sociology and anthropology for the study of human behaviour in and around organisations.

LEVELS OF ANALYSIS OF OB

"Organisational behaviour is the field that seeks knowledge of behaviour in organisational settings by systematically studying individual, group and organisational processes." Thus, organisational behaviour focuses on three levels of analysis, viz., individuals, groups, and organization. OB provides a way for understanding human behaviour in the organisation. OB provides for understanding human behaviour in all the directions in which human beings interact. Thus OB can be understood at the individual level, interpersonal level, group level and intergroup level.

1. **Behaviour at the Individual Level:** Organisations are made up of their individual members. The individual is a central feature of organisational behaviour and a necessary part of any behavioural situation. The behaviour of human beings provides for analysing why and how an individual behaves in a particular way. Human behaviour is a complex phenomenon and is affected by a large number of factors - psychological, social, cultural, and others. OB integrates these factors to provide simplicity in understanding human behaviour.
2. **Behaviour at Group Level:** Though people interpret any thing at their individual level, they are often modified by group pressures which thus becomes a force in shaping human behaviour. Thus individuals should be studied in group also. Research in group dynamics has contributed vitally to OB and shows how a group behaves in its norms, cohesion, goals, procedures, communication pattern, leadership, and membership. These research results and furthering managerial knowledge of understanding group behaviour which is very important for organisational moral and productivity.
3. **Behaviour at Organisational Level**

   (a) ***Behaviour at Interpersonal Level:*** Human behaviour can be understood at the level of interpersonal interaction. Such interpersonal interaction is normally in paired relationship which represents man's most natural attempt at socialization. When one focuses on the influence of one's peer and its effect in working relationship, or examines the superior-subordinate relationship, it is obvious that the two-person relationship is inevitable in the organisation. OB provides means for understanding these interpersonal relationships in the organisation. Analysis of reciprocal relationship, role analysis, and transactional analysis are some of the common methods which provide such understanding.

   (b) ***Behaviour at Intergroup Level:*** The organisation is made up of many groups that develop a complex of relationships to build its process and substance. Understanding the effect of group relationships is important for managers in today's organisation. Intergroup relationship may be in the form of cooperation or competition. The co-operative relationships help the organisation in achieving its objectives. OB provides means to understand and achieve co-operative group relationships through interaction, rotation of members among groups, avoidance of win-lose situation, and focus on total group objectives.

1.6 ORGANISATION AS A SOCIAL SYSTEM

A social system is s complex set of human relationships interacting in many ways. There is no limitation in these interactions. In a system every small group is a subsystem.

Organisations may be well studied and analysed if it is taken as a system. In an organisation its parts and sub-parts are orderly arranged according to a certain pre-decided plan. An organisation is basically a combination of parts, subsystems. Every part may have many subparts. Every subsystem (different groups and departments) have similar features as the parent organisation. An organisation is a system of mutually dependent parts, having many subsystems.

Parts and subparts of an organisation are mutually related to each other, through interaction parts and subparts are interactive within the organisation as well as outside the organisation. Change in one part will definitely effect other parts directly or indirectly.

In a social system of organisation, system not only the totality of parts and sub-part but their proper arrangement is also very important. So now it is clear that an organisation is a system of interdependent framework in which its various subparts are arranged.

Physical systems can be identified very easily because they have boundary, which is clearly visible. However in case of a social system, the boundary is not visible because here it is nothing like a distinct line or wall. In case of human organisations all the controllable factors come under social system while all the uncontrollable factors come as External factors.

1.7 UNIT EXERCISES

Short Answers

Q1. What is orgnisational Behaviour? Discuss its nature.

Q2. "The purpose of OB is to explain, predict and control behaviour." Discuss.

Q3. Define Organisation and Organisation Behaviour.

Q4. Explain "organisation as a social system".

Long Answers

1. Define Organisation and Organisation Behaviour. Is it true that all behaviour is caused and reasons are known.
2. What are the features of organization as a system? Why should organizations be studied from the perspective of systems approach?
3. What is meant by organizational typology? Explain typologies of organizations based on their functions and primary beneficiary.
4. How can organizations be differentiated on the basis of primary beneficiaries? Discuss the usefulness of this typology.

Chapter 2

Concept of Individual Behaviour

2.0 INTRODUCTION

The nature of human behaviour is complex and in understanding the behaviour of people, they should be studied in their totality by taking a total man concept. This concept is essentially a combination of all factors affecting human behaviour. It recognises that any attempt at generalisation usually falls short of the mark because people are different. If both individual and environmental variables are considered, there can be (I) differences in behaviour in an individual over time (intra-individual) and (ii) differences in behaviour among individuals given the same set of stimuli (inter-individual).

2.1 OBJECTIVE

After studying this unit we should be able to :

- explain perception, learning and personality of the people
- describe attitude of the people.

2.2 CONCEPT OF INDIVIDUAL BEHAVIOUR

Individual behaviour means some concrete action by a person. For instance, how a teacher behaves in the class reflects his behaviour. The behaviour of an individual is influence by various factors. Some of the factors lie within himself, e.g., his instincts, personality traits, internal feelings, etc, while some lie outside him comprising the external environment of which he is a part, e.g., weather conditions, events conveying some information, and other peoples' behaviour that directly influence his behaviour. Thus, individual behaviour is not a self-induced phenomenon, but is affected by the larger environmental system, e.g., group, family, and the society within which one functions.

Human Behaviour as a Function of Person and Environment

According to Kurt Lewin, human behaviour (B) is a function of both person (P) and environment (E)

$$B = f\ (P \text{ X } E)$$

Thus, behaviour of an individual is determined by (1) his personal characteristics, and (2) the environmental setting in which he operates. For instance, the performance of a nurse in a hospital is affected by both personal and environmental characteristics. Personal or individual characteristics of a nurse include education, skills, experience, health, age, background, aptitude, value system, perception, etc. Environmental factors under which a nurse functions include patients, other nurses, doctors and hospital staff, physical facilities, monitoring devices, etc.

Individual Differences

Each person in the world is individually different. The idea of individual differences comes originally from psychology. From the day of birth, each person is unique; and experiences after birth tend to make him even more different. The law of individual differences states that management can motivate employees by treating them individually. There can be no standard technique of dealing with all individuals.

Every individual may behave differently to the same stimulus under the given environment. And a person may respond differently to a given stimulus under different environment. This is because of the differences among individuals. People differ in age, sex, attitudes, background, education, perception, intelligence, value system, physical features, etc. There may be many possible combinations of these characteristics. That is why, placed in accident, the doctor will like to provide first-aid to the victims immediately and hospitalize them, if necessary; the traffic controller will engage himself in analyzing the violation of traffic rules and an anti-social element will try to remove the belongings of the persons involved in the accident. Therefore, it is essential to recognize individual differences while dealing with any human relation problem. The value of any generalization about human behaviour will always be subject to individual differences.

Environmental Factors

Behaviour of an individual is influenced by environmental variables to a great extent. These include possibility of rewards, nature of supervision, relation with fellow workers, types of tools and machines, quality of working conditions, etc. Environment acts on the individual eliciting a response which is determined by his individual characteristics. Sometime, the situational variables have a significant influence on the behaviour of an individual. In such cases, environmental variables may be modified to create conditions conducive to desirable behaviour.

2.3 DETERMINANTS OF INDIVIDUAL BEHAVIOUR

Human behaviour is the result of interaction between individual characteristics and the characteristics of the environment in which the behaviour occurs. Each person with a unique combination of characteristics is different from all others. Some of these characteristics are inherited from birth and others are learned over time. Personal characteristics remain inside the person whereas environmental ones outside the person. These personal and environmental characteristics serve as the foundations of human behaviour.

The list of such factors are as follows :

I. Personal Biographical Factors

1. Sex
2. Age
3. Education
4. Abilities
5. Marital Status

II. Psychological Factors

1. Personality
2. Perception
3. Attitudes

4. Values
5. Learning

III. General Environmental Factors
1. Economic Conditions
2. Political Situations
3. Cultural Values
4. Social Norms

IV. Organizational Factors
1. Physical Facilities
2. Organizational Structure and Design
3. Leadership Styles
4. Reward System

I. Personal Biographical Factors

Every individual has certain inherited characteristics which can't be changed by external forces. These include the following:

1. **Sex:** Sex has a profound impact on one's behaviour at work. It affects turnover and absenteeism. Historically, our society has placed home and family responsibility on the females. When a child is ill or some one needs to await the electrician or plumber, it is often woman who has to abstain from work.
2. **Age:** Age has an important impact on performance, turnover, absenteeism and satisfaction. With advances in age, employee's performance tends to deciine. The older one grows, less likely he/she becomes to quit the job due to decreasing propensity to move from one job to another and from one place to another. The absenteeism rate among the older/aged is likely to be higher mainly due to poor health associated with old age.
3. **Education:** Education has its effect on individual behaviour largely through the level and type of education. Increased level of education serves to increase an individual's expectations about positive outcomes such as more satisfying job, higher income level, and "good life." Disillusionment occurs when outcomes do not match expectations.
4. **Abilities:** These refer to an individual's capabilities to perform his job. An individual's abilities are of two kinds, namely, (a) intellectual, and (b) physical.

   (a) ***Intellectual Abilities:*** The abilities required to perform mental work-are known as mental abilities. They include number aptitude, verbal comprehension, perceptual speed and inductive reasoning. The degree of intellectual abilities required will normally depend upon the level in the organization where the individual is working.

(b) ***Physical Abilities:*** These include stamina, strength and similar skills. Physical abilities are more important for doing less skilled and more standardized jobs in the lower levels of the organization.

5. **Marital Status.** Married employees are believed to show higher consistency in their behaviour. Rates of absenteeism and labour turnover are lower among them. They are supposed to be more satisfied with their jobs. Very possibly, the need for a steady job and regular income by the married employees explains the above type of behaviour.

II. Psychological Factors

Psychological factors refer to individual's characteristics and attributes (though not observable) that can affect individual's behaviour. There are several psychological factors, but the important ones include personality, perception, attitudes, values and learning.

III. Environmental Factors

Environmental factors consist of such variables as economic conditions, social and cultural norms which are outside an individual. Political factors also affect individual behaviour. The environment consists of all aspects of the physical world that can be seen, heard, felt or touched. The social environment of an individual includes relationship with family, friends, co-workers, supervisors and subordinates. The behaviour of others (as distinct from the individual's relationship with them) is also part of an individual's social environment. Political stability/instability and the actions of political leaders create political environment.

IV. Organizational Factors

Individual behaviour is influenced by a wide variety of organizational systems and resources. Systems such as the organizational structure and hierarchy strongly influence and constrain both what individuals do and how they do. In addition, individual behaviour is influenced by various types of resources provided by the organization such as advice and directions from leaders, physical support in terms of facilities and technology. The important organizational factors affecting human behaviour are explained below:

(a) ***Physical Facilities:*** The physical facilities such as lighting, ventilation, air-conditioning, painting on walls, space provided for each employee, equipment, etc. have their influence on employee behaviour and performance.

(b) ***Organization Structure and Design:*** Human behaviour is influenced by the way, in which the different groups and departments in the organization are set up and the way in which the reporting relationships and lines of communication are established among different positions in the organization. The behaviour and performance of an individual is influenced by where that person fits into the overall structure and design of the organization.

(c) ***Leadership:*** The role of leadership and supervision is to provide direction, assistance, advice and coaching to individual members. The leader behaviour is, therefore, a potential source of influence on an individual.

(*d*) ***Reward Systems:*** Organizations establish reward systems to compensate their employees. The behaviour and performance of an individual is influenced by the reward system which may include both financial and. non-financial rewards.

2.4 PERCEPTION

Human beings are constantly attacked by numerous sensory stimulations including noise, sight, smell, taste etc. The critical question in the study of perception is why the same universe is viewed differently by different persons? The answer is the perception. Different people perceive the universe differently.

> "Perception can be defined as a process by which individuals organise and interpret their sensory impressions in order to give meaning to the their environments".
>
> —***S. P. Robbins***

Perception is defined as the process by which an individual selects, organizes, and interprets stimuli into a meaningful picture of the world. A stimulus is any unit of input. Sensory receptors are the human organs as the eyes, ears, nose, mouth and skin, they receive the sensory input. These sense y functions are to see, hear, smell, taste, and feel. The study f perception is largely the study of what we subconsciously add to or subtract from raw sensory inputs to produce our own private picture of the world.

According to **Kolasa,** the perception involves two basic elements :

(a) Perception is the process of selection or screening which prevents us from processing irrelevant or disruptive information.

(b) There is organisation implying that the information which is processed has to be ordered and classified in some logical manner which permits us to assign meaning to the stimulus situations.

Factors Influencing Perception

Following factors influence the perceptual mechanism :

External Factors

These includes:

(*a*) ***Intensity:*** High intensity increases the chances of selection. If the message is bright, if sentences are underlined, it gets more attention than in normal case. The greater the intensity of stimulus, the more likely it will be noticed. An intense stimulus has more power to push itself our selection filters than does the weak stimulus.

(*b*) ***Size:*** Size establishes dominance and overrides other things and thereby enhances perceptual selection. The bigger the size of perceived stimulus, higher is the probability that it is perceived.

(c) ***Frequency:*** A repeated external stimulus is more attention getting than a single one. A stimulus, that is repeated, has a better chance of catching us. Repetition increases our sensitivity and alertness to the stimulus. Thus, the greater the frequency with which a sensory stimulus is presented, the greater the chances we select it for attention. Repetition is one of the most frequently used techniques in advertising and is the most common way of getting our attention. Repetition aids in increasing the awareness of the stimulus.

(d) ***Status:*** Perception is also influenced by the status of perceiver. High status people can exert influence on perception of employees than low status people.

(e) ***Contrast:*** Stimuli, that contrasts with the surrounding environment, are more likely to be selected for attention than the stimuli that blends in. A contrasting effect can be caused by colour/size or any other factor that is unusual. The contrast principle states that external stimuli that stands out against the background or which are not what are expecting, will receive their attention. The contrast effect also explains why a male person stands out in a crowd of females.

(f) ***Repetition:*** A repeated message is more likely to be perceived than a single message. Work instructions that are repeated tend to be received better. Marketing managers and advertisers use this principle in order to get the customers' attention. As noted by **Morgan** and **King** "a stimulus that is repeated has a better change of catching us during one of the periods when our attention to a task is waning. In addition repetition increases our sensitivity or alterness to the stimulus".

Internal Factors

These includes :

(a) ***Needs and desires:*** The needs and motives of the people play a vital role in perception. Perception of a frustrated person would be entirely different than that of a happy going person. People at different level of needs and desires perceive the same thing differently. Power seekers are more likely to notice power related stimuli. Socially oriented people pay attention to interpersonal stimuli. People will likely to notice stimuli relevant to current active motives and compatible with major personality characteristics.

(b) ***Experience:*** Experience and knowledge have a constant bearing on perception. Successful experiences enhance and boost the perceptive ability and lead to accuracy in perception of a person where as failure erodes self confidence.

(c) ***Personality:*** Personality is another important factor that has a profound influence on perceived behaviour. Optimistic people perceive the things in favourable terms while pessimistic beings in negative term. According to **Maslow,** "that between these two extremes there exist a category who can see things more accurately and subjectively. Research on the effects of individual personality on perception reveals many truths."

1. Thoughtful individuals do not expose by expressing extreme judgments of others.
2. Persons who accept themselves and have faith in their individuality perceive things favourably.
3. Secured individuals tend to perceive others as warm, not cold.

(d) ***Learning:*** Learning is an important factor in developing perceptual sets. A perceptual set is basically what a person expects from the stimuli on the basis of his clearing and experience relative to same or similar stimuli. This is also known as cognitive awareness by which the mind organises information and forms

Perceptual Process/Elements of Perception/Perceptual Mechanism

Perception is the process that operates constantly between us and reality. Perception process involves the following five steps (Fig. 8.2) :

Stimulus

Step-I—Stimulus: Perception initiates with the presence of the stimulus situation.

Step-II—Registration: It involves the physiological mechanism, both sensory and neutral. Obviously, an invidividual's physiological ability to hear and see determines his perception.

-t-Reaction

Step-III—Interpretation : It is the highly crucial sub process. Without the interpretation of the perceived events, the perceived world would be meaningless. Interpretation is subjective and judgmental process. In organisations, interpretation is influenced by many factors such as halo effect, stereotyping, attribution, impression and inference.

Step-IV—Feedback : It is important for interpreting the perceptual event data. In the work settings, the psychological feedback, which is likely to affect a subordinate's perception, may be in the form of a variation in the tone of the voice of the superior.

Step-V—Reaction : Perception ends in reaction or response which may be in the overt or covert form.

2.5 PERCEPTUAL ERRORS AND DISTORTION

Quite often, errors creep into the perceptual interpretation of individuals because of short-cuts in judging others or events. The errors may arise due to selective perception, projection, stereotyping, halo effect, impression, inference, attribution, etc. Such errors usually creep in while appraising the performance of subordinates or forming impressions of others. The following section deals with the perceptual errors and explains how perceptual distortion could be avoided.

(i) ***Selective Perception:*** People differ in terms of their needs, motives, interests, etc. They tend to perceive what is in accordance with their needs, motives and interests. Sometimes, they

distort meanings so that they may fit with what they want. If a man feels very threatened or insecure, everything around him will appear to be a potential source of danger.

People are more likely to pay attention to those aspects of their environment which they anticipate or expect rather than those they do not anticipate or expect. And people tend to anticipate what they are familiar with. Thus, *they selectively interpret what they see on the basis of their background, interests, attitudes and experience.* Take for example, a doctor, a mechanic and a policeman who saw an automobile accident happen right in front of them. Because of their experience in particular fields, each one will probably notice certain things about the accident - things that will stand out for each. The doctor will see the condition of the people involved in the accident, whether they need medical help and ambulance. The mechanic will notice the condition of the car, how much damage has taken place. The policeman might see who violated a traffic rule. Thus, each might select from the total event the aspects he thought were significant.

Perception is basically a selective process. As people can see only limited amount of information in the environment, they are characteristically selective. By selection, certain aspects of stimuli are screened out and others are admitted. Those which are admitted remain in the awareness of the people and those which are screened out fall below the threshold. There are a number of factors which affect selectivity. These include : needs and motives, beliefs, expectations, perceptual defence.

(ii) Projection: It means *attributing one's own traits or characteristics to the people being judged.* The tendency to attribute one's own characteristics to other people can distort perceptual judgments about others. This may be particularly true regarding undesirable traits which the perceiver possesses but fails to recognise in himself. For example, an individual who is himself not very energetic may see others as lazy or may explain their lack of achievement as resulting from their unwillingness to work hard. One who is dishonest may be suspicious of others and may perceive dishonest intentions in others where they do not exist. People who are afraid may interpret others' behaviour as fearful or anxious.

When a manager engages in projection, he compromises his ability to respond to individual differences. He tends to see people as more homogeneous than they really are. In order to avoid this error in judging others, the manager should be conscious of his weakness of overlooking differences among people.

(iii) Stereotyping: *Judging people on the basis of the characteristics of the group to which they belong is called "stereotyping".* The word 'stereotype' was first used by Walter Lippmann to perception. It was basically applied for *ethnic prejudice.* Now it is often used as a short-cut to predicting the behaviour of people. Some examples of common stereotypes are that Americans are materialistic, Japanese are nationalistic, and Germans are industrious.

Stereotyping is the tendency for a person's perception of another to be influenced by the social group to which he belongs. In perceiving another, a person is likely to categorise the other according to some salient group characteristics such as sex, race, religion, nationality, occupation or organizational affiliation. The individual's experiences with others in the category in which he has placed them lead him to believe that they have certain traits in common. Generalisations based on stereotyping make assimilation easier since it permits to maintain consistency. It becomes less difficult to deal with an unmanageable number of stimuli if we use stereotypes. But the danger lies in incorrect stereotyping. For example, all politicians are not self-serving or all salespersons are not aggressive. Exceptions may always be there. This fact must be considered while judging a person based on the generally accepted traits of a group to which he belongs.

(iv) Halo Effect: It refers to the tendency a/drawing a general impression about an individual based on a single characteristic such as intelligence, sociability or appearance. This is a very common type of error committed by managers while evaluating the subordinates. Halo error creeps in when the manager or rater allows one aspect of a man's character or performance to influence his entire evaluation.[7] It is the tendency of many raters to let the rating they assign to one characteristic excessively influence their ratings on all subsequent characteristics. A rater may tend to give an employee approximately the same rating on all factors. This error can be recognised quite easily on factor scales. The rating scale technique of performance appraisal is particularly susceptible to the halo effect. One way of minimising the effect of halo error is to have manager judge all his subordinates on a single factor or trait before going to the next. In this manner, he can consider all of the men relative to a standard or to each other on each trait.

Halo effect takes place in all walks of life. For instance, a teacher may award higher marks to those students who are more social. In employment interview, candidates with vocal skills may be given higher weightage. A communication from an important person tends to be overrated and the same from an ordinary person may be discounted.

(v) Impression (Recency Effect): People often form impression of others on the first sight. Even before knowing any of their personality traits, they start having impression and making assessment of individuals they meet for the first time. This sometimes leads to perceptual distortion because first impression need not be the last impression. If a new employee in an industrial organization is judged on the basis of his first impression on the superior, it will be a great injustice to such an employee.

(vi) Inference: There is a tendency on the part of some people to finite others on limited information. For example, an employee might be sitting at his desk'throughout the working hours without doing anything, but it may be inferred that he is sincere towards his duties. Thus, performance appraisal must not be based on half-cooked or incomplete information. In the above case, the productivity and the behaviour of the concerned employee towards customers, fellow employees and others must also be taken into consideration.

(vii) Performance Expectation or Self-fulfilling Prophecy: Based on expectations, some bias in perception may creep in. In many cases it has been found that people try to validate their perceptions of reality (or expected performance) when those perceptions are faulty. For instance, if a manager expects good results from his people, they are not likely to let him down. Thus, expectations become reality. This is called **self-fulfilling prophecy** or pygmalion effect, i.e., people's expectations determine their behaviour.

If the boss inaccurately perceives the capability of a subordinate and the resulting expectations cause the subordinate to show performance as perceived by the boss, it is called self fulfilling prophecy. It states that expecting certain things to happen shapes the behaviour of the perceiver in such a way that the expected is more likely to happen. Because the boss expected better performance from the subordinate, the former may start rating the latter higher or the latter does better because of former's expectations. Thus, our expectations affect the way we interact with others such that we get what we wish for (self-fulfilling prophecy).

(viii) Attribution: When people give cause and effect explanation to the observed behaviour, it is known as attribution. Perception is distorted sometimes by the efforts of the perceiver to attribute a causal explanation to an outcome. There is a tendency for the individuals to attribute their own behaviour to situational factors, but explain the behaviour of others by their personal dispositions.

When a person observes an event in an organization, his evaluation of and reaction to other's behaviour may be highly influenced by his perception. A nurse who drops a tray of medicine will be excused if the incident is perceived as caused by slippery floor; chastised if it is viewed as caused by her clumsiness ; and perhaps fired if it is viewed as a deliberate act. Similarly, increased profitability of a plant may be attributed to installation of new machines, efficient handling of resources, or to the rising market.

The attribution theory suggests that when we observe an individual's behaviour, we attempt to determine whether it was internally or externally caused. Internally caused behaviour .is believed to be under the control of the individual. Externally caused behaviour is seen as resulting from outside causes. In other words, the person is seen as forced into the behaviour by the situation. If an employee is late for work, the supervisor may relate it to oversleeping which is an internal interpretation. But if coming late is attributed to a major traffic jam on the way, it is called external attribution.

Perceptual distortion occurs because of attribution on two counts : (1) fundamental attribution error and (2) self-serving bias. When we make judgments about the behaviour of other people, we have a tendency to underestimate the influence of external factors and overestimate the influence of internal or personal factors. This is called the fundamental attribution error which can explain why a sales manager may be prone to attribute the poor performance of sales agents to laziness rather than the innovative product line introduced by a competitor. There is also a tendency for individuals to attribute their successes to internal factors like ability or effort while putting the blame for failure on external factors like luck. This is called self-serving bias.

(ix) Perceptual Set: Previously held beliefs about objects influence an individual's perception of similar objects. This is called perceptual set. For example, a manager may have developed the general belief and attitudes that workers are lazy and shirkers, and that they want to gain whatever is possible from the organization without giving their best to it. His subsequent perceptions will be influenced by this set when he meets a group of workers. The manager tends to interpret the behaviour of workers according to his mental set.

2.6 MANAGERIAL IMPLICATION OF PERCEPTION

A manager is primarily concerned with the achievement of organisational objectives through specified behaviour of its member. Perception affects the outcome of behaviour. This is so because people act on the basis of what they see. Hence, in understanding behaviour, the managers must recognize that facts people do not perceive as meaningful usually will not influence their behaviour, whereas the things they believe to be real, even though factually incorrect or non-existence, will influence it. Thus the understanding of human perception, particularly in the organisation setting, is important in understanding and controlling the behaviour. In an organisational setting, perception is important in various activities. However, there are three major areas which require special attention so far as the perceptual accuracy is concerned. There are : interpersonal working relationship, selection of new employees, and performance appraisal.

1. **Interpersonal Working Relationship:** Organisations are intended to bring about integrated behaviour. Therefore, managers in the organisation need to know whether or not members share similar or at least compatible perceptions. If any do not, the problems of the organisation are greater and will require that efforts are made to make perceptions more compatible. Misperceptions usually lead to strained relation and may even result in open conflict among people.
2. **Selection of Employees:** Organisations typically select new employees on the basis of selection tests, interviews and reviews of the applicants' backgrounds. In many instances, much of the information is vague, and managers are subject to many of the perceptual problems when they make the selection decisions. The major areas of problems in this case are that (i) the managers' emotional state may vary from day to day causing unfair perceptions of the same applicants; and (ii) there may be strong tendencies towards logical error and stereotyping specially during initial interviews.
3. **Performance Appraisal:** The appraisal of a subordinate's performance is highly affected by the accuracy of a manager's perceptions. The major areas of concern in this context are : (i) managers may have tendencies to positively evaluate some employees because they are better liked, or are on favoured tasks, or are particularly noticeable; and (ii) because of halo effects, performance evaluation will be affected adversely.

Developing Perceptual Skills

Looking into the need for correct perception, it is imperative that people in the organisation develop skills to perceive correctly. For this purpose, various attempts can be made. Though it cannot be said with certainty that these measures will bring perfectly correct perceptions because these may have their limitations these can help in increasing the degree of correct perception. Following attempts can be made to have better perception.

1. **Perceiving Oneself Accurately:** One of the major reasons why people misperceive others is that they fail to perceive themselves accurately. Therefore, the important thing

which a person must do is that he should understand him more accurately. The more accurate he understand himself, the more accurate he can perceive others. The concept of Johri Window as discussed in Chapter 9 must be applied by people and attempts must be made to increase awareness about self. Some common practices that can be adopted in this context are mutual trust, better interpersonal interaction, open communication with others, etc.

2. **Enhancing Self-concept:** Self concept is normally a function of how successfully people accomplish the things they attempt to do. When people handle roles where they can exhibit and enhance their competence and be successful, they will develop a basic sense of self-esteem and have positive self-regard. When self-concept is developed and people have acquired a positive self-regard, they are apt to respect others more and perceive them more accurately. Maslow contends that self-actualising individuals have more accurate perceptions about themselves than those who are not self-actualising. This correct perception about oneself will tend to perceive others more correctly as discussed above.
3. **Having Positive Attitudes:** Attitudes also affect perception. Unless managers can take positive attitude to whatever situation they find themselves and see the things from a positive angle, their perceptions are likely to be distorted. Therefore, managers must be aware to their personal biases, make concerted efforts to be as unbiased as possible, make conscious efforts to get rid of any negative feelings they may have of others. All these will put managers in their proper perspective and thus enhance their perceptual skills.
4. **Being Empathic:** Empathy means being able to see a situation as it is experienced by others. This is putting your feet in another's shoes. A person can understand the problem in true perspective when he looks at it from others' point of view also. This may help the person to understand other side of the problem and hence more clear perception of the problem. This may occur only when the people can be sensitive to the needs of others and perceive situations from their point of view as well before making final decisions.
5. **Communicating More Openly:** Lot of misperception arises in the organisation because of lack of adequate communication, undue reliance on one-way communication. Therefore, managers should take steps for making communication effective so as to ensure that right message reaches at the right place at right time. This may help not only the managers to understand the organisational situations in much better perspective but employees can also look at the situations in much better way and any misperceptions may be dispelled.
6. **Avoiding Common Perceptual Distortions:** As discussed earlier, there are some factors which affect perception adversely like hallo effect, stereotyping, attribution, first impression, etc. In order to have better perception of the situation, people in the organisation should guard themselves specially against these common biases. This may be possible if they put continuous efforts and make the decisions only after careful analysis of the situation.

2.7 LEARNING

Learning is a continuous process. It occurs all the time. Learning is any relatively permanent change in behaviour that occurs as a result of experience. We can say that the changes in the behaviour indicate that learning has taken place and that learning is a change in behaviour.

The definition of learning highlights the following **characteristics** of learning :

1. Learning involves change. This may be good or bad from an organisational point of view. People can learn unfavourable behaviours as well as favourable behaviours.
2. The change must be relatively permanent. Temporary changes may be only reflexive and fail to represent any learning.
3. Learning takes place when there is a change in actions. A change in an individual's thought processes or attitudes, if accompanied by no change in behaviour, would not be learning.
4. Some form of experience is necessary for learning. This may be required directly through observation or practice or it may result from indirect experiences such as that acquired through reading.

2.8 STEPS IN LEARNING PROCESS

There are four steps for the learning to take place :

Step-1—Input: There should be a stimulus which is clearer to the learner. In work settings, unless the employee understands the messages communicated by the management, he is unlikely to be affected in the appropriate direction as intended by the communication.

Step-2—Response : Response means the act which the learner has to perform. He should be allowed and encouraged to practice the performance response.

Step-3—Motivation : There must be a motivation or drive before there can be any learning. Motivation involves interest & the attitude to learn, he is likely to learn even though he possesses adequate capacity to learn and understand what is being taught.

Step-4—*Reinforcement* : Reward or incentive refers to what satisfies a motive. If the person is not rewarded or does not perceive the likelihood of the reward in near future, he stops learning and even tends to unlearn the skills which he already possesses.

These steps in learning have a direct bearing on training in organisational settings.

Training can be effective if these steps are adhered to. Management often takes into account only stimulus and response but ignores the actual motivation of the trainee and requirement for giving a feeling of adequate forthcoming reward.

2.9 THEORIES OF LEARNING

Four theories have been offered to explain the process by which we acquire pattern of behaviour. These theories are :

(a) Classical conditioning
(b) Operant conditioning (Instrumental conditioning)
(c) Cognitive theories
(d) Social learning theory.

(a) Classical Conditioning: It is a type of conditioning where an individual responds to some stimulus that would not invariably produce such a response. Classical conditioning grew out of experiments to teach dogs to salivate in response to ringing of the bell, conducted by Russian psychologist, **Ivan Pavlov.**

A simple surgical procedure allowed Povlov to measure accurately the amount of saliva secreted by a dog. When Povlov presented the dog with a piece of meat, the dog exhibited a noticeable increase in salivation. When Pavlov withheld the presentation of meat and nearly rang a bell, the dog has no salivation. Then Pavlov proceeded to link the meat and the ringing of the bell. After repeatedly hearing the bell before getting the food, the dog began to salivate nearly at the sound of the bell even if no food was offered. In effect, the dog learned to respond, that is to salivate to the bell.

The meat was an unconditioned stimulus. It invariably caused the dog to react in a specific way. The reaction that took place whenever the unconditioned stimulus occurred, was called as unconditioned response. The bell was the artificial stimulus or conditioned stimulus. While it was originally neutral when the bell was paired with the meat (an unconditioned stimulus), it eventually produced a response when presented alone. It is the conditioned response. This describes the behaviour of the dog salivating in reaction to the bell alone.

Using these concepts, we can summarize the classical conditioning. Learning a conditioned response involve building up an association between a conditioned stimulus and an unconditioned stimulus. Using the paired stimuli, one compelling and other one neutral, the neutral one becomes a conditioned stimulus and hence takes on the properties of the unconditioned stimulus.

Classical conditioning is passive. Something happens and we behave in a specific way. It is elicited in response to a specific, identifiable event. As such, it can explain simple reflexive behaviours. But most behaviour, particularly the complex behaviour of individuals in organisation, is emitted rather than elicited. It is voluntary rather than reflexive. For example, employees choose to arrive at work on time, ask their superior for help with problems. The learning of these behaviours is better understood by looking at operant conditioning.

(b) Operant Conditioning: Operant is defined as behaviour that produces effects. Operant conditioning given by **Skinner** suggests that individuals emit responses that are rewarded and will not emit reponses that are either not rewarded or not punished. Operant conditioning is a voluntary behaviour and it is determined, maintained and controlled by its consequences. In contrast, respondent behaviour is an involuntary response to an environmental stimulus.

Operant conditioning acts on environment to produce consequences. It is basically assumed that man's behaviour is determined by environment and individuals learn by producing alteration in their environment. Operant conditioning presupposes that human beings explore their environment and act upon it. In classical conditioning the sequence of event is independent of subject's behaviour. In operant conditioning, reinforcement is given only when the correct response is made. According to **Skinner,** the consequences determine the likelihood that the given operant will be performed in the future. To change behaviour, the consequences of that behaviour must be changed.

Operant conditioning is a powerful tool for managing people in organisations. Most behaviours in organisations are learned, controlled and altered by the consequences, i.e. operant behaviours. Management can use the operant conditioning process successfully to control and influence the behaviour of the employees by manipulating its reward system. If one expects to influence behaviour, he must also be able to manipulate the consequences.

Four types of reinforcement strategies can be employed by managers to influence the behaviour of the employees :

(i) Positive Reinforcement

(ii) Negative Reinforcement

(iii) Extinction

(iv) Punishment.

(i) Positive Reinforcement: It strengthens and increases behaviour by the presentation of the desirable consequence (reward). Positive reinforcer is a reward that follows behaviour and is capable of increasing the frequency of the behaviour. Effective reinforcer must meet the two conditions :

(a) The reward should be contingent upon the rate of performance.

(b) The reward should be matched with the need or the desire of the performer.

There are two types of positive reinforcer :

(a) Primary reinforcers

(b) Secondary reinforcers

(a) Primary reinforcers such as food, water and sex are of biological importance in that they are innately satisfying and have effects which are independent of past experiences. Primary enforcers must be learned.

(b) Secondary reinforcers such as job advancement, recognition, praise and esteem result from previous association with a primary reinforcer.

In order to apply reinforcement procedure successfully, management must select reinforcers that are sufficiently powerful and durable.

(ii) Negative Reinforcement: The threat to punish rather than to give reward is called as negative reinforcement. Negative reinforcers also serve to strengthen desired behaviour responses leading to their removal or termination. Negative reinforcement is employed to increase the frequency of a response by removing a noxious consequence. People learn a negatively reinforced behaviour through an avoidance learning process. Skinner approach is primarily based on the principles of the positive reinforcement only.

(iii) Extinction: It is an effective method of controlling undesirable behaviour. It refers to non-reinforcement. It is based on the principle that if the response is not reinforced, it will eventually disappear. For example, a teacher ignores a noisy student, the student may drop the attention getting behaviour. Extinction is less painful than punishment because it does not involve the direct application of an aversive consequence. Students who perform well are praised quite often by the teachers. If they begin to slack off and turn out poor performance, the teacher may try to modify their behaviour by withholding praise. Extinction is a behavioural strategy that does not promote desirable behaviours but can reduce undesirable behaviours. If the students eventually show the good work, the teacher may again praise them (positive reinforcement) but if the poor performance is again resulting in, extinction will be re-employed.

(iv) Punishment: It is a control device employed in the organisations to discourage and reduce annoying behaviours. It can take either of the two form :

(a) These can be withdrawal or termination of a desirable or rewarding consequence.

(b) There can be an unpleasant consequence after a behaviour is performed.

Punishment reduces the response frequency; it weakens behaviour. The use of abrasive control is the most controversial method of modifying behaviour because it produces undesirable by-products.

Instrumental learning theorists believe that learning occurs through a trial and error process, with habits formed as a result of repeated rewards received for certain responses or behaviours. This model of learning applies to many situations in which consumers learn about products, services and retailers.

Critics of instrumental learning theory point out that a considerable amount of learning takes place in the absence of direct reinforcement, either positive or negative. We do not have to be arrested to know that we would obey the law. Individuals learn a great deal through a process, psychologists call modelling or observational learning (vicarious learning). They observe the behaviour of others, remember it and imitate it. Instrumental theorists argue that children learn in this way because they can envision a reward, and, therefore, imitate the behaviour that leads to it. But critics maintain that instrumentalists confuse learning and performance (behaviour). Both children and adults learn a great deal that they do not act upon. Moreover, they may learn merely for the sake of learning, not for the sake of rewards. The belief that learning is a function of thinking, of mental processes, is known as cognitive theory.

(c) ***Cognitive Theory:*** The theory was given by **Tolman.** He held that learning involves a relationship between cognitive environmental cues and expectations. He evolved and tested this theory through controlled experiments using rats in the laboratory. He showed that rats learned to run through a complicated maze towards a goal (food). It was observed that rate developed expectations at every choice point in the maze. Thus, they learned to expect that certain cognitive cues related to the choice point could ultimately lead to food. In situations where rats got the food, the relationship between the cues and expectancy was strengthened and learning look place. **Tolman** approach is also called as stimulus-stimulus approach. These experiments embarrassed the behaviouristic learning theorists. Reinforcement failed to predict rats' behaviour and it was no longer a pre-requisite to learning. One stimulus led to another stimulus rather than classical S—R or operant R—S interpretation. Indeed, the rats' behaviour was purposive. In other words, they learned a cognitive map to determine how to reach food.

Tolman made significant contributions to learning theory by forcing the behaviouristic theorists to evolve highly complex explanation of behaviour and indicating the need to include cognitions in a mediating role between the environmental stimulus and the behaviour. These theories exerted a strong effect on early human relations movement.

(d) Social Learning Theory: Individuals can also learn by observing what happens to other people and just by being told about something as well as by direct experiences. For example, what we learn comes from watching models i.e., from our parents, teachers, peers, superiors and so forth.

While social learning theory is an extension of operant conditioning, that is, it assumes that behaviour is a function of consequences. It also acknowledges the existence of observational learning and the importance of perception in learning. People respond to how they perceive and define consequences, not to the objective consequences themselves. The influence of models is central to the social learning viewpoint. Four processes have been found to determine the influence that a model will have on an individual.

These are :

(i) Attentional processes

(ii) Retention processes

(iii) Motor reproduction processes

(iv) Reinforcement processes.

(i) Attentional Processes: People only learn from a model when they recognize and pay attention to its critical features. We tend to be most influenced by models that are attractive, repeatedly available and we think are important or we see as similar to us.

(ii) Retention Processes: A model's influence will depend on how well the individual remembers the model's action, even after the model is no longer readily available.

(iii) Motor Reproduction Processes: After a person has seen a new behaviour by observing the model, the watching must be converted to doing. This process then demonstrates that the individual can perform the modelled activities.

(iv) Reinforcement Processes: Individuals will be motivated to exhibit the modelled behaviour, if positive incentives or records are provided. Behaviours, that are reinforced, will be given more attention, learned better and performed more often.

2.10 PERSONALITY

The term 'personality' has been derived from the Latin term per sona which means to 'speak through'. The Latin term denotes the masks worn by actors in ancient Greece and Rome. Common usage of the word 'personality' signifies the role which the person (actor) displays to the public.

Though the term personality is frequently used by people but there does not seem to be any consensus about its meaning. It may mean different things to different people. To some, it means a general sum of traits or characteristics of the person; to others, it refers to a unitary mode of response to life situations. Thus there prevails a great deal of controversy over the meaning of personality.

In psychology, the term 'personality' is interpreted in different ways by different theorists. For example, Carl Rogers views personality in terms of self, an organized, permanent, subjectively perceived entity which is at the very heart of all our experiences. Gordon Allport defines personality as what an individual really is, as an internal 'something' that guides and directs all human activities. Still another conception is that of Freud, who describes the structure of personality as composed of three elements-the id, ego, and super ego.

According to Gordon Allport, "Personality is the dynamic organization within the individual of those psychological systems that determine his unique adjustment to his environment" In the words of Floyd L. Ruch, "Personality includes external appearance and behaviour, inner awareness of self as a permanent organizing force and the particular pattern or organization of measurable traits, both inner and outer"

A comprehensive definition of personality is given by Fred Luthans. In his words, personality means how a person affects others and how he understands and views himself as well as the pattern of inner and outer measurable traits, and the person-situation interaction. How a person affects others depends upon his physical appearance (such as height, weight, facial features, colour, etc.) and behaviour (such as courteous, friendly, expressive, cooperative, etc.). Thus, personality represents the 'whole person' concept. It includes perception, learning, motivation and more.

DETERMINANTS OF PERSONALITY

The factors which shape the personality of an individual are discussed as under:

1. Biological Factors

(a) ***Heredity:*** It means the transmission of the qualities from ancestor to descendant through a mechanism lying primarily in the chromosomes of the germ cells. Physical stature, facial attractiveness, sex, temperament, muscle composition, reflexes, etc. are inherited from one's parents. However, the importance of heredity varies from one personality trait to another. For example, heredity is generally more important in determining a person's temperament than his values and ideals.

(b) ***Brain:*** There is a general feeling that brain plays an important role in the development of one's personality. However, no conclusive proof is available so far about the nature of relationship between the brain and personality.

(c) ***Physical features:*** An individual's external appearance may have a i tremendous effect on his personality. Some people give relatively higher weightage to the physical features of an individual while defining his personality. Such factors include height, weight, colour, facial features, etc. of the individual. Good physical appearance is an asset for the job of a sales person and public relations.

2. Family and Social Factors

The development of individual's personality is also influenced by his " family and other social groups. The infant acquires those behaviour patterns that are customary and acceptable to the standards of the family and the community where the family lives. The status of the family in the society influences individual's perception about self, others, work, money, etc.

Family and social factors shape a person's personality through the processes of socialisation and identification. Socialisation is a process by which an infant acquires, from the enormously wide range of behavioural potentialities that are open to him at birth, those behaviour patterns that are customary and acceptable to the family and social groups. Socialisation process starts with initial contact between mother and her new infant. Later on, other members of the family and social groups influence the socialisation process.

The identification process occurs when a person tries to identify himself with some person whom he feels ideal in family. Generally a child in the family tries to behave like his father or mother. The identification process can be examined from three different perspectives. First, identification can be viewed as the similarity of behaviour (including feelings and attitudes) between the child and the model. Second, identification can be looked as the child's motives or desires to be like the model. Third, it can be viewed as the process through which the child actually takes on the attributes of the model.

3. Situational Factors

An individual's personality may change in different situations. The demands of different situations may call for different aspects of one's personality. Therefore, we should not look at the personality factor in isolation. Although certain generalisations can be made about personality, there exist significant individual differences which are further influenced by situational factors.

The relationship of the above factors affects the formation and development of personality. Physiological inheritance is entirely an internal contribution. Group and the culture are the early environmental factors that influence later behaviour. Family and the social setting during early stages of education are the important factors which influence the initial formation of personality. Whatever the child learns lasts for life time. Later in life, it is the peer groups of primary affiliations at work, social activities, etc. which shape the personality of an individual.

2.11 PERSONALITY THEORIES

Personality theories can be grouped under the following five categories :

(a) Trait theory

(b) Freud theory

(c) Adler and Jung theories

(d) Social learning theories

(e) Holistic theories

(a)Trait Theory: A personality trait can be defined as "an enduring attribute of a person that appears constantly in a variety of situations."

(i) Individual can be described in terms of construction of traits such as affiliation, achievement, anxiety, aggression and dependency.

(ii) Trait distinguishes one personality from another.

(iii) The traits and the amount of each trait that a person has is assumed to be stable fairly and the differences in personality and behaviour between two individuals is assumed to be the result of the differences in the amount of each that each person has.

Thousands of words in English language refer to the characteristics of behaviour of traits. But the fundamental question is how to reduce them to small number of meaningful traits. One technique is the factor analysis. It is a complex statistical technique for reducing large number of personality traits into small number of independent traits. The technique has the advantage of reducing several hundred test responses. **Norman** provided the different descriptive objective pairs of words for the same kind to trait

(b) Freud Theory: Freud contributed significantly towards the understanding of human behaviour through his concept of unconsciousness. According to Freud, human mind is composed of three elements (i) the preconscious (ii) the conscious and (iii) the unconscious. The items in the mind that can be recognized only through Freud association method are preconscious. The conscious element is concerned with thoughts, feelings, beliefs and desires that we can learn about ourselves through intro-inspection. The unconscious is basically concerned with ideas and wishes that can not be learned through intro-inspection but can be determined from hypnotism, dreams and Freudian Therapecific Techniques. According to Freud, the conscious is guided by a reasoned reality principle and the unconscious is guided by the famous hedonist principle of pleasure. Freud developed an organisation of personality consisting of three structures within the human mind—*the id, the ego* and *the super ego.* These parts of the mind are primarily responsible for originating human actions and reactions and modifications.

Id *:* Id is the original and the most basic system of human personality. It consists of everything psychologically that is inherited and present at the time of the birth. At the base of the Freudian theory lies the id that is primitive, instinctual and governed by the principles of greed and pleasure. Id represents a store house of all instincts, containing in its dark depths all wishes, desires and unconsciously direct and determine our behaviour. Id is largely childish, irrational, never satisfied, demanding and destructive of others. Id is the foundation upon which all other parts of the personality are erected.

Ego : As an individual learns to separate the unreality from reality in childhood, the ego develops. The ego is the reality oriented part in thinking, it is largely practical and works in an executive capacity. Ego is rational and logical and in essence it is the conscious mediator between the realities of the world and the id's demand. It constantly works to keep a healthy psychological balance between id's impulsive demands and super ego's restrictive guidance. Ego regulates and integrates the inner motives and conflicting demands, defends the person by using defence mechanisms and masters the person's goals. The ego develops by creating an effective perceptual mechanism that enables a person to adjust to the reality principle viz. tolerance of tension, expectation of punishment, awareness of things and associated inhibitions of actions. The most important characteristics of ego is that it has the ability to distinguish between mental images and actual sources of tension release, and it responds to the real sources of tension reduction. If the ego succeeds, the individual is content, otherwise he will be dissatisfied and have a mental stress, ambivalence and burn out.

Super ego: It represents noblest thoughts, ideals, feelings that are acquired by a person from his parents, teachers, friends, religion, organisation and colleagues etc. As a child grows and absorbs parental and cultural attitudes and values, he develops a super ego. It is also labelled as *'ego-ideal'* that tells the individual what is acceptable. The primary concern of super ego is to determine whether the action proposed by ego is the right or wrong so that the individual acts in accordance with the values and standards of the society. If people violate the prohibitions of super ego, they may feel guilty.

In Freudian theory of personality, the instinctual drives of id and super ego constantly battle each other and seek to breakout of bonds of reason—the ego. As a person becomes torn between this conflict, a friction develops and results in anxiety, an ominous feeling that all is not well. Anxiety creates tension and such as a person resorts to defensive mechanism in order to reduce tension.

(c) Adler And Jung Theory: **Adler** emphasized the thrust for superiority as a drive which motivates the individual. He developed the concepts of compensation and the inferiority complex based on the drive for power. Individuals, who are weak in one area of work tend to excel in another area of work, Alder stressed social relationships instead of innate or biological factors. This as well as his stress on individual uniqueness, style of life and the creative self bring him close to modern theorists who consider themselves as psychoanalytic in approach.

Jung developed analytical psychology stressing the unconscious aspect of psychoanalysis. He postulated the collective unconsciousness. According to him, personality is based on predisposing patterns borrowed by the individual from his ancestors. His collective unconscious extends back through previous generations to the dawn of history. It is his notion of heredity transference of acquired features which is the least acceptable to modern theorists. Despite in stress in the past, Jung asserted that the operation of an individual's personality is as much future oriented as rooted in the past. To the extent he asserted that the individual was not bound to the past but could effectively build his future as a dynamic optimist.

(d) Social learning theory: The theory considers the situation as an important determinant of behaviour as against trait theories which assume that personality is characterized by the enduring traits of an individual. According to this theory, an individual's action in a given situation, individual's appraisal of the situation and post reinforcement to behaviour are somewhat similar situations. When the situation they encounter are relatively stable, individuals behaviour will be more or less consistent.

The main focus of the learning approach is on the patterns of behaviour the individual learns in coping with environment. Some behaviour patterns are learned or acquired through direct experience. Responses can also be acquired or learned without direct reinforcement. Social learning theorists believe that reinforcement is not necessary for learning but they accept the view that reinforcement facilitates learning by focussing attention. According to social learning school, much of the human learning is vicarious or observational.

Reinforcement, though not necessary for learning, is very crucial for the performance of learned behaviour. The assumption of this theory is that people behave in the ways likely to produce reinforcement. An individual's repertoire of learned behaviours is extensive; the particular action chosen for specific situation depends upon the expected outcome. The reinforcement that controls the expression of learned behaviour may be:

(i) Direct: Refers to the social approval or disapproval or alleviation of aversive conditions and other tangible rewards.

(ii) Vicarious: Refers to observation of some one else receiving reward or punishment for similar behaviour.

(iii) Self-administered: Refers to evaluation of one's own performance with self praise or reproach.

Of all these, self administered reinforcement theory plays a vital role in social learning theory.

(e) Holistic Theories: **Kolasa** has grouped several theorists under a common title—*Holistic theorists.* They include holistic, organismic and field theorists who stress on the totality and interrelatedness of all kinds of human behaviour. In spite of the common aspect of emphases on the individual as a whole, they differ in many ways.

Maslow has focused on the concept of needs derived from the positive and optimistic dimensions of the individual's total functioning. He has structured several levels of needs *i.e.* the hierarchy of needs. His concept of self actualization need is of great significance. His concept of hierarchy of needs has been greatly relied upon to understand human behaviour in organisational settings.

Rogers visualizes personality in terms of the organism (or of the whole individual) functioning in a phenomenal field (or the entire experience). The patterns of perceptions in this field provide the basis for the self which seeks to become consistent with itself and its environment. If this is not possible for any reason, the organism is exposed to threats. Based on his approach, a new school of thought, called Phenomenology, has developed. This viewpoint assumes that the reality for the individual consists of what he perceives in his field or experiences instead of things as they factually are.

Herzberg approach considers man in his two aspects. One aspect of the man is 'Adam' or the animal nature which aims to avoid the pain of adjustment to the environment, while the other aspect is Abraham, which motivates him to achieve and add to his existence. The Adam aspect of man possesses hygiene needs which are satiated through salary, working conditions and fringe benefits. The Abraham aspect of man involves needs, which are motivators, including those related to psychological growth of the individual in work settings, job enlargement, etc.

Lewin (field theorists), interprets Lumen behaviours and depicts the individual's personality in a perceptual field in physical units. The field has been considered on the psychological life space of the individual with forces attracting or diverting him in respect of a goal.

Festinger has postulated cognitive dissonance as a motivating condition in the individual. As soon as two cognitions of an individual are inconsistent with each other, he tends to change one of them to adhere to the other, minimising the dissonance.

Personality and Behaviour

Each man's personality reveals itself in the way he works with his superior, his subordinates, and other people. As a result, when the incumbent on a job changes, everyone has to adjust to a whole series of changes in the way work is accomplished. The result is that the organization functions differently from the way the designers of the structure envisioned, and what organization really is reflects the personality of those who hold key jobs. This affects the individual performance, and consequently organisational performance. Some of the important personality factors that determine what kind of performance will be achieved or what kind of behaviour is exhibited at work are self concept and self esteem, need patterns, machiavellianism, locus of control, tolerance for ambiguity, type A and B personalities, introversion-extroversion, and work-ethic orientation.

1. **Self Concept and Self Esteem:** Self concept is the way individuals define themselves as to who they are and derive their sense of identity. Self esteem denotes the extent to which they consistently regard themselves as capable, successful, important, and worthy individuals. Self esteem is an important personality factor that determines how managers perceive themselves and their role in the organization. People with high self esteem tend to take on more challenging assigments and contribute significantly to the organisational effectiveness if the organisation rewards them suitably for their contributions.
2. **Need Patterns:** According to the personality characteristics, there are four types of needs that people have at work. These are needs for achievement, affiliation, autonomy, and dominance. Those who have high need for achievement engage themselves proactively in work behaviour in order to feel proud about their achievements and successes; those

having high need for autonomy like to work in an environment with less close supervision; and those with high need for dominance are very effective in an environment where they can actively enforce their legitimate authority.

3. **Machiavellianism:** Machiavellianism refers to manipulation of others as a primary way of achieving one's goals. Mach scale measures the extent to which an individual tends to be machiavellian. People with high score on mach scale, tend to be cool, logical in assessing the system around them, willing to twist and turn facts to influence others, and try to gain control of people, events, and situations by manipulating the system to their advantage.
4. **Locus of Control:** Locus of control means whether people believe that they are in control of events, or events control them. Those who have internal locus of control believe that they control and shape the course of events in their lives; those who have external locus of control tend to believe that events occur purely by chance or because of factors beyond their own control. Former category of people seek opportunities for advancement, and rely more on their abilities and judgement at work; while latter category of people remain mostly inactive and allow the events occur on their own.
5. **Tolerance for Ambiguity:** Based on personality characteristics, some people can tolerate high level of ambiguity without experiencing undue stress and still function effectively while people who have a low tolerance for ambiguity may be effective in structured work setting but it is almost impossible to operate effectively when things are rapidly changing and much information about the future turn of events is not available. Generally managers have to work in an environment full of uncertainty because of rapid change; therefore, they have to develop high level of tolerance for ambiguity.
6. **Type A and B:** Personality has been grouped into two categories denoted by alphabets A and B. Type A people always feel a sense of time urgency, are highly achievement-oriented, exhibit a competitive drive, and are impatient when their work is slowed down for any reason. Such people are more prone to heart attack. On the other hand, type B people are easy-going, do not have urgency for time and do not experience the competitive drive.
7. **Introversion and Extroversion:** Introversion is the tendency in individuals which directs them to turn inward and experience and process feelings, thoughts and ideas within themselves. Extroversion refers to the tendency in individuals to turn outward of themselves searching for external stimuli with which they can interact. Introverts are quiet, reflective and intellectual people who prefer to interact with a small intimate circle of friends. They are more likely to be successful when they can work on highly abstract ideas such as research and development in a relatively quiet atmosphere. Extroverts, on the other hand, are sociable, lively, gregarious, and seek outward interaction. They are likely to be more successful working in the sales activities, publicity department, personal relations unit, and so on where they can interact face to face with others.

8. **Work-ethic Orientation:** People may have different work-ethic orientation. The extremely work-ethic oriented people get greatly involved in the job and live up to being described as living, eating and breathing the job. For such people, work becomes the only consideration of satisfaction and they have very little outside interests. On the other hand, people with low work-ethic orientation try to do the minimum that is necessary to get without being fired on the job. For effective organisations, people with high work-ethic orientation are necessary as compared to extremely high or low work-ethic orientation because the extremely high work-ethic oriented people will burn their energy too quickly creating lot of health problems thus affecting long-term organisational effectiveness adversely, while people with low work-ethic organisational effectiveness adversely, while people with low work-ethic orientation will not be able to achieve anything meaningful for the organisation.

Based on the above discussion, some conclusions can be drawn about the desirable personality characteristics for effective managers. Apart from possessing the necessary managerial skills and abilities, managers need to have high level of self concept, high level of tolerance for ambiguity. A type of personality, good mix of needs for achievement, affiliation and power, internal locus of control, are relatively extroverts, and have high work-ethic orientation.

2.13 UNIT EXERCISES

Short Answers

Q1. Define personality.

Q2. How does learning differ from maturation?

Q3. Explain the concept of individual beheviour?

Q4. What is cognitive learning?

Q5. "Learning leads to change in human behavior." Comment

Long Answers

Q1. Define personality. What are the major factors which shape the personality of an individual.

Q2. What do you understand by personality traits? Explain by giving examples

Q3. How does learning differ from maturation? Discuss the factors, which affect learning.

Q4. "Learning theory can be used to explain behaviour and to control behaviour." Explain the validity of the statement.

Q5. Explain the various theories of personality. Which of them is convincing to you and why?

CHAPTER 3

Individual's Role in Society

3.0 INTRODUCTION

In general every individual plays some role in society. It may happen that some individual is very important to the society while other one is less important in one or many terms. To a great extent individual's role in society depends on the individual's attitude also.

Attitudes are a major factor affecting behaviour. They influence the perception of objects and people, exposure to and comprehension of information, choice of friends, co-workers and so on. The importance of attitudes in understanding psychological phenomenon was given formal recognition early in the history of social psychology. From the time of the concept's entry into the language of psychology until now, interest in attitudes has been strong and growing. However, over the years attitudes have been studied with differing emphases and methods. For example, between the 1920s and up to World War II the attention of attitude researchers was directed principally towards definitional issues and attitude measurement. In addition, there were studies concerned with relationship of attitudes to some social variables. World War II brought with it a growing concern about the place of the attitude concept in understanding prejudice, particularly anti-Semitism. This period also brought the measurement of attitudes and opinions concerning various facts of soldiering and war. After the war, the subject of attitudes was taken up by academicians, particularly in the context of attitude change. Till now, the researchers have developed a loosely structured theoretical framework formulating the psychological processes underlyings attitude change and the direct application of the study of attitudes to contemporary social problems.

3.1 OBJECTIVES

Main objectives of the study of this unit is to:

- To know what exactly is the role of an individual in society
- To know the attitude of an individual

3.2 NATURE OF INDIVIDUAL DIFFERENCES

Individual differences may be reflected in individual's different types of behaviour – conformity, differences in rate of learning and development, interaction with people having different types of personality characteristics, productivity and any such type of behaviour. Such differences range along a continuum from desirable to undesirable. With respect to work, individuals differ in the following respects :

1. People differ in the importance they attach to intrinsic rewards to the job. People with different psychological make-ups respond differently to challenging versus routine jobs. Some people prefer challenging jobs that afford the expression of the scope for higher abilities. As against this, there may be people who prefer job security and routine operations in their jobs. Thus, different people attach different degrees of importance to rewards and kinds of job they would like to perform.

2. People differ in the type of compensation plan they want or desire. Some people like to work under time-wage system while others prefer to work under piece-wage system or incentive system involving compensation based on productivity.
3. People differ in the style of supervision. Some people prefer to provide necessary imputs for important decisions and like to be their own boss to the maximum extent. On the other hand, some people may not like such working and may depend mostly on others for decision – making. Similarly, people respond differently to different styles of leadership and supervision. Some may prefer to work under autocratic style while others work more effectively under democratic or laissez-faire style.
4. People differ in their preferred schedules of work hour. Some people awake early in the morning, start their working and go early in the bed. Some people do exactly opposite of this.
5. People differ in their tolerance for stress and ambiguity. Some people do better in stressing and ambugious situations as such situations may bring out their best and they feel the situations as challenging. Others may not bear such stresses for long.

3.3 CAUSE OF INDIVIDUAL DIFFERENCES

The variability in behaviour is the consequence of a combination of different factors. All these factors affect the human behaviour in one way or the other. Various such factors can be presented in the following figure :

Individual Differences

Individual variables

1. Physiological variables
   Age
   Sex
   Physiological Characteristics
   Heredity
2. Psychological variables
   Intelligence
   Learning
   Personality
   Attitudes
   Motivation
3. Socio-cultural variables
   Value systems
   Cultural background

Situational variables

1. Organisational variables
   Type of organisation
   Type of supervision
   Training
   Type of incentives
   Social environment at work place
2. Physical and job variables
   Methods of work
   Design of work
   Condition of work equipment
   Physical work environment

The behaviour is a result of total effects of several variables – individual and situational. The difference in the behaviour of two individuals at a given moment of time can be interpreted in the context of these two factors. If one can measure both the behaviour and specific variables that are associated with it, then it would be possible to quantify the effect of several variables as related to the behaviour. The quantification of such variables may lead to take positive actions so that desirable behaviour results. For example, if situational variables have significant impact on the behaviour, it may be possible to modify these variables in order to create a situation that is conducive to more acceptable behaviour. Similarly, many of the individual factors may be modified to achieve more desirable behaviour in a given situation.

No doubt, psychologists agree that both these factors are important. However, a disagreement revolves around the comparative importance of each of them. Thus to understand the complexity of human behaviour and to develop an appropriate and meaningful model, both the factors should be taken into account. Thus the human behaviour model should show these two variables as integrating components rather than as separate entities.

Individual Variables

An individual is affected by the physiological, psychological and sociocultural variables. Therefore, in order to identify the individual differences, these three variables must be identified.

(i) ***Physiological variables:*** The human being possesses certain biological endowments which are vital to his behaviour. Various physiological characteristics of heredity, sensory organs, physical build-up, nervous system determine the outcome of his behaviour. However, a person is not merely a conglomeration of organs, nerves, bones,muscles, and brain but a much more comples. As such, these factors are essential to his maintenance and adjustment but play a relatively minor role in shaping his behaviour.

(ii) ***Psychological variables:*** Psychological factors are more important in shaping the behaviour of a person. From the moment of birth, psychological processes – perception, learning, and motivation – become integral part. These processes do not operate as isolated, separate entities any more than do the biological mechanisms of the body. Various psychological processes, taken as a whole, are included in the concept of personality and this plays a very important role in shaping human behaviour.

(iii) ***Socio-cultural variables:*** Socio-cultural variables affect human behaviour as he learns many behaviours from his society and cultural institutions. Since individuals may come from different society and cultural background, they may reflect different types of behaviours.

All these variables – physiological, psychological, socio-cultural-taken together will make a particular individual unique and distinct as compared to others and, therefore, his behaviour is likely to be different than others.

Situational Variables

Besides individual variables, situational variables also affect human behaviour. In an organisation context, such variables may be various types of organisational practices like nature of organisation, supervision, training, incentives, and social environment at work place; or physical and job variables like methods of work, design of work, condition of work, equipment, and physical environment of work. These variables may act either as facilitating factors or restraining factors and consequently an individual is likely to depict a behaviour accordingly. The situational variables may be important as the same individual is likely to behave differently in different situations.

3.4 IMPLICATIONS OF INDIVIDUAL DIFFERENCES

The understanding of variation in human beings that causes each individual different from every other and gives rise to the variation in the performance at the work-place is important from managerial point of view. Individual differences mean that management can achieve the desired behaviour from individuals by treating them differently. In fact, it is almost impossible to develop one theory about the nature of man, fit every one into it, and develop an approach to management which will ensure absolute results at all times with all people. Thus management must analyse how differences in individuals can be used in most appropriate manner. Schein has visualised this approach as such. 'Perhaps the most important implication is that the successful manager must be a good diagnostician and must value a spirit of inquiry. If the attributes and motives of the people under him are so variable, he must have the sensitivity and diagnostic ability to be able to sense and appreciate the differences. Second, rather than regard to the existence of differences as a painful truth to be wished away, he must also learn to value the diagnostic process which reveals differences. Finally, he must have the personal flexibility and the range of skills necessary to vary his own behaviour. If the needs and motives of his subordinates are different, they must be treated differently.

Individual differences have great importance in the organisations because different individuals with different qualities and capacities are required to perform various fuctions. If the work is to be the best in quality and quantity, it is essential that each operation is performed by the individuals best qualified to perform it. The understanding of individual differences not only solves the problem of assignment of activities to them but also helps in taking best out of them by motivating and leading them accordingly.

Considering the differences among people at work, Porter and Lawler have visualised the future organisation to be highly individualised. They view that organisations in future will accept a wide variety of management, structures and technologies so as to accommodate the individual differences because a single organisation is likely to offer variety of jobs to suit different individuals. In a research study in Texas Instrument it was observed that a particular type of person likes a particular type of management practices which is as follows :

(i) Tribalistic : People who prefer directive, strong leadership from their boss

(ii) Ego-centric : People who desire to work alone in their own entrepreneurial style

(iii) Socio-centric : People who seek social relationship that their job provides

(iv) Existential : People who strive for growth and self-fulfilment needs especially through their work.

Similarly, people with different personality characteristics are suitable for different jobs. Thus, understanding individual differences may provide clue to management to design organisation structure, adopt leadership and motivation techniques and develop control systems so as to serve the needs of different individuals adequately.

3.5 MODELS OF MAN

Individual differences, as discussed earlier, cause difference in behaviour. In dealing with human beings, either understanding or influencing their behaviour, management makes some assumptions about them consciously or unconsciously. Managerial effectiveness in dealing with people will depend on the degree to which its assumptions fit the actual situations. Historically, the assumptions about people in the organisations have largely reflected philosophical positions on the nature of man and have served as the justification for the particular organisation. Whole of managerial actions have depended on such assumptions over period of time. However, such assumptions have shown great variations and unanimity has eluded. These have given many models of man in terms of basic nature, his behaviour and consequently different managerial strategies in dealing with him. Schein has identified four models of man : rational-economic man, social man, self-actualising man, and complex man. These models are roughly in order of their historical appearance. To this may be added one more identified by Whyte, that is, organisation man. This model can be fitted very well in between social man and self-actualising man. A brief description of these models is presented below.

Rational-Economic Man

The rational-economic man model is the oldest one. It is based on the doctrine of maximising of self-interest by man. There are two elements in this maximisation. First, man is able to calculate the cost of his efforts for getting any inducement. Similarly, he can also calculate the value of the inducement which he receives from his efforts. Second, he is able to evaluate all the alternatives as well as he is able to know all the alternatives available. Thus he maximises his need satisfaction in terms of marginal efforts being equal to marginal inducement for work. Thus following assumptions can be made about rational-economic man in respect of his behaviour :

1. Man is primarily motivated by economic incentives and he is willing to do things which maximise his economic returns.
2. The feelings of the man are essentially irrational and must be controlled in order to achieve rationality and self-interest.
3. In the context of organisation individual relationship, the organisation controls the economic incentives and man remains mostly passive.
4. Since man's feelings will interfere his rationality, the organisation can be designed in such a way that it controls his feelings and consequently avoids unpredictability in his behaviour.

The rational-economic model, though comes primarily from economist, psychologists have studied this model for predicting human behaviour. For example, McGregor's assumptions of Theory

X reflect this model wherein he has suggested that managers may have certain assumptions about human behaviour and design their activities accordingly to control human beings. A detailed description of these assumptions has been given in Chapter 8.

The kinds of assumptions a manager makes about people will greatly determine the actions he takes in motivating and controlling people. In simple rational-economic model, people can be induced to produce more by providing economic incentives. This works very simply, that is, people are engaged by the organisation for productive purpose. It will continue to give them incentives till it is receiving matching contributions from them. Beyond that, the organisation is not responsible. For example, the piece-rate system is based directly on this assumption. The people will produce more to get more money. By more production, both organisation and people are happy and this can go on regular basis. In this case, there is no conflict between people and organisation because both are satisfying their needs simultaneously through the in-built mechanism of the organisation-people relationship.

This model is based on classical organisation theory. As will be noticed in Chapter 18, the classical models of designing organisation structures and processes have various shortcomings and do not suit the present-day organisations. The economic incentives can work till man is not reasonably satisfied by the need of money. Though money is such a factor that its need can never be satisfied because it may purchase many things through which people may satisfy their other needs; within organisational context, the role of money is to maintain the people in the organisation and beyond tat it is not able to provide incentives to people, as will be seen later. Therefore, whole assumptions of rational economic model of man are not sufficient for understanding and predicting his behaviour.

Social Man

Social man concept is based on the doctrine that man being part of the society, is influenced by social forces and seeks satisfaction of those needs which are in tune with maintaining his social relationships. This is the basic crux of human relations approach in management. The following assumptions can be made about social man :

1. Man is basically motivated by his social needs and all his efforts are directed to get this satisfaction by maintaining relationship with others.
2. Man is more responsive to group pressure and sanction rather than the control and pressure put by management in the organisation because he values social relationship higher than his economic motives which are directly controlled by management.
3. He will obey and comply management's order so long as these are in conformity with satisfaction of his social needs.
4. As a result of industrialisation, specialisation, and rationalisation, the work has become meaningless which develops more alienation, frustration, and conflict. Therefore, management should change and organise work in such a way that it provides more belongingness not only in terms of interpersonal and group relationships, but also man's relationship with his job.

Social man concept is the invention of many researches which behavioural scientists have carried out from time to time beginning from famous Hawthorne Experiments, as discussed in the previous chapter.

The type of managerial strategy that can be applied in the case of social man is quite different as compared to rational economic man. This has many implications for management. First, the manager should not concentrate only on the output achieved by the people but he should also focus his attention on people themselves. Thus a drastic change in various styles is required. Second, instead of being concerned with motivating and controlling people with economic incentives, the manager should be concerned with people's feelings about their belongingness. This requires a change in the organisation structure based on specialisation and division of labour to a more democratic and free organisation structure. Third, since groups are basis of organisation and individual interaction, man's behaviour should be analysed and motivated in terms of groups and not on individual basis. Fourth, instead of being creator of work and controller of behaviour, the manager should act as facilitator and sympathetic supporter. Thus whole system is directed towards people.

Organisation Man

Organisation man is an extension of social man. William Whyte, who has given the concept of 'organisation man', believes that the value of loyalty to the organisation and co-operation with fellow workers is important for man. A man who believes and acts in this way is, according to him, an organisation man. This concept is based on the idea of sacrificing individuality for the sake of the group and the organisation. Though this idea was earlier suggested by Henry Fayol when he suggested the subordination of individual interest to the general interest, he did not emphasis the concept of social ethic in behaviour. Whyte suggests that social ethic guides organisation man which is based on three major propositions :

1. The group is the source of creativity. The individual by himself is isolated and meaningless; only when he collaborates with others does he create. Individual helps to produce a whole that is greater that the sum of its parts.
2. Belongingness is the ultimate need of the individual. There should be no conflicts between man and society because what is normally considered conflict is merely misunderstanding and breakdown in communication.
3. The science achieves the goal of belongingness. By applying the methods of science, the obstacles to consensus can be eliminated and an equilibrium can be created where society's needs and the needs of the individual are one and the same.

Organisation man emphasises that there is no conflict between organisation and individual. Even if there is any, it can be overcome by sacrificing the individual interest in favour of organisational interest. However, assumption behind this proposition is that the organisation will take care of individual interest. Its implication is that management will design its various actions which will satisfy the people. People will not see their interest differently as the organisation is there to take care of their interest.

Self-actualising Man

Self-actualising man concept is a further extension of social man and organisation man models. The assumption of social man concept about the nature of work that it has become meaningless because of high degree of division of labour and specialisation is true. But the self-acutualising man concept differs in suggesting the way through which man overcomes the limitations of work. As against the formation of social groups as the basis for satisfaction, self-actualising man assumes that man's inherent need is to use his capabilities and skills in such a way that he should feel develop a sense of creating certain things. Thus there is a conflict between self-actualising man and formal organisation because it does not allow him to satisfy his self-actualising needs. The managers normally take following assumptions about self-actualising man :

1. The various needs of man can be put in hierarchy. For example, Maslow has put various needs in a hierarchy-physiological, safety, belongingness, esteem, and self-actualising. Any unsatisfied need is a motivating factor for man. Since he attempts to satisfy his needs according to this hierarchy, he takes self-actualisation as his ultimate goal as most of his needs are satisfied reasonably in that order. Thus he tries to make a sense and meaning in his work.
2. Man moves from immaturity to maturity in self-actualising himself. In this process, there will be various changes in his behaviour.
3. Man is primarily self-motivated and self-controlled. Therefore any incentives and control imposed externally will not threaten him and result in less mature adjustment.
4. There is often a conflict between formal organisation designed on traditional thinking and self-actualising man because the organisation is based on the assumptions of immature personality. However, if the man is left free, he will try to put in his maximum efforts.

These assumptions are mostly based on McGregor's Theory Y and Argyris's immaturity-maturity theory, though McGregor's Theory Y goes beyond these assumptions. The type of managerial actions that will be required for satisfying self-actualising man will be those suitable for social man with some additional features. For example, groups may be only one source of satisfaction of self-actualising man. People in the organisation will require more autonomy, incentives based on intrinsic factors, and participation throughout the organisational processes. These features create a normal involvement on the part of people to release a greater potential for commitment to organisational goals and creative efforts in the pursuit of those goals.

Complex Man

The various models of man, discussed above, are simplistic assumptions of people and their behaviour. They assume that man will behave according to certain set pattern. If the condition for behaviour is given, the behaviour of man can be understood and predicted depending upon the assumptions made. However, researches have demonstrated that it is not so. First, there are many complex variables which determine human behaviour. These variables themselves are quite unpredicatable. Secondly, even if cause-effect relationship is established between variables and behaviour, it is not necessary that everyone will behave accordingly because of individual differences, as discussed earlier. Thus human being is quite complex and our assumption about predictability of human behaviour specified in the beginning of this chapter that it is not possible to predict human behaviour completely and accurately holds good. Following assumptions can be made about complex man :

1. Man is motivated by complex variables. No doubt, his needs can be arranged in certain hierarchy but this hierarchy cannot be universal. There can be many overlapping needs and the degree to which man will seek satisfaction to various needs. Thus it is not necessary that man will try for self-actualisation.
2. Man is capable of learning many motives out of interaction with the organisation. Thus his total need pattern will be determined by his initial needs as well as needs developed by organisational contacts.
3. There are variations among people in the same organisation. Such variations may be in terms of their need pattern, their behaviour, and consequently the need for control and direction.
4. The understanding of human needs may not be the final step in understanding human behaviour because of the absence of a direct cause-effect relationship between need and behavoiur. For example, a person may behave differently as compared to another person having same set of needs.
5. Man can behave diversely if we take into account his need pattern, lack of direct cause effect relationship between need and behavoiur and individual differences. Thus man can respond to various managerial actions but the way of reaction is not uniform. This will depend upon his motives and abilities, nature of task, and nature of incentives – financial and non-financial.

Complex man presents the real picture of human behaviour. This has replaced the simplistic model of man. The manager can take clue for managerial actions in two ways : First, he must realise that there is no action which can be utilised successfully in all the situations. This is the basic theme of contingency approach which is fast developing in organisational analysis. This puts emphasis on the manager being good diagnostician and must value the spirit of enquiry. Second, he should differentiate people on the basis of various factors and must adopt actions which may affect different people. It means he can not simply design a system and assume that it will work. Rather, he must review it in terms of its effectiveness by taking feedback from various sources. This will enable him to find out whether he is proceeding correctly of otherwise. A suitable action, then, can be taken before the situation goes out of control.

Most behaviour in the organisation can be understood by taking assumptions of complex man. Though this model is quite complex, it indicates the real situation and emphasises that human behaviour is not as simple as is assumed. The whole chapters of this part will be directed for understanding this complex behaviour. However, before that, it is desirable to identify what are the forces which put limits on rationality because various models of man reject the assumption of rational-economic man. This rejection is in terms of total behaviour of human being.

3.6 CONCEPT OF ATTITUDES

It is necessary to be precise in defining attitudes, because the variety of published definitions and descriptions is almost endless. Like any other cocept, attitudes may also be defined in two ways-conceptual and operational. Even there is quite a difference in the conceptual definition of the term attitude, and divergent points of view regarding the concept of attitude have developed. The researchers on attitudes tend to define the term on two major aspects : set and readiness, and effect and evaluation.

When the term attitude first entered in the field of social phenomenon, it was natural to conceive of attitude as a tendency, set, or readiness to respond to some social object. For the first time, Allport noted that all the definitions of attitude which he had observed contained the words 'readiness', 'set' (tendency to respond), or 'disposition to act'. Even Allport has used these terms is defining attitude. He defines attidude as a 'mental and neural state of readiness, organized through experience, exerting a directive or dynamic influence upon the individual's response to all objects and situations with which it is related. From this point of view, attitude implies a heightened responsiveness to certain stimuli.

Many researchers have defined attitude in terms of effect and evaluation. For example, Krech and Crutchfield define attitude as an 'enduring organisation of motivational, emotional, perceptual, and cognitive processes with respect to some aspect of the individual's world. Thus attitudes are beliefs imbued with emotional and motivational properties and are expressed in a person's favourability towards an object. The evaluative nature of attitudes is also emphasized by Katz and Scotland when they define attitude as 'a tendency or predisposition to evaluate an object or symbol of that object in a certain way. Evaluation consists of attributing goodness-badness or desirable-undesirable qualities to an object.

Apart from conceptual approach, there is operational approach in defining the term attitude. The concept of attitude is operationalised in a number of ways but in most cases, studies rely on some kind of questionnaire to measure attitudes. Taking attitudes from this point of view, only evaluative aspect of attitudes has been taken into account. For example, Fishbein has noted that most measures of attitudes tap an underlying dimension of favourability-unfavourability and, therefore, attitudes should be regarded as synonymous with evaluating meaning. Thus in practice, 'the term attitude often is used in a generic sense to any reports of what people think or feel or the ways in which they intend to act.

Attitude, Opinion and Belief

There are certain other terms, such as opinion and belief, which are used quite closely with attitudes. However, there is a basic difference in these terms. An opinion is generally the expression of one's judgement of a particular set of facts, an evaluation of the circumstances presented to him. Thurstone defines opinions as expressions of attitudes. However, Kolasa observes that 'an opinion is response to a specifically limited stimulus, but the response is certainly influenced by the predisposition with which the individual is operating, that is, the attitude structure. Undoubtedly attitudes are basic to opinions as well as to many other aspects of behaviour. Although attitudes tend to be generalized predisposition to react in some way towards objects or concepts, opinions tend to be focused on more specific aspects of the object or the concept. McCormick and Tiffin observe that 'the measurement of attitudes is generally based on the expressions of opinions. But we should distinguish between attitude scale which, like a thermometer or barometer, reflects the generalized level of individuals' attitudes towards some object or concept, and opinion surveys, which typically are used to elicit the opinions of people toward specific aspects of, for example, their work situation.

A difference can also be made between attitude and belief. A belief is 'an enduring organisation of perceptions and cognitions about some aspects of individuals' world'. Thus belief is a hypothesis concerning the nature of objects, more particularly, concerning one's judgement of the probability regarding their nature. In this sense, belief is the cognitive component of attitude which reflects the manner in which an object is perceived. Kolasa observes that 'beliefs are stronger than opinions; we hold them more firmly than we do the more changeable evaluations of minor or transitory events represented by opinions. Beliefs are less affected by the pra or con positions fundamentl in attitudes than are opinions, but all three aspects may influence the others.

The difference between attitudes, opinions, and beliefs exist on conceptual basis. Most researchers believe that these three terms are so closely tied that it is difficult to separate them except on a limited conceptual basis. In the literature, often, there is considerable amount of overlapping in these three terms. Most psychologists, however, believe that attitudes are more fundamental to human behaviour than are the related aspects. For this reason, more attempts have been made to analyse attitudes as compared to others.

Attitudes and Behaviour

As discussed earlier, individual's behaviour is not a simple and direct stimulus-response relationship, rather it is affected by the individual concerned, as is explained by S-O-B model. The work situation is interpreted by the individual, and attitudes play an important part in which the situation is interpreted. Only after individual's interpretation and comparison does the response occur. This means that response expected of a purely objective and rational consideration of the work situation and its characteristics may not be the actual response of the individual. His response depends completely on how he interprets the situation and on his own personal attitudes towards the situation. Obviously attitudes are an important consideration because of their central position in the process transforming work requirements into effort. Attitudes have been thought as serving four functions and thereby affecting the behaviour : (i) utilitarian or instrumental, (ii) ego defensive, (ii) value orientation and (iv) knowledge.

(i) ***Instrumental:*** Attitudes serve as a means to reach a desired goal or to avoid an undesired one. Instrumental attitudes are aroused by the activation of a need or cues that are associated with the attitude object and arouse favourable or unfavourable feelings.

(ii) ***Ego-defensive:*** The ego-defensive function of attitudes acknowledges the importance of psychological thought. Attitudes may be required and maintained to protect the person from facing threats in the external world or from becoming aware of his own unacceptable impulses. Ego-defensive attitudes may be aroused by internal or external threat, frustrating events, appeals or to the build-up or repressed impulses, and suggestions by authoritarian sources. The attitudes influence his behaviour by affecting his perception of the situation accordingly.

(iii) ***Value Orientation:*** The value-orientation function takes into account attitudes that are held because they express a person's values or enhance his self-identity. These attitudes arise by conditions that threaten the self-concept, appeals to reassert the person's self-image, or by cues that engage the person's values and make them salient to him.

(iv) ***Knowledge:*** The knowledge function of attitudes is based on a person's need to maintain a stable, organized and meaningful structure of the world. Attitudes that provide a standard against which a person evaluates aspects of his world serve the knowledge function too.

These functions of attitudes affect the individual's way of interpreting the information coming to him. Since attitudes intervene between work requirements and work responses, information about how people feel about their jobs can be quite useful in prediction about work response. Thus these types of attitudes can portray areas of investigation for making the individual and the organisation more compatible.

3.7 THEORIES OF ATTITUDE FORMATION

A great number of theories have been proposed to explain attitude formation and change. Although these theories have many limitations they provide useful thinking about the processes underlying attitude formation. These theories are organized into major grouping according to the nature of the psychological processes postulated to underlie formation and change of attitudes. These theories may broadly be classified into three categories, cognitive-consistency theories, functional theories and social judgement theories. however, there is frequent discontinuity between various groupings because related approaches have focused on different sets of phenomena. Nevertheless, such classification is valid from practical point of view.

Cognitive Consistency Theories

Attitudes do not exist in isolation: indeed, a complex structure results which appears to have at its heart a consistent tendency to maintain balance and resist change from influences of various types. In general, these theories are concerned with inconsistencies that arise between related beliefs, bits of knowledge, and/or evaluations about an object or an issue. Though various consistency theories differ in several respects, including the form of inconsistency about which they concerned, all of them have in common the idea that the psychological tension created by this unpleasant state leads to attempts at reducing the inconsistency. There are four important theories under this grouping.

1. Balance Theory: The basic model of balance theory has been provided by Heider. The theory is concerned with consistency in the judgement of people and or/ or issues that are linked by some form of relationships. there are three elements in the attitude formation: the person, other person, and impersonal entity. Two generic types of relationships are considered to exist between the elements: linking or sentiment or effect, while unit relationships express the fact that two elements are perceived as belonging together. Both linking and units relations can be positive and negative. In a three element system, balance exists if all three relations are positive or if two relations are negative and one is positive. Imbalance exists if all three relations are negative or if two relations are positive and one is negative. People tend to perceive others and objects linked to them so that the system is balanced. Thus if a perceiver likes a source who favour a certain position on an issue, the balancing process induces the perceiver to favour that position too. The balanced states are stable and imbalanced states are unstable. When imbalanced states occurs, te psychological tension created motivates the person to restore balance cognitively by changing the relations. Thus a person's attitude towards an object depend on his attitudes towards a source who is linked with the object.

The basic model of Heider has been criticized on some grounds. For example, the theory does not consider the degree of linking or unit relationship nor the relevance to the perceiver of the elements and relations. Consequently, there are no degrees f balance or imbalance, and it is no possible to make quantitative predictions about the degree of attitude change.

In an extension of balance model, Abelson has suggested four methods in which a person can resolve imbalance in cognitive structures: denial, bolstering, differentiation, and transcendence. Denial involves denying relationship when imbalance occurs. Bolstering involves adding element in the structure, that is adding another issue in the main issue. Differentiation involves splitting one of the elements into two elements that are related in opposite ways to other elements in the system and negatively related to each other. Transcendence involves combining elements into larger, more super ordinate units from a balanced structure. These processes occur in hierarchy so that a person's attempts to resolve imbalance in the ordering are discussed. The ordering is based on the assumption that the person will attempt with the least effortful resolution first. This theory helps in understanding the role of persuasive communication and interpersonal attractiveness in changing the attitudes.

2. Congruity Theory: Osgood and Tannenbaum have proposed the congruity theory of attitudes which is similar to the balance theory. The focus of the theory is on changes in the evaluation of a source and a concept, that are linked by an associative or dissociative assertion. Congruity exists when a source and concept that are positively associated have exactly the same evaluations and when a source and concept that are positively associated have exactly the same evaluations and when a source and concept that are negatively associated have exactly the oppositive evaluations attached to them. Congruity is a stable state and incongruity is unstable one. As such, incongruity leads to attitude change, and the theory states how much attitudes towards the source and towards the concept change in order to resolve the incongruity.

3. Affective Congnitive Consistency Theory: This theory, propounded by Rosenberg, is concerned with the consistency between a person's overall attitude or effect towards an object or issue and his beliefs about its relationship to his more general values. Rosenberg has related attitudes to one aspect of cognitive structure-means-end relationship between the object or issue and the achievement of desired and undesired values or goals. The theory is also called structural because it is concerned mainly with what happens within the individual when an attitude changes. It proposes that the relationship between the affective and the cognitive components of the attitude change when an attitude is altered.

The theory postulates that a person's effect towards or evaluation of the attitude object tends to be consistent with this congnitive structural component. When there is inconsistency beyond a certain level of tolerance, the individual is motivated to reduce the inconsistency and thereby to change one or both components to make them more consistent. The theory, thus, suggests that changes in the affective component produce changes in the cognitive component in order to bring about consistency between the two. The theory also suggests that persuasive communication conveys information about how the attitude object or issue furthers the attainment of certain desirable ends or conveys persuasive material that result in a re-evaluation of the goals themselves.

4. Cognitive Dissonance Theory: The cognitive dissonance theory, proposed by Festinger, has had by far the greatest impact on the study of attitudes. At first sight, this theory may appear similar to the affective-cognitive theory. The difference between the two is that this theory (dissonance) tends to tie in the third component of the attitudes (behavioural tendency) with cognitions about the attitude object. Rather than dealing with only one belief, this theory deals with relationship a person's ideas have with one other. It states that there are three types of relationshis between all cognitions : dissonance, consonance, and irrelevance. Cognitions are dissonant whenever they are incompatible; or if they are opposed to one's experience about the relationship of events. Cognitions are consonant when one follows from the other on the basis of logic or experience. Cognitions are totally irrelevant when two events are not interrelated. The presence of dissonance gives rise to pressures to reduce or eliminate the dissonance and avoid the further increase of dissonance. Dissonance varies in magnitude. The total amount of dissonance is a function of the proportion of relevant elements that are dissonant with one another relative to the total number of consonant and dissonant elements, each weighted by the importance of the elements for the person. Higher the degree of dissonance, higher would be the attempt to reduce it. Dissonance is reduced through three methods : changing a behavioural cognitive element, changing an environmental element, and adding a new cognitive element.

The basic model of Festinger applies to several situations affecting behaviour of persons. In each behaviour, the person experiences dissonance when he engages in behaviour contrary to his attitudes. Since magnitude of dissonance is a function of the relative number and important elements, the amount of justification a person has for engaging in the attitude-discrepant behaviour is an important determinant of the amount of dissonance he experiences. Justification adds consonant element to the otherwise dissonant situation. For example, when a person has to choose among a number of alternatives, he experiences conflict before the decision. After the decision, he experiences dissonance because the positive features of rejected alternatives and negative features of selected alternative dissonant with the choice. To overcome this dissonance, the justification process starts. Dissonance-reducing changes have the net effect of increasing the valuation of the chosen alternative and decreasing the valuation of rejected alternatives.

Functional Theory

Functional theory considers how attitudes and efforts are related to the motivational structure of the individual. The theory focuses on the meaning of the influence situation in terms of both the kinds of motives that is arouses and the individual's method of coping and achieving his goals. An understanding of the functions served by attitudes is important for attitude change procedure since a particular method may produce change in individuals whose attitudes serve one particular function, but may produce no change in an opposite direction in individuals for whom the attitudes serve a different function.

The most prominent person who visualised functional theory is Katz and he suggests four functions of attitudes : utilitarian or instrumental function, ego-defensive, value orientation, and knowledge, as discussed earlier. It can be seen that there is some similarity in parts of this theory to cognitive dissonance theory. What Katz points out is that when an attitude serves an adjustive function one of the two conditions must prevail before it can be changed; (i) the attitude and the activities related to it no longer provide the satisfaction they once did; or (ii) the individual's level of aspiration has been raised. Shifts in the satisfaction which come from behaviours bring with them changes in the attitudes. When new behaviours inconsistent with attitudes bring satisfaction these attitudes then must be adjusted. However, Katz functional theory has not stimulated much research except for the work on changing ego-defensive attitudes.

Kelman has given another approach about the functional approach of attitudes. His theory is directed towards the types of social relationships that occur in social influence situations. Kelman has distinguished three processes of attitude formation and change compliance, identification, and internalization. These processes derive functional meaning primarily from their emphasis on the motivational significance of the individual's relationship to the influencing agent, or from the differing types of social integration that they represent. Compliance occurs when an attitude is formed or changed in order to gain a favourable reaction from other differing types of social integration that they represent. Compliance occurs when an attitude is formed or changed in order to gain a favourable reaction from other person or group. Identification occurs when a person forms or changes his attitude because his adoption helps him establish or maintain a positive self-defining relationship with the influencing agent. Internalisation involves adopting an attitude because it is congruent with one's overall value system. The individual perceives the content of the induced attitude as enhancing his own values. This approach makes an important contribution towards an understanding of the conditions that influence the maintenance and stability of attitude change.

Social Judgement Theory

The social judgement theory, formulated originally by Sherif and Hoveland, attempts to explains how existing attitudes produce distortions of attitudinally related objects and how these judgements mediate attitude change. Accordingly, a person's own stand on an issue, that is, initial attitude, serves as an anchor for the judgement of attitudinally related stimuli. The person's initial attitude on an issue provides a point of reference against which he evaluates other opinions. These views can be considered in terms of attitudinal continuum and can be considered as comprising latitudes. The latitude of acceptance, which is the range of opinions the individual finds acceptable, encompasses the opinion that best characterizes his own stand. The attitude of rejection, which is the range of opinions the individual finds objectionable, encompasses the opinion he finds most objectionable. The attitude of non-commitment is the range of opinions that the person finds neither acceptable nor unacceptable.

2.8 FACTORS IN ATTITUDE FORMATION

The attitudes are learned. Though there are different approaches as how learning works and is acquired by individuals, generally it is held that individuals learn things from the environment in which they interact. Thus for attitude formation, all those factors must be taken into account from which people learn. Such factors may be analysed in terms of groups. Starting from the family as a group, an individual moves in a close group, then to larger groups, and finally to the society as a whole. Apart from these groups the individual's psychological make-up, particularly his personality, is also responsible for shaping h is behaviour and attitudes. Thus in order to understand the various factors and how they affect the attitudes, both these category of factors should be analysed.

1. Group Factors: The influence of groups on the attitudes of individuals is inversely proportional to the distance of the group from the individual. From this point of view, three types of groups have different types of effect on the attitudes of a person.

(i) Family: The term family may be used in a variety of ways : it may include a nuclear family which means the immediate group of father, mother, and children; an extended family which includes nuclear family and other relatives. Both these types of family have influence on the attitudes of individuals. In fact, when a person starts learning anything about the world, he learns it through his mother which is known as the process of socialization. In this socialization process, he learns and forms attitudes also. Gradually, when the child grows up he comes in contact with others in the family but does not make significant contact with persons outside his family. Family has two important roles. First, other family members have certain personality characteristics, evaluate criteria, and attitudes, and the family as a whole has certain attitudes and values which are shared by all other persons. Second, family mediates the influence of larger social systems on the individual's attitudes, values, and personality characteristics. As an individual interacts with other family members, he simultaneously both influences the personality characteristics and attitudes of others and in turn is influenced by others. Since a family is a primary group, the attitudes of family member tend to converge and are typically more homogeneous than would be the case if they were not in the family.

(ii) Reference Groups: The awareness and learning of behaviour alternatives is accomplished efficiently through the influence of reference groups. A reference group is any interacting aggregation of people that influences an individual's attitudes of behaviour. This group may include family or other types of groupings, either primary or secondary groups. Reference groups serve important inputs to an individual's learning of his attitudes and awareness of alternative behaviours and life style. This happens through the process of socialization. Socialisation, as discussed earlier, is a process by which a new member learns the value system, the norms, and the required behaviour patterns of the society, organisations, or groups in which he is entering. Though all groups with which an individual makes contact have influence on his attitudes, the values and norms of the primary groups play a very important role in influencing attitudes, opinions, and beliefs of the members of the group.

(iii) Social Factors: The social classes have important influence on individual's attitudes. They have the important task of transmitting cultural behaviour patterns to specific groups and families. They define the expectations of society for groups of people and for families within the groups. The family then transmits these cultural expectations to the individual. Thus social classes restrict behaviour between individuals of differing social classes, specially in intimate relationships. People have their close relationships with people of similar classes, which tends to restrict attitude formation in similar patterns of other members. This is so because attitudes and values provide goals which aid alternative evaluation and provide motivation for research and evaluation. These are transmitted differently among social classes.

2. Personality Factors: Personality factors are important in attitude formation. However, many personality characteristics themselves are determined by group and social factors, as discussed earlier. Personality differences between individuals are very important concomitant of the discussion of attitudes. This area has been the subject of great interest of research and study, particularly with respect to broader area of prejudice and social functioning. Various studies show that there is positive relationship between different personality factors and attitudes. Adrono et al show that there was a coherent pattern of ethnocentric attitudes including anti-Semitism among persons having authoritarian personality. The ethnocentrics stuck to the straight and narrow, holding conventional values, not being able to accept certain socially unacceptable impulses and, therefore, in the main, projecting these on others. McClosky has found a relationship between personality correlates of conservatism and liberalism. He found that the conservative attitudes characterized these at the lower end of the intelligence scale with less education and with less awareness of current events. Various other research studies also show positive relationship between personality variables and particular attitudes. Since personality itself is influenced by various group and social factors as well as heredity factors, in understanding attitude formation, these factors, particularly former ones, must be analysed.

3.9 ATTITUDE MEASUREMENT

Attitudes are subjective attributes of people. They can be regarded as constructs in the sense that they are conceptualizations of human qualities that are formed on the basis of either rational consideration of statistical evidence. Thus, people may vary along each of a number of attitudinal dimensions. Keeping this measurement aspect into consideration, the attitudes might be defined operationally by describing the measurement systems that psychologists use to measure attitudes. Attitude measurement, developed largely by social psychologists, is concerned with efforts to tap these attitude measurement. In pulling together numerous methods dealing with attitude measurement, Summers uses the following organisation which, in effect, is classification of methods of attitude measurement : (i) self-report (usually elicited with questionnaires dealing with beliefs, feelings, and behaviours); (ii) indirect tests (such as projective techniques and disguised approaches); (iii) direct observation techniques; and 9iv) psychological reaction techniques. However, attitude measurement of employees in organisations is most commonly carried out with self-respect questionnaires. Measurement of attitudes based on questionnaires uses several scaling methods. There are three types of attitude scaling which are commonly used in attitude measurement : Thurstone type of scale, Likert scale, and semantic differential.

The Thurstone type of scaling goes back to the early work of Thurstone and Chave, who collected a large number of statements relating to the area in which attitudes were to be measured. These statements may be relating to any object about which attitudes are to be measured. The statements are both favourable and unfavorable, and are placed in 11 piles, with most favourable statement being placed in pile 11. Other statements are placed in between, their position depending on the degree of favourability or unfavourability. The scale is then presented to the respondents. Each respondent checks the statement with which he agrees. His attitude score is then based either on the average or the median scale of the statements that he has checked.

Soon after Thurstone scale, Likert experimented with certain other varieties of attitude scales. Likert's attitude scale uses five points. The statement relating to the measurement of attitudes is given to the person concerned and he is asked to check one of the five points given for every statement. These points show degree of agreement or disagreement with the given statements. The Likert scale is considered better as compared to Thurstone because of several positive facts. For example, in this scaling, there is not much problem in making numerous statements because for every aspect, only one statement is required which will show both positive and negative degrees. Seiler and Hough refer to Likert scaling as equally or more reliable than the Thurstone, and faster, and equally or more valid.

The semantic differential, an attitude scaling technique that lends itself to various applications, was developed by Osgood, Suci, and Tannenbaum. Semantic differential means the successive allocation of a concept to a point in the multidimensional space by selection from among a set of given scaled semantic alternatives. For any given purpose it consists of several or many pairs of opposite adjectives or phrases, with scale values n between. In using this scale, the respondent marks the position along each scale that reflects his attitude to the attitude object. Scale values (often ranging from 1 to 7) are associated with the different responses and individual's attitude score usually is the sum of these.

Apart from these measures of attitudes, certain other scales have also been developed. These include the Guttman technique, the error-choice method, and the sentence completion method.

3.10 ATTITUDE CHANGE

There is often a paradox of attitudes in that people need them to provide stability to social world yet world is a changing one and people must change their attitudes appropriate to the situation. The attitude change appropriate to organisational requirement is more important because attitudes affect behaviour and only a certain behaviour is desirable from organisation point of view. Organisations adopt a number of techniques for changing attitudes of their members so that their behaviour corresponds with the organisational requirement. However, whatever the techniques for attitudes change are adopted, they can be effective only if basic characteristics of attitudes and their nature are kept in consideration. Though various theories of attitude formation and change have been presented earlier which help in understanding attitudes and the techniques through which they can be changed, the change techniques can be more effective, if three basic factors are considered adequately : (i) the characteristics of attitudes; (ii) the personality of attitude holder; and (iii) the group affiliation of the attitude holder. These factors have been derived from two sources : theory of attitude formation and the factors affecting attitude formation.

1. Characteristics of Attitudes: In understanding attitude change, the analysis of attitude characteristics is an important element. Theories of attitudes suggest numerous types of their characteristics. Such characteristics may be (i) extremeness of the attitude, (ii) multiplexity, (iii) consistency, (iv) interconnectedness, (v) consonance of the attitude cluster of which the focal attitude is a part, (vi) the number and strength of the needs which are served by the attitude, and (vii) centrality of related values. Taking these characteristics of attitudes, there may be two types of attitude change : congruent and incongruent. The congruent change involves an increase in the strength of an existing attitude, either to make a positive attitude even more fa\vourable or to make a negative attitude more strongly negative. An incongruent change is one in which the direction of change is opposite to the originally held attitude. Congruent change is easier to produce than incongruent one-specially when the attitude held is extreme, central in the attitude system, and interconnected with supporting attitudes.

Another characteristic involved in changebility of attitudes is their simplicity. The number of facts involved in the cognition and the number of facts to which it is related make the attitude simple or complex. It is more likely to produce change in simple attitude than the complex one. The degree of interconnectedness determines the changeability of attitudes. Usually, attitudes which are strongly supported by other attitudes are more resistant to change. Similarly, depending on how many social wants support them and the strength of these wants, the attitudes may be more or less changeable. Attitudes which reflect the core or principal component of an individual's personality would most likely be very resistant to change.

2. Personality of Attitude Holder: The personality factor of attitude holder are also important in attitude change in the sense that some persons are more persuable as compared to others. This is so because of personality differences. Such differences change the nature of attitudes because attitudes are subjective qualities. Persuasibility is the tendency of a person to accept a persuasive communication. It commonly refers to a response to a direct influence attempt. Several personality factors suggest different types of persuasibility. First is level of self esteem of the person. The more inadequate a person feels and the more social inhibitions he has, the more likely is he to be persuasible. People with a great deal of confidence in their own intellectual ability are not only more resistant to change but more willing to expose themselves to discrepant information.

Related to the personality factors, there is a style of thinking referred to as close minded or dogmatism. Dogmatism is a form of authoritarianism where there is admiration of those in authority and hatred for those opposed to authority. There is a strong belief in the cause and a decreasing tendency to admit that other causes might be valid. Dogmatism is a relatively closed system in which the beliefs and disbeliefs are isolated from one another. It tends to be organised around some central authority theme which must be protected at all costs. In dogmatism, there is high degree of rejection of opposing beliefs, a relatively low level of interconnection among belief systems, and complex cognitions about positively valued objects as against congnitions about negatively valued objects.

In such case attitude change is often resisted. However, personality factors should not be overemphasised in attitude change because the change makes much more sense in the context of total change attempt situation.

3. Group Affiliation: Individuals often express their attitudes in terms of groups. This is more so in the case of less extreme attitudes. This is so because membership in the group prevents existing attitudes from being disturbed by filtering the information. As will be discussed later, one of the powerful bonds which holds the group together is the fact members think alike. Information likely to cause dissonance or inconsistency is either omitted or perceived according to group together is the fact that members think alike. Information likely to cause dissonance or inconsistency is either omitted or perceived according to group norms with some modification or is rejected or considered irrelevant. Though people are not always exposed to information in the concept or groups and information which may change their attitudes impinges upon them from many sources, even outside the group, their membership still influences the way the new information is perceived. This is particularly true of primary groups, such as family, friendship group, etc.

3.11 METHODS OF ATTITUDE CHANGE

Various methods have been adopted for attitude change. Cohen has classified them into four categories : Communication of additional information approval and disapproval of particular attitude, group influence, and inducing engagement in discrepant behaviour. However, in some way or the other, all these methods involve introducing discrepancies among the elements making up the individual's attitude in the hope that elements will be rebalanced through changing the affective component of the attitude. Thus, in practice, the central variable in attitude change is the feeling component associated with the attitude object. Thus from organisation's point of view, a manager may take the following actions in bringing out change in the attitudes of organisational members. Such as course of action may be in the form of group action, persuasion through leadership , persuasion through communication, and the influence of total situation. These factors have been taken for detailed analysis in later chapters. The group influence has been discussed in the next chapter while other methods are discussed in the next part.

3.13 UNIT EXERCISE

Short Answers

Q1. Explain the meaning of 'attitude' and 'values'.

Q2. What are the sources of values?

Q3. How are attitude formed?

Q4. How can attitudes be measured?

Q5. Write a short note on organizational commitment.

Long Answers

Q1. What is the concept of attitude? How do attitudes differ from opinions and beliefs.

Q2. What are the various factors which affect attitude formation?

Q3. What do you mean by attitudes? Explain the types of attitudes.

Q4. Explain the features of attitudes. What are the sources of attitudes.

Q5. How are attitudes formed? How can attitudes be measured.

CHAPTER 4

Leadership

4.0 INTRODUCTION

The problem of leadership has been one of man's major concerns since the days of antiquity. Leadership was a matter of concern even in biblical times. The children of Israel needed someone to guide them out of their bondage in Egypt, and Moses stepped forward to lead them in their journey to the promised holy land of Israel. In the 20th century, Great Britain needed the leadership of Winston Churchill to successfully combat her enemies in the 2nd World War. In the same way Franklin D Roosevelt provided leadership to the American people, Adolph Hitler in Germany, Stalin in USSR and M.K. Gandhi in India.

Coming to the business enterprises, people working there need leaders, who could be instrumental in guiding the efforts of groups of workers to achieve the goals of both individuals and the organization. Leadership is a process of influence on a group.

Leadership is the ability of a manager to induce subordinates to work with confidence and zeal. Peter F Drucker considers "leadership" as a human characteristic which lifts a man's vision to higher sights, raises a man's performance to higher standards and builds man's personality beyond its normal limitations.

4.1 OBJECTIVES

This lesson is intended to discuss the concept and importance of leadership and group decision making in an organisation. After studying this lesson you will be able to:

(i) know meaning and nature of leadership

(ii) describe leadership styles and patterns

(iii) know kinds of leadership skill

(iv) describe the importance of leadership in an organisation

(v) understand types and functions of leadership styles

(vi) know about the leadership committee and importance of group decision making

4.2 DEFINITIONS AND MEANING OF LEADERSHIP

Leadership is a great quality and it can create and convert anything. There are many definitions of leadership. Some of the definitions of leadership are reproduced below:

"Leadership" according to Alford and Beatty "is the ability to secure desirable actions from a group of followers voluntarily, without the use of coercion".

According to Chester I Barnard, "It (leadership) refers to the quality of the behaviour of the individual whereby they guide people on their activities in organized efforts".

According to Terry, "a leader shows the way by his own example. He is not a pusher, he pulls rather than pushes".

According to Koontz and O'Donnell - Managerial leadership is "the ability to exert interpersonal influence by means of communication, towards the achievement of a goal. Since managers get things done through people, their success depends, to a considerable extent upon their ability to provide !eadership".

In the words of R.T. Livingston - Leadership is "the ability to awaken in others the desire to follow a common objective".

According to the Encyclopedia of the Social Sciences - "Leadership is the relation between an individual and a group around some common interest and behaving in a manner directed or determined by him".

According to Peter Drucker - Leadership "is not making friends and influencing people i.e., salesmanship. Leadership is the lifting of man's vision to higher sights, the raising of man's performance to higher standards, the building of man's personality beyond its normal limitations".

According to Louis A Allen - "A leader is one who guides and directs other people. He gives the efforts to his followers a direction and purpose by influencing their behaviour".

In the words of Theo Haimann - "Leadership is the process by which an executive imaginatively directs, guides and influences the work of others in choosing and attaining specified goals by mediating between the individuals and the organization in such a manner that both will obtain maximum satisfaction".

In the words of James Gibbon - Leadership is "a process of influencing on a group in a particular situation at a given point of time and in a specific set of circumstances that stimulates people to strive willingly to attain organizational objectives, giving them the experience of helping attain the common objectives and satisfaction with the type of leadership provided".

According to Katz and Kalm - "In the descriptions of organizations, no word is used with such varied meanings. The word leadership is sometimes used to indicate that it is an attribute of personality; sometimes, it is used as if it were a characteristic of certain positions, and sometimes as an attribute of behaviour".

From the above definitions we can conclude that leadership is a psychological process of influencing followers (subordinates) and providing guidance, directing and leading the people in an organization towards attainment of the objectives of the enterprise.

4.3 NATURE OR CHARACTERISTIC FEATURES OF LEADERSHIP

1. **Leadership implies the existence of followers:** We appraise the qualities of leadership by studying his followers. In an organization leaders are also followers for e.g.:- Supervisor works under a branch head. Thus, in a formal organization a leader has to be able to be both a leader as well as a follower, and be able to relate himself both upward and downward.
2. **Leadership involves a community of interest between the leader and his followers:** In other words, the objectives of both the leader and his men are one and the same. If ome other purpose, it is no leadership.
3. **Leadership involves an unequal distribution of authority among leaders and group members:** Leaders can direct some of the activities of group members, i.e., the group

members are compelled or are willing to obey most of the leader's directions. The group members cannot similarly direct the leader's activities, though they will obviously affect those activities in a number of ways.

4. **Leadership is a process of Influence:** Leadership implies that leaders can influence their followers or subordinates in addition to being able to give their followers or subordinates legitimate directions.

5. **Leadership is the function of stimulation:** Leadership is the function of motivating people to strive willingly to attain organizational objectives. A successful leader allows his subordinates (followers) to have their individual goals set up by themselves in such a way that they do not conflict with the organizational objectives.

6. **A leader must be exemplary:** In the words of George Terry - "A Leader shows the way by his own example. He is not a pusher, he pulls rather than pushes".

   According to L.G. Urwick - "it does not what a leader says, still less what he writes, that influences subordinates. It is what he is. And they judge what he is by what he does and how he behaves". From the above explanation it is clear that a leader must set an ideal before his followers. He must stimulate his followers for hard and sincere work by his personal behaviour. In other words a leader must set an exemplary standard before his followers.

7. **A Leader ensures absolute justice:** A leader must be objective and impartial. He should not follow unfair practices like favouritism and nepotism. He must show fair play and absolute justice in all his decisions and actions.

4.4 LEADERSHIP STYLES AND PATTERNS

Tannenbaum and Schmidt have described the range of possible leadership behavior available to a manager. Each type of action is related to the degree of authority used by the boss and to the degree of freedom available to his subordinates in reaching decisions. The figure below shows the different leadership styles and patterns.

Leadership Styles

1. **The Manager makes decision and announces it:** It is an extreme form of autocratic leadership whereby decisions are made by the boss who identifies the problem, considers alternative solutions, selects one of them and then reports his decision to his subordinates for implementation.

2. **The Manager sells his decisions:** It is a slightly improved form of leadership wherein the manager takes the additional step of persuading the subordinates to accept his decision.

3. **The Manager presents his ideas and invites questions:** There is greater involvement of the employees in this pattern. The boss arrives at the decision, but provides a full opportunity to his subordinates to get fuller explanation of his thinking and intentions.

4. **The manager presents a tentative decision subject to change:** Herein the decision is tentatively taken by the manager but he is amenable to change and influence from the employees.
5. **The manager may present the problem, get the suggestions and then take his own decision:** Herein sufficient opportunity is given to the employees to make suggestions that are coolly considered by the Manager.

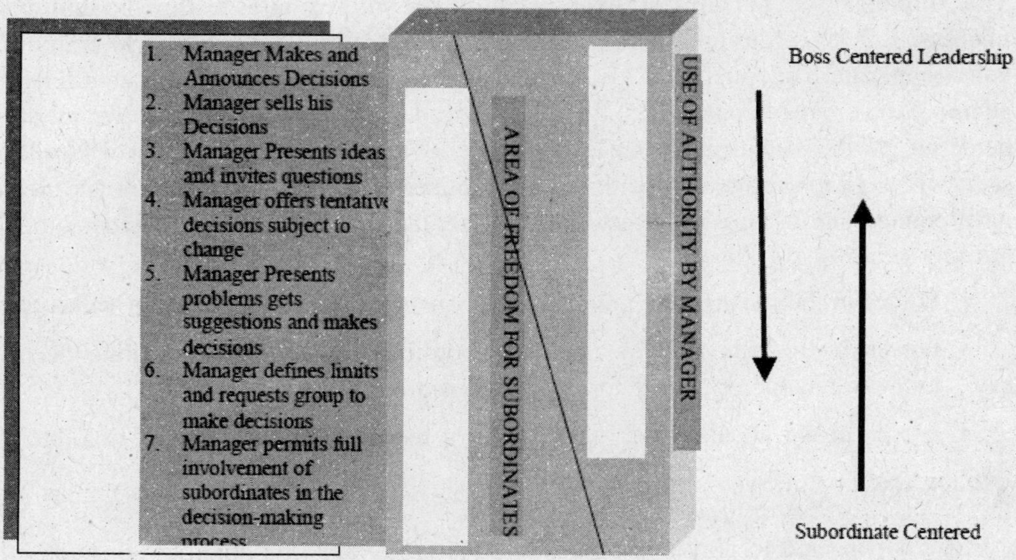

Figure 4.1: Range of leadership styles

Leadership Styles

1. **The Manager makes decision and announces it:** It is an extreme form of autocratic leadership whereby decisions are made by the boss who identifies the problem, considers alternative solutions, selects one of them and then reports his decision to his subordinates for implementation.
2. **The Manager sells his decisions:** It is a slightly improved form of leadership wherein the manager takes the additional step of persuading the subordinates to accept his decision.
3. **The Manager presents his ideas and invites questions:** There is greater involvement of the employees in this pattern. The boss arrives at the decision, but provides a full opportunity to his subordinates to get fuller explanation of his thinking and intentions.
4. **The manager presents a tentative decision subject to change:** Herein the decision is tentatively taken by the manager but he is amenable to change and influence from the employees.

5. **The manager may present the problem, get the suggestions and then take his own decision:** Herein sufficient opportunity is given to the employees to make suggestions that are coolly considered by the Manager.
6. **The Manager may define the limits and request the group to make a decision:** A manager of this style of management lets the group have the right to make the decision. The subordinates are able to take the decision to the limits defined by the manager.
7. **The Manager may permit full involvement of the subordinates in the decisionmaking process:** It is often designated as 'Democratic' leadership. Leadership style refers to the behaviour pattern adopted by a leader to influence the behaviour of his subordinates for attaining the organizational goals. As different leadership styles have their own merits and demerits, it is difficult to prefer one leadership styles to another. Γhe selection of a leadership style will depend on the consideration of a number of factors. Tannenbaum and Schmidt have pointed out the important factors that affect the choice of a style of leadership. They are:
   - Forces in the manager i.e., the manager's personality, experience and value system.
   - Forces in the subordinates i.e., the subordinates readiness for making decisions, knowledge, interest, need for independence etc.
   - Forces in the situation i.e., complexity of the problem, pressure of time etc.

4.5 LEADERSHIP SKILL

The leader is expected to play many roles and therefore, must be qualified to guide others to organizational achievement. Although no set of absolute traits or skills may be identified, the individuals who possess abilities to lead others must have certain attributes to help them in performing their leadership rolls. In a broad way the skills which are necessary for an industrial leader may be summarized under four heads:-

(a) Human skill

(b) Conceptual skill

(c) Technical skill and

(d) Personal skill.

Human Skill

A good leader is considerate towards his followers because his success largely depends on the co-operation of his followers. He approaches various problems in terms of people involved more than in terms of technical aspects involved. A leader should have an understanding of human behaviour. He should know people; know their needs, sentiments, emotions, as also their actions and reactions to particular decisions, their motivations etc. Thus, a successful leader possesses the human relations attitude. He always tries to develop social understanding with other people. The human skill involves the following:-

(a) ***Empathy:*** A leader should be able to look at things objectively. He should respect the rights, belief and sentiments of others. He should equip himself to meet the challenges emanating from the actions and reactions of other people. The leader should be empathetic towards his followers so that he can carefully judge their strengths, weakness, and ambitions and give them the attention they deserve.

(b) ***Objectivity:*** A good leader is fair and objective in dealing with subordinates. He must be free from bias and prejudice while becoming emotionally involved with the followers. His approach to any issue or problem should be objective and not based on any pressure, prejudice or preconceived notions. Objectivity is a vital aspect of analytical decision making. Honesty, fairplay, justice and integrity of character are expected of any good leader.

(c) ***Communication Skill:*** A leader should have the ability to persuade, to inform, stimulate, direct and convince his subordinates. To achieve this, a leader should have good communication skill. Good communications seem to find all responsibilities easier to perform because they relate to others more easily and can better utilize the available resources.

(d) ***Teaching Skill:*** A leader should have the ability to demonstrate how to accomplish a particular task.

(e) ***Social Skill:*** A leader should understand his followers. He should be helpful, sympathetic and friendly. He should have the ability to win his followers confidence and loyalty.

Conceptual Skill

In the words of Chester Barnard -"the essential aspect of the executive process is the sensing of the organization as a whole and the total situation relevant to it". Conceptual skills include -

(a) The understanding of the organization behaviour,

(b) Understanding the competitors of the firm, and

(c) Knowing the financial status of the firm.

A leader should have the ability to look at the enterprise as a whole, to recognize that the various functions of an organization depend upon one another and are interrelated, that changes in one affect all others. The leader should have skill to run the firm in such a way that overall performance of the firm in the long run will be sound.

Technical Skill

A leader should have a thorough knowledge of, and competence in, the principles, procedures and operations of a job. Technical skill involves specialized knowledge, analytical skill and a facility in the use of the tools and techniques of a specific discipline. Technical competence is an essential quality of leadership.

Personal Skill

The most important task of the leader is to get the best from others. This is possible only if he possesses certain qualities.

These personal skills include-

(a) ***Intelligence:*** Intellectual capacity is an essential quality of leadership. Leaders generally have somewhat higher level of intelligence than the average of their followers.

(b) ***Emotional Maturity:*** A leader should act with self-coincidence, avoid anger, take decisions on a rational basis and think clearly and maturely. A leader should also have high frustration tolerance. According to Koontz and O'Donnell - "Leaders cannot afford to become panicky, unsure of themselves in the face of conflicting forces, doubtful of their principles when challenged, or amenable to influence".

(c) ***Personal Motivation:*** This involves the creation of enthusiasm within the leader himself to get a job done. It is only through enthusiasm that one can achieve what one wants. Leaders have relatively intense achievement type motivational drive. He should work hard more for the satisfaction of inner drives than for extrinsic material rewards.

(d) ***Integrity:*** In the words of F.W Taylor - "integrity is the straight forward honesty of purpose which makes a man truthful, not only to others but to himself; which makes a man high-minded, and gives him high aspirations and high ideals".

(e) ***Flexibility of Mind:*** A leader must be prepared to accommodate other's viewpoints and modify his decisions, if need be. A leader should have a flexible mind, so that he may change in obedience to the change in circumstances. Thomas Carle has said - "A foolish consistency is the hobgoblin of a little mind". In sum, a leader must have a dynamic personality, intellectual attainment, amiable disposition, unassuming temperament and knowledge of how to deal with his followers.

Difference between Leadership and Management: Leadership is different from management. The main differences between these two terms are:-

1. A manager is required to plan, organize, direct and control. But a leader is one who gets others to follow him.
2. A manager depends on his authority. But a leader depends on his confidence and goodwill. He inspires enthusiasm.
3. Management is concerned with the formulation of broad policies to guide the operations of an enterprise. But leadership is concerned with the initiation of action for the accomplishment of the goals.
4. An individual is a leader in the true sense if he is accepted as a leader by the group. A manager is appointed and he derives his authority by virtue of his office.
5. Management is associated with the organized structure. But leadership may be associated with unorganised groups.

4.6 IMPORTANCE OF LEADERSHIP

The importance of leadership in an organization cannot be denied. People working in an organization need individuals (leaders) who could be instrumental in guiding the efforts of groups of workers to achieve goals and objectives of both the individuals and the organization. The leader guides the action of others in accomplishing these tasks. A good leader motivates his subordinates, creates confidence and increases the morale of the workers. In the words of Peter F Drucker - "Good leadership is a must for the success of a business but the business leaders are the scarcest resources of any enterprise". The following points highlight the importance of leadership:-

1. Leadership is the process of influencing the activities of an individual or a group towards the achievement of a goal.
2. An effective leader motivates the subordinates for higher level of performance.
3. Leadership promotes team - spirit and team - work which is quite essential for the success of any organization.
4. Leadership is an aid to authority. A leadership helps in the effective use of formal authority.
5. Leadership creates confidence in the subordinates by giving them proper guidance and advice.

The history of business is full of instances where good leaders led their business concerns to unprecedented peaks of success .To quote George R Terry - " The will to do is triggered by leadership and lukewarm desires for achievement are transformed into burning passe.. for successful accomplishments by the skilful use of leadership."

4.7 FUNCTIONS OF A LEADER

According to Peter Drucker - "An effective leader is one who can make ordinary men do extraordinary things, make common people do uncommon things. Leadership is a lifting of a man's sights to a higher vision, the raising of man's standard to a higher performance, the building of a man's personality beyond its normal limitations." This view point of Peter Drucker stresses the leaders' obligation to attain organizational goals and gives attention to the needs of the individuals who are his subordinates. The important functions of a business leader may be briefly summarized as follows:-

1. **To take the initiative:** A leader initiates all the measures that are necessary for the purpose of ensuring the health and progress of the undertaking in a competitive economy. He should not expect others to guide or direct him. He should lay down the aims and objectives, commence their implementation and see that the goals are achieved according the predetermined targets.
2. **He identifies group goals:** A leader must always help the group identify and attain their goals. Thus, a leader is a goal setter.

3. **He represents the organization:** A leader represents the organization and its purpose, ideals, philosophy and problems to those working for it and to the outside world .In other words, leaders is true representative of the entire organization.
4. **He acts as a arbitrator:** When groups experience internal difference, whether based on emotional or intellectual clashes, a leader can often resolve the differences. He acts as an arbitrator to prevent serious group difference.
5. **To assign reasons for his action:** It is a delicate task of leaders to assigns reason to his every command. He has to instruct things in such a way that they are intelligible to all concerned and their co-operation is readily forthcoming.
6. **To interpret:** He interprets the objectives of the organization and the means to be followed to achieve them; he appraises his followers, convinces them, and creates confidence among them.
7. **To guide and direct:** It is the primary function of the leader to guide and direct the organization. He should issue the necessary instructions and see that they are properly communicated.
8. **To encourage team work:** A leader must try to win the confidence of his subordinates. He must act like the capital of a team.
9. **He manages the organization:** Last, but not the least, he administers the undertaking by arranging for the forecast, planning, organization, direction, coordination and control of its activities.

4.8 TYPE OF LEADERS

The different types of leadership styles are:-

1. Autocratic or task Management Leadership,
2. Participative or democratic leadership,
3. Laissez faire or Free-rein Leadership, and
4. Paternalistic Leadership.

Autocratic or Task Management Leadership

The autocratic Leader gives order which he insists shall be obeyed. He determines polices for the group without consulting them, and does not give detailed information about future plans, but simply tells the group what steps must they take. In other words, an autocratic leader is one who centralizes the authority in himself and does not delegate authority to his subordinates. He is dictatorial by nature, and has no regard for the subordinates. He drives himself and his subordinates with one thought uppermost in his mind - action must produce results. An autocratic close the entire planning and cells upon his subordinates to execute what he has planned. An Autocratic leader operates on the following assumptions:

(a) An average human being has inherent dislikes of work and will avoid it if he can.

(b) His assumption is that if his subordinate was intelligent enough, he would not be in that subordinate position.

(c) He assumes that unintelligent subordinates are immature, unreliable and irresponsible persons. Therefore, they should be constantly watched in the course of their work.

(d) As he has no regard for his subordinates, he gets the work done by his subordinates through negative motivation i.e. through threats of penalty and punishment. Thus under this style all decision-making power is centralized in the leader. The autocratic leader stresses his prerogative to decide and order and subordinates obligation to do what they are told to carry out. He does not give subordinates the freedom to influence his behaviour.

Types of autocratic leadership

Strict autocratic leaders: A strict autocratic relies on negative influence and gives orders which the subordinates must accept. He may also use his power to disperse rewards to his group.

Benevolent Autocrat: The benevolent is effected in getting high productivity in many situations and he can develop effective human relationship. His motivational style is usually positive.

Manipulative Autocrat: A manipulative autocratic leader is one who makes the subordinates feel that they are participating in decision making process even though he has already taken the decision.

Participative or Democratic Leadership

A democratic leader is one who consults and invites his subordinates to participate in the decision making process. He gives orders only after consulting the group; sees to it that polices are worked out in group decisions and with the acceptance of group. The manager largely avoids the use of power to get a job done. He behaves that a desired organizational behaviour can be obtained if employees' needs and wants are satisfied. Therefore, he not only issues orders but interprets them and sees to it that the employees have the necessary skill and tool to carry out their assignments. He assigns a fair work lead to his personal and recognizes the job that is well done; there is a team approach to the attainment of organizational goals. He recognizes human value for greater concern for his subordinates. A participative leader operates on the following assumptions:

(a) Subordinates are capable of doing work and assuming the responsibility if they are given opportunities and incentives.

(b) Subordinates are supervised, guided and aided rather then threatened and commanded to work.

(c) Mistakes are not viewed seriously. The assumption is that disciplinary action breeds discontent and frustration among employees and creates an unhealthy work environment.

Laissez Faire or Free-rein Leadership

A free-rein leader does not lead, but leaves the group entirely to itself. The leader avoids using power and interest the decision making authority to his subordinates. He does not direct his subordinates and there is complete freedom for the subordinates. Group of members work themselves and provide their own motivation. The manager exits as a contact man with outsiders to bring for his group the information and resources it needs to accomplish its job. A free-rain leadership operates on the following assumption:

(a) He follows the rule of minimum exposure to accountability.

(b) He relieves himself of responsibilities and is ready to blame his subordinates if something goes wrong.

(c) He has no clear idea of the goals to be attained.

(d) He is more security conscious than status conscious.

This mode of direction can produce good and quick results if the subordinates are highly educated and brilliant people who have a will to go ahead and perform their responsibility.

Paternalistic Leadership

Under this type of leadership, the leader assumes that his function is fatherly. His attitude is that of treating the relationship between the leader and his groups that of family with the leader as the head of the family. The leader works to help to work to help, guide, protect and keep his followers happily working together as members of a family. He provides them with good working condition, fringe benefits and employee services. It is said that employees under such leadership well work harder out of gratitude.

4.9 LEADERSHIP COMMITTEE

A committee is a small group of people formed from a larger group of employees assigned with a particular task. A committee member may be appointed or the employee concerned may also volunteer to become a member. The ideal size of a committee for most of the tasks is 3 to 5 persons. The first person named in a committee is usually considered as the chairman of the committee.

Selecting Members for a Committee

In selecting committee members we have to remember the contribution that participating members can make to the committee. The following guidelines may be followed in selecting a committee member:

- He/She should be interested in the work to be done.
- He/She should honour the appointment and be committed to the job.
- The person should have special skills needed for the job.

- He/ She should not be overloaded with conflicting commitments.
- He/She should be willing to contribute to the group.
- The chairman should consider him/her as useful and desirable for the committee.
- He/She should be compatible with other members and should cooperate with them.

Selecting the Chairman for the Committee

Utmost care is needed in selecting the chairman of the committee than in selecting its members. The chairman has the primary responsibility to give leadership to the group and to stimulate them to their higher productivity both individually and as members of the group. He/ She should be able to organise the individual members into a working group.

It is always desirable to have a chairman who had previously served as a member of a committee or has had similar experience. The chairman may also be chosen for his/ her ability to lead the group. The one who proposes an idea or alternatively, the committee may select the leader by themselves.

4.10 UNIT EXERCISE

Short Answers

Q1. Define leadership.

Q2. Why is leadership important?

Q3. Explain autocratic leadership.

Q4. What is task centred leadership?

Q5. Enumerate the traits of a good leader.

Long Answers

Q1. "A good leader is one who understands his subordinates, their needs and their sources of satisfaction". Comment.

Q2. What is leadership? Discuss the trait theory and situational theory of leadership.

Q3. Critically examine the different approaches to the study of the leadership behavior. Is there one best style of leadership?

Q4. What is meant by leadership style? How will you secure effective leadership behavior? Is there one best style of leadership in the management of an organization?

Q5. Is the manager of a group always its leader? What does the existence of leadership substitutes tells us about the role of leadership? Discuss.

CHAPTER 5

Communication

5.0 AIMS AND OBJECTIVES

The purpose of this lesson is to know the meaning, functions, types and importance of communication in an organisation. After study this lesson you will be able to:

(i) understand meaning, importance and functions of communication

(ii) describe steps involved in communication process

(iii) know the downward, upward and lateral communication in the organisation

(iv) describe patterns of direction (communication network)

(v) differentiate between formal and informal action communication within an organisation

(vi) describe barriers to effective communication.

5.1 INTRODUCTION

Communication is the exchange of messages between people for the purpose of achieving common meanings. Unless common meanings are shared, managers find it extremely difficult to influence others. Whenever group of people interact, communication takes place. Communication is the exchange of information using a shared set of symbols. It is the process that links group members and enables them to coordinate their activities.

Therefore, when managers foster effective communication, they strengthen the connections between employees and build cooperation. Communication also functions to build and reinforce interdependence between various parts of the organization. As a linking mechanism among the different organizational subsystems, communication is a central feature of the structure of groups and organizations. It helps to coordinate tasks and activities within and between organizations.

5.2 DEFINITIONS OF COMMUNICATION

Whenever a group of people interact, communication takes place. Communication is the exchange of information using a shared set of symbols. It is the process that links group members and enables them to coordinate their activities. Therefore, when managers foster effective communication, they strengthen the connections between employees and build cooperation. The term "communication" is derived from the Latin word "communis" which means "common". This stands for the sharing of ideas in common. It is the process of passing information and understanding from one person to another.

According to Theo Haimann, "Communication, fundamental and vital to all managerial actions, is the process of imparting ideas and making oneself understood by others".

According to Dalton McFarland, "Communication may be broadly defined as the process of meaningful interaction among human beings. More specifically, it is the process by which meanings are perceived and understandings are reached among human beings".

According to Louis A Allen, "Communication is the sum of all the things one person does when he wants to create understanding in the mind of another. It is a bridge of meaning. It involves a systematic and continuous process of telling, listening and understanding". In the words of Newman and Summer, "Communication is an exchange of fact, ideas, opinions or emotions by two or more persons".

According to Hudson, " Communication in its simplest form is conveying of information from one person to another".

According to Charles E Redfield, communication is "the broad field of human interchange of facts and opinions and not the technologies of telephone, telegraph, radio and the like".

According to Koontz and O'Donnell, "Communication, is an intercourse by words, letters symbols or messages, and is a way that the organization members shares meaning and understanding with another".

In the words of Jacques, "Communication is the sum total of directly and indirectly, consciously and unconsciously transmitted feeling, attitudes and wishes".

In the words of Mockler, "Communication is the process of passing information, ideas or even emotions from one person to another".

In the words of Kelly, "Communication is a field of knowledge dealing with systematic application of symbols to acquire common information regarding an object or event".

In the words of Brown, communication is "a process of transmitting ideas or thoughts from one person to another, for the purpose of creating understanding in the thinking of the person receiving the communication".

According to Sigmund, Communication is "the transmission and reception of ideas, feelings and attitudes both verbally and non-verbally eliciting a response. It is a dynamic concept underlying all lands of living systems".

According to Ordeay Tead, "Communication is a composite:

- Of information given and received,
- Of learning experience in which certain attitudes, knowledge and skills change, carrying with them alternations of behaviour,
- Of a listening effort by all involved,
- Of a sympathetic fresh examination of issues by communicator himself,
- Of a sensitive interaction of points of view – leading to a higher level of shared understanding and common intention".

It should be clear from the above definitions that communication is not merely sending or receiving message. It is much more than that. It includes proper understanding of message, its acceptance and action on it. Unless common meanings are shared, managers find it extremely difficult to influence others. Communication is a critical part of every manager's job. Without effective communication, even the most brilliant strategies and the best-laid plans may not be successful. As a result, it is not surprising that high-level executives, as well as managers at other levels, often mention effective communication skills, both oral and written, as crucial elements for managerial success. Communication is thus an attempt to share understanding by two or more persons. It is a two-way process and is completed when there is some response from the receiver of information. It has two basic objectives:

1. To transmit message, ideas or opinions, and
2. To create an impression or understanding in the minds of the receiver of information.

5.3 IMPORTANCE OF COMMUNICATION

Communication is an indispensable activity in all organizations. No organization can think of its existence without effective communication. That is why, Chester Bernard remarked, "the first executive function is to develop and maintain a system of communication". An organization's very survival depends on its employees' ability to communicate with one another and with the members of its environment. The free flow of ideas and information is an essential ingredient in the drive for quality and continuous improvement. The organization relies on communications to learn what its customers want, to foster

cooperation among its employees, and to identify and adapt to changes in the environment. An effective communication system is essential to pass messages, ideas and information for explaining objectives and plans, controlling, performance and taking corrective action.

The importance of communication in management can be judged from the following:

1. Gaining acceptance of policies, winning cooperation of others, getting instructions and ideas clearly understood and bringing about the desired changes in performance are dependent upon effective communication.
2. Communication helps the management in arriving at vital decisions. In its absence, it may not be possible for the top-level management to come in closer contact with each other and discuss the important problems pertaining to the organization.
3. Constant communication with personnel helps the management to remain informed about their problems, difficulties and grievances. Appropriate steps can be taken in time to remove the worker's difficulties. Conflicts often arise because of communication gap. They can be averted by setting up a regular arrangement of keeping contact with the workers through communication media.
4. Communication is quite essential for coordination, which is the essence of effective management. It brings about mutual understanding between the personnel at all levels and fosters the spirit of cooperation. In the words of Mary Crushing Niles, "Good communications are essential to coordination. They are necessary upward, downward and sideways, through all the levels of authority and advise for the transmission, interpretation and adoption of policies, for the sharing of knowledge and information, and for the more subtle needs of good morale and mutual understanding".

5. Greater, better and cheaper production are the aims of all managers. In today's organizations; the information passes through a variety of filters and there is always a chance for misinterpretation. An effective system of communication can play a vital role in avoiding this illusion. The employees should be told clearly what exactly to do and the way in which an instruction is to be carried out. In this process certain directions are to be given, certain feelings must be expressed and a certain amount of interpersonal perceptions must be exchanged. In the words of Shobhana Khandwala, "For this, management has to sell ideas, motivate the workers to work with a will, and build up higher morale in the company. Communication, as an influence, process, plays a vital role here. It becomes, thus, a part of education, propaganda, leadership and guidance function of the management".
6. Under an effective system of communication it is quite convenient for the employees to express their grievances, and bring all their problems to the notice of the management. Proper communications between the interested parties reduce the point of friction and minimize those that inevitably arise. Hence by effective communication, a group having 'skill' and 'will' to do is to be built up.
7. Communication helps in securing the largest possible participation or consultation in decision making, planning and general administration. This will give democratic character to managerial process and strengthen the morale of the staff.

5.4 FUNCTIONS OF COMMUNICATION

Communication serves four major functions within an organization.

5.4.1 Control

Communication acts to control the employees' behaviour. Organizations have authority hierarchies and formal guidelines that employees are required to follow. The control mechanism can work only when the communication – oral and written, is effective. Informal communication also controls behaviour.

5.4.2 Information

Communication is a vital necessity to an organization, just as the bloodstream is to the person. It is essential that information must be communicated to the managers on the basis of which the plans can be developed; these plans must be communicated to the operating managers and employees.

5.4.3 Motivation

Communication fosters motivation by clarifying to employees what is to be done, how well they are doing and what can be done to prove performance if it is unsatisfactory.

5.4.4 Emotional Expression

Communication provides a release for the emotional expression of feelings and for fulfillment of social needs. Employees show their frustrations and feelings of satisfaction through communication.

5.5 COMMUNICATION STYLES

When people communicate, they differ not only in non-verbal behaviours and language but in the degree to which they provide and seek information. Such differences constitute various communication styles. A popular model for describing differences in communication style is the Johari window developed by Joseph Luft and Harry Ingham. The name Johari is derived from the first names of its developers. The Johari window is a grid that describes tendencies for facilitating or hindering interpersonal communication.

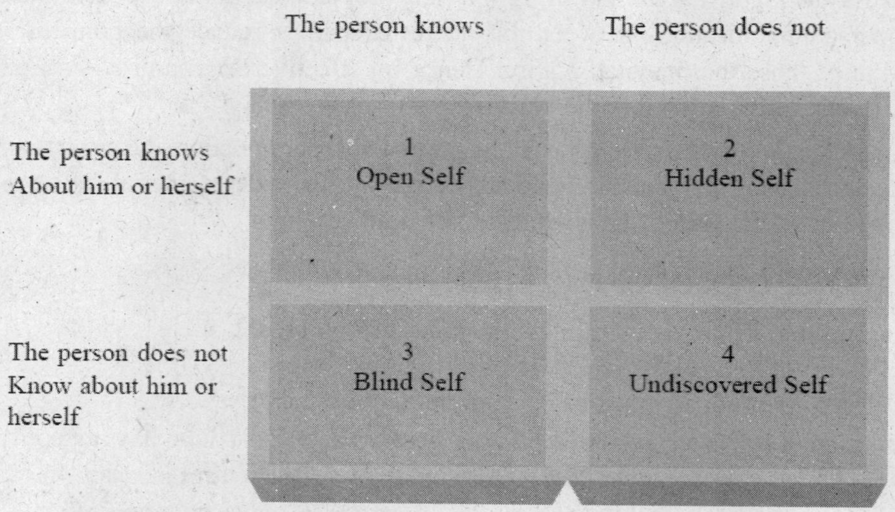

Fig. The Jojari Window

The model classifies an individual's tendencies to facilitate or hinder interpersonal communication along two dimensions: exposure and feedback. Exposure is defined as the extent to which an individual openly and candidly divulges feelings, experiences, and information when trying to communicate. Feedback is the extent to which an individual successfully elicits exposure from others. As shown in the figure above, these dimensions translate into four "windows" – open self, hidden self, blind self and undiscovered self.

1. **Open Self:** The open self is the arena information known to the person and to others. A large arena results from behaviour that is high in both exposure and feedback. There would generally be openness and compatibility and little reason to be defensive. This type of interpersonal relationship would tend decrease interpersonal conflict.
2. **Hidden Self:** In this situation the hidden information is known to the person but not to others; it encompasses those things or feelings that we are aware of but don't share with

others for fear they will think less of us or possibly use the information against us. Very large hidden knowledge can cause problems if the person expends too much effort in keeping secrets or others if suspicious about the lack of disclosure.

There is potential interpersonal conflict in this situation because the person may keep his or her true feelings or attitudes secret and will not open up to the others.

3. **Blind Self:** The blind self are information known to others but not to yourself. This is the result of no one ever telling you or because you are defensively blocking them out. The person may be unintentionally irritating to the other. The other could tell the person but may be fearful of hurting the person's feelings. Such a configuration is rarely total human resources. Furthermore, the person is likely to make many blunders, reflecting insensitivity to others. As in the "hidden self", there is potential interpersonal conflict in this situation.
4. **Undiscovered Self:** The undiscovered self includes feelings, experience, and information that neither you nor others are aware of. It arises from lack of communication. A manager whose unknown area is very large tends to be an autocratic leader, perceived as aloof. Employees may have trouble discerning what this person wants. In other words, there is much misunderstanding and interpersonal conflict and is almost sure to result. The Johari window only points out possible interpersonal styles. It does not necessarily describe but rather helps analyze possible interpersonal conflict situations. The National

Training Laboratory (NTL) recommends seven guidelines for providing feedback for effective interpersonal relations. These guidelines given below can help to decrease the potential for interpersonal conflict.

5.6 THE COMMUNICATION PROCESS

Communication is important in building and sustaining human relationships at work. It cannot be replaced by the advances in information technology and data management that have taken place over the past several decades. Communication can be thought of as a process or flow. Before communication can take place, a purpose, expressed as a message to be conveyed is needed. It passes between the sender and the receiver. The result is transference of meaning from one person to another.

The figure below depicts the communication process. This model is made up of seven parts: (1) the communication source, (2) encoding, (3) the message, (4) the channel, (5) decoding, (6) the receiver, and (7) feedback.

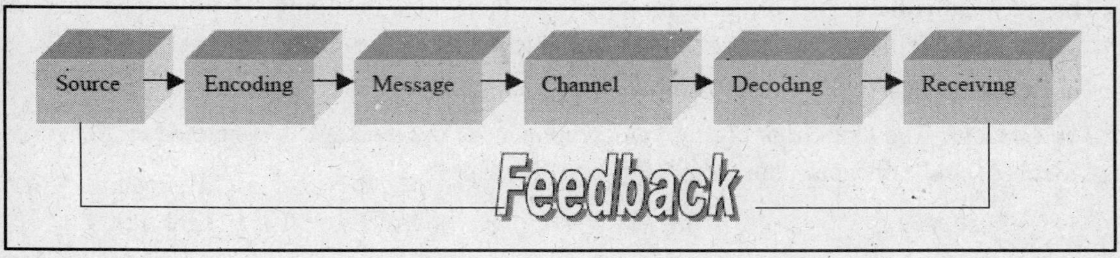

5.6.1 Source

The source initiates a message. This is the origin of the communication and can be an individual, group or inanimate object. The effectiveness of a communication depends to a considerable degree on the characteristics of the source. Aristotle believed that acceptance of the source's message could be increased by:-

- Pathos – Playing on the emotions of the receiver.
- Logos – Generating logical arguments or
- Ethos – Asking for message acceptance because the source is trustworthy.

The person who initiates the communication process is known as sender, source or communicator. In an organization, the sender will be a person who has a need or desire to send a message to others. The sender has some information which he wants to communicate to some other person to achieve some purpose. By initiating the message, the sender attempts to achieve understanding and change in the behaviour of the receiver.

5.6.2 Encoding

Once the source has decided what message to communicate, the content of the message must be put in a form the receiver can understand. As the background for encoding information, the sender uses his or her own frame of reference. It includes the individual's communication view of the organization or situation as a function of personal education, interpersonal relationships, attitudes, knowledge and experience.

Three conditions are necessary for successful encoding the message.

Skill: Successful communicating depends on the skill you posses. Without the requisite skills, the message of the communicator will not reach the requisite skills; the message of the communicator will not reach the receiver in the desired form. One's total communicative success includes speaking, reading, listening and reasoning skills.

Attitudes: Our attitudes influence our behaviour. We hold predisposed ideas on a number of topics and our communications are affected by these attitudes.

Knowledge: We cannot communicate what we don't know. The amount of knowledge the source holds about his or her subject will affect the message he or she seeks to transfer.

5.6.3 The Message

The message is the actual physical product from the source encoding. The message contains the thoughts and feelings that the communicator intends to evoke in the receiver.

The message has two primary components:-

The Content: The thought or conceptual component of the message is contained in the words, ideas, symbols and concepts chosen to relay the message.

The Affect: The feeling or emotional component of the message is contained in the intensity, force, demeanour (conduct or behaviour), and sometimes the gestures of the communicator.

According to **D.K Berlo** - "when we speak, the speech is the message. When we write, the writing is the message. When we paint, the picture is the message. When we gesture, the movements of our arms, the expressions on our faces are the message".

5.6.4 THE CHANNEL

The actual means by which the message is transmitted to the receiver (Visual, auditory, written or some combination of these three) is called the channel. The channel is the medium through which the message travels. The channel is the observable carrier of the message. Communication in which the sender's voice is used as the channel is called oral communication. When the channel involves written language, the sender is using written communication. The sender's choice of a channel conveys additional information beyond that contained in the message itself. For example, documenting an employee's poor performance in writing conveys that the manager has taken the problem seriously.

Channel	Required Source of Activity	Required Receiver Activity	Some Examples
1.Auditory	Speaking Use of mechanical sending device	Listening	Telegraph signals Radio Telephone conversations
2. Visual	Action	Observing	Ship-to-shore visual signals. Hand signals Color emphasis Flag waving
3.Written	Composition	Reading	Reports Company policy manuals Books
4.Auditory-visual combination	Speaking and action	Listening and observing	Television, movies Ballet Students listening to a lecture
5.Visual-written combination	Action and composition	Observing and reading	Billboard advertising Magazines Newspapers Transit advertising
6.Auditory-written combination	Speaking and composition	Listing and reading	Students following handouts provided by the instructor

5.6.5 Decoding

Decoding means interpreting what the message means. The extent to which the decoding by the receiver depends heavily on the individual characteristics of the sender and receiver. The greater the similarity in the background or status factors of the communicators, the greater the probability that a message will be perceived accurately. Most messages can be decoded in more than one way. Receiving and decoding a message are a type of perception. The decoding process is therefore subject to the perception biases.

5.6.6 The Receiver

The receiver is the object to whom the message is directed. Receiving the message means one or more of the receiver's senses register the message - for example, hearing the sound of a supplier's voice over the telephone or seeing the boss give a thumbs-up signal. Like the sender, the receiver is subject to many influences that can affect the understanding of the message. Most important, the receiver will perceive a communication in a manner that is consistent with previous experiences. Communications that are not consistent with expectations is likely to be rejected.

5.6.7 Feedback

The final link in the communication process is a feedback loop. Feedback, in effect, is communication travelling in the opposite direction. If the sender pays attention to the feedback and interprets it accurately, the feedback can help the sender learn whether the original communication was decoded accurately. Without feedback, one-way communication occurs between managers and their employees. Faced with differences in their power, lack of time, and a desire to save face by not passing on negative information, employees may be discouraged form providing the necessary feedback to their managers.

5.7 DIRECTIONS OF COMMUNICATION IN THE ORGANIZATION

Within organizations, there are three directions in which communications flow: downward, upward and laterally (horizontal).

5.7.1 Downward Communication

Downward communication involves a message travelling to one or more receivers at the lower level in the hierarchy. The message frequently involves directions or performance feedback. The downward flow of communication generally corresponds to the formal organizational communications system, which is usually synonymous with the chain of command or line of authority. This system has received a great deal of attention from both managers and behavioural scientists since it is crucial to organizational functioning.

5.7.2 Upward Communication

In upward communication, the message is directed toward a higher level in the hierarchy. It is often takes the form of progress reports or information about successes and failures of the individuals or work groups reporting to the receiver of the message. Sometimes employees also send suggestions or complaints upward through the organization's hierarchy.

The upward flow of communication involves two distinct manager-subordinate activities in addition to feedback:

(a) The participation by employees in formal organizational decisions.

(b) Employee appeal is a result against formal organization decisions. The employee appeal is a result of the industrial democracy concept that provides for two-way communication in areas of disagreement.

Stimulating Upward Communication

Although most managers agree on the need for upward communication, it is often not clear what actions can be taken to stimulate it. Given this situation, it is important to develop ways to stimulate upward communication. Planty and Machaver give the following suggestions.

Stimulating Upward Communication

1. **Coverage must be systematic and balanced:** While spontaneous communication is often useful, efforts at stimulating upward communication must be planned, systematic, and balanced. The planning requirement assures that communication is not left to chance, while the balance requirement attempts to prevent upward communication originating from only a few sources. Many times only the most vocal organizational members are heard, whereas the less vocal may have important things to say as well.

   In following these principles, management obtains information from a wider variety of sources, and communication is not limited to crisis situations. The old adage "no news is good news" does not hold for upward organizational communication.

2. **The flow of communication must be directed:** Communication that is not directed to the proper receivers becomes rumour and finds its way through the organization according to who will listen. Proper directed communication, however, reaches those individuals who are in a position to take action. Employees who are dissatisfied and wish to communicate with management must be directed to the correct channels, and these channels should be known to everyone.

3. **Listening must be sensitive:** Because of the fundamental nature of hierarchical systems, employees may be conditioned to tell management what they think management wants to hear rather than what they actually feel. Complaints are often disguised in ways that prevent them from being obvious to the listener. Consequently, management must attempt to respond not only to the spoken word, but to the meaning of the words. To a large degree, the sensitivity of the manager determines the amount and type of communication that is directed upward from subordinates.

4. **Listening must be objective:** Upward communication will be selective and infrequent if employees think their communications are not being perceived in an objective fashion. It is easy for managers to show more interest in favorable communication than unfavorable or seek out those employees who will agree with them and ignore those who do not. Objectivity in upward communication means that management must make a conscious effort to avoid these biases.
5. **Listening implies action:** Communication is not an end in itself but a means to an end. While listening to employees is certainly important, unless some kind of action is forthcoming, the listening function loses its value. In some cases, listening itself can give the employee the impression that action will be taken, and management must be cautious not to leave the impression that communication efforts guarantee results.

If, for example, employees offer suggestions for work improvements that cannot be implemented, they should be told why.

If properly utilized, upward communication is potentially one of the most useful managerial practices. Upward communication keeps managers aware of how employees feel about their jobs, co-workers and the organization in general. Managers also rely on upward communication for ideas on how things can be improved.

5.7.3 Lateral Communication

When takes place among members of the same work group, among members of work groups at the same level, among managers at the same level or among any horizontally equivalent personnel, we describe it as lateral communications. In lateral communication, the sender and receiver(s) are at the same level in the hierarchy. Formal communications that travel laterally involve employees engaged in carrying out the same or related tasks. The messages might concern advice, problem solving, or coordination of activities.

The direction of communication in organizations explained above is summarized in the figure below.

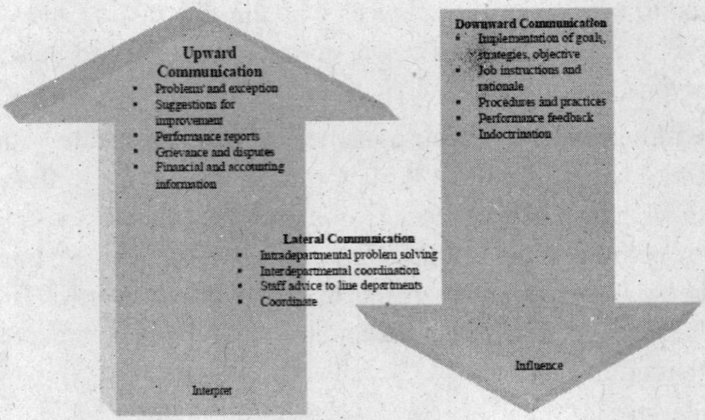

Directions of Communication in Organization

5.8 COMMUNICATION NETWORKS

A communication network is the pattern of directions in which information flows in the organization. Channels of communication (networks by which information flows) are either formal networks or informal networks. Formal networks follow the authority chain and are limited to task-related communications. The informal network (grapevine) is free to move in any direction, skip authority levels, and is as likely to satisfy group members' social needs as it is to facilitate task accomplishments.

The basic types of communication networks are shown in the figure below:

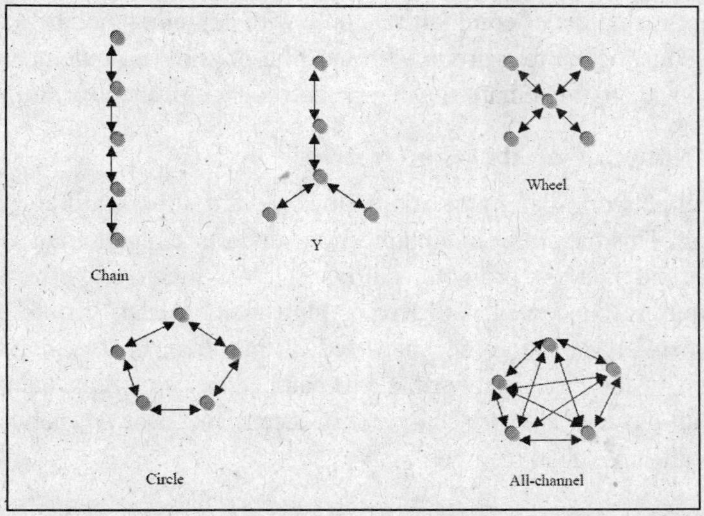

Chain Network

In chain network, communication travels up and down through the hierarchy. Each person communicates with only the person directly above or below in terms of reporting relationships. The chain network rigidly follows the formal chain of command.

Y Network

In the Y network, the flow of communication resembles an upside down Y; information flows upward and downward through the hierarchy, widening to encompass the number of employees reporting to a supervisor.

Wheel Network

In a wheel network, information flows to and from a single person. Employees in the group communicate primarily with that person rather than with each other. Such a communication network is a fast means of getting information to employees, since the person at the hub of the wheel can do so directly and efficiently. The wheel network relies on the leader to act as the central conduit (channel) for the entire group's communication.

The chain network, the Y network and the wheel network are fairly centralized in that most messages must flow through a pivotal (essential, crucial) person in the network. In the wheel network, the most centralized, all messages must flow through the individual at the centre of the wheel. In the chain network, some members can communicate with more than one member of the network, but the individual in the centre of the chain still tends to emerge as the controller of the messages. In the Y network, the member at the fork of the "Y" usually becomes the central person in the network.

Circle Network

In a circle network, employees communicate only with adjoining members of the organization. The circle network is analogous to a group working in a physical arrangement such that workers can communicate with their immediate neighbour but not with others in the group.

The All-Channel Network or the Star Network

In an all-channel network, communications flow upward, downward and laterally among all members of the group. This pattern of communication supports an egalitarian, (equal, unrestricted) participative culture and fosters (promote, cultivate) cross-functional efforts. The all-channel network is best if you are concerned with having high member satisfaction. The circle network and the all-channel network are more decentralized in that there is freer communication among the various members. In the circle network, each member can communicate with the individual on either side. The all-channel network is the most decentralized of the networks; each member can communicate with any other member.

5.9 INFORMAL COMMUNICATION

Informal communication is communication outside the organization's formally authorized channels. Informal communication includes all messages transmitted in the work setting other than those that are generated specifically to fulfil work-related assignments. The nature of such communication is nowhere described in the formal communication systems, but the organization could not survive without it.

5.9.1 The Grapevine

The network for much informal communication is the organization's grapevine. Grapevines develop in organizations to handle communications that the formal channels of communication do not handle. It typically supplements or replaces the organizational hierarchy as the means for transmitting communication. The grapevine serves as an excellent source of information about employee attitudes as well as an emotional outlet for workers. Thus, grapevine is likely to be strong during uncertain times and in organizations that limit the low of information to employees through formal channels. Also, employees may participate in a grapevine to help meet social needs.

The development of grapevines is inevitable. Although grapevines are neither good nor bad in themselves, the messages they carry are subject to distortion as messages transmitted from one human link to another become progressively more garbled (distorted: confused). Their content is misinterpreted, abbreviated, embellished (overstated) and selectively transmitted in terms of what the sender believes the receiver wants or needs to know. Since the original message may be only partially true, it is not surprising that the grapevine is sometimes referred to as a rumour mill. The information that travels through a grapevine typically takes the form of gossip (belief about other people) and rumours (efforts to predict future events).

The Grapevine has three main characteristics

(a) It is not controlled by management.

(b) It is perceived by most employees as being more believable and reliable than formal communiqués issued by top management.

(c) It is largely used to serve the self-interests of these people within it.

The network of a grapevine typically takes on one of the patterns shown in the figure below:

Single Strand (each tells one other)

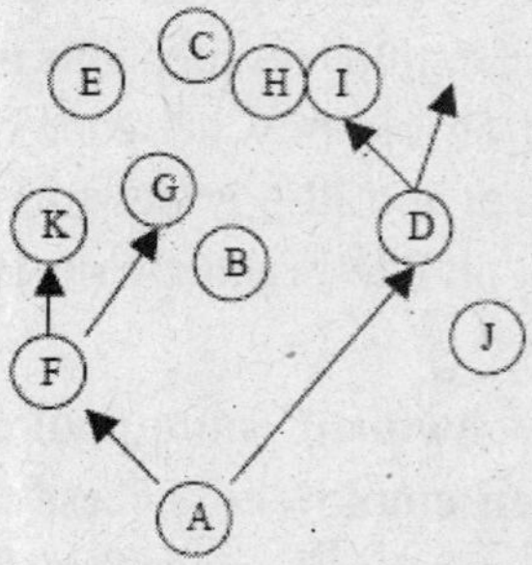

Probability
(each randomly tell others)

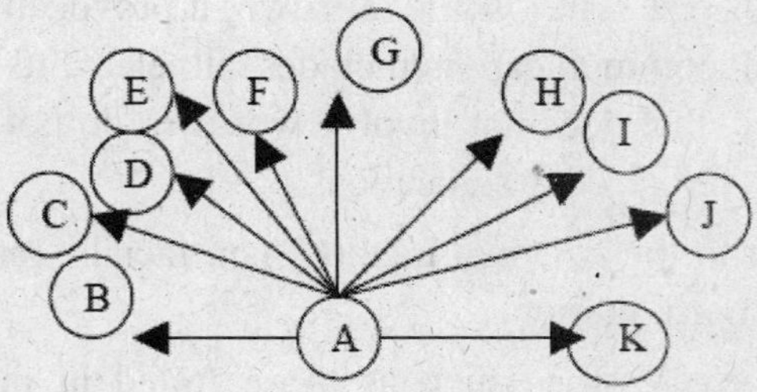

Gossip (one tells all)

Grapevine Patterns

(i) ***Single Strand:*** In the single-strand chain, communication moves serially from person A to B to C and so on.

(ii) ***Gossip Chain:*** With gossip chain, person A seeks out and tells others.

(iii) ***Probability Chain:*** When following the probability chain, person A spreads the message randomly as do individuals F and D.

(iv) ***Cluster Chain:*** In cluster chain, person A tells three selected individuals and then one of these tells three others.

Despite the fact that grapevines sometimes create difficulties when they carry gossip and false rumours, they are a fact of life in organizations and it is unrealistic of managers to think that they can eliminate grapevines.

The Old-Boy Network

The old-boy network is another network for informal communication. It is an exclusive group that wields power through shared information. In an old-boy network, members share information to help one another along in their careers. An old-boy network differs from other kinds of informal alliances among groups of employees in that its members have control over much of the organizations resources. Belonging to an old-boy network can be advantageous to its members, but from an organization's perspective, an old-boy network can be harmful. It limits some employees' access to information and prevents the organization from readily tapping the potential of people outside the network.

Organizations that view their entire pool of employees as a source of competitive advantage therefore seek to broaden employees' access to information. The more the organization's goals, strategies, performance and staffing needs are communicated through formal channels, and the more the organization listens to its employees, the less important are informal channels such as old-boy networks.

5.10 NON-VERBAL COMMUNICATION

Non-verbal communication is communication by means of elements and behaviours that are not coded into words. A glance, a star, a smile, a frown, a provocative body movement - they all convey meaning. Nonverbal communication includes all elements of communication, such as gestures and the use of space, that does not involve words or do not involve language. Porter has defined four aspects of non-verbal communications:

1. **Physical:** Pertaining to the personal method, i.e., facial expressions, tone of voice, sense of touch, smell and body motion.
2. **Esthetics:** Creative expressions such as those found in music, dancing or any of the creative arts.

3. **Symbolic:** Conveying messages through symbolic representations of reality; includes religious, status or ego-building symbols.
4. **Sign:** Mechanical means of conveying messages such as bills, buzzers, locks on doors, etc.

The important categories of non-verbal communication include:-

Proxemics

Proxemics refers to the influence of proximity and space on communication. The study of an individual's perception and use of space, including territorial space, is called proxemics. Territorial space refers to bands of space extending outward from the body. These bands constitute comfort zones. In each comfort zone, different cultures prefer different types of interaction with others. Typically there are four zones of territorial space.

(a) ***Intimate Zone (touching to two feet):*** This space is normally reserved for closest family and friends. In this zone, we interact with spouses, significant others, family members and others with whom we have an intimate relationship.

(b) ***Personal Zone (two to four feet):*** Family and friends may enter this zone without causing discomfort. Friends typically interact with this distance.

(c) ***Social Zone (four to twelve feet):*** The person comfortably interacts with others in this zone. Most business transactions take place within the social zone. We prefer that business associates and acquaintances interact with us in this zone.

(d) ***Public Zone (twelve feet to as far as the person can hear and see):*** This is the most distant zone at which communication can occur. Most of us prefer that strangers stay at least 12 feet from us, and we become uncomfortable when they move closer. Lectures and other formal presentations take place within this zone.

In general, a person who moves into a closer zone of personal space is signalling a desire for greater closeness. When the receiver of this non-verbal message interprets it as a request for more closeness than is desirable, the receiver probably will feel uncomfortable and try to move away. Territorial space varies greatly across cultures. People often become uncomfortable when operating in territorial space different from those in which they are familiar.

Kinesics

Kinesics is the study of body movements, including posture. Like proxemics, kinesics is culturally bound; there is no single universal gesture. Kinesics behaviour refers to body movements, such as gestures, facial expressions, eye movements and posture. We often draw conclusions regarding people's feelings about an issue, not only from their words but also from their non-verbal behaviour, such as their facial expressions.

(a) ***Facial Expressions:*** The face is a rich source of nonverbal communication. The face often gives unintended clues to emotions the sender is trying to hide. Although smiles have universal meaning, frowns, raised eyebrows, and wrinkled foreheads must all be interpreted in conjunction with the actors, the situation and the culture.

(b) ***Eye Behaviour:*** Eye behaviour are used to add cues for the receiver. Eye contact can enhance reflective listening, and it varies by culture. In India, a direct gaze indicates honesty and forthrightness. Appropriate use of eye contact signals interest in the other person.

(c) ***Gestures:*** Some people use gestures extensively; others communicate little through this channel. In India, the handshake is a widely used gesture. People often use the handshake as a source of information about another person's characteristics. A strong, firm handshake is seen as a sign of confidence and enthusiasm.

Paralanguage

Paralanguage refers to vocal aspects of communication that relate to how something is said rather than to what is said. Voice quality, tone of voice, laughing, and yawning fit in this category. People make attributions about the sender by deciphering (make sense of; interpret or decode) paralanguage cues. Rapid, loud speech may be taken as a sign of nervousness or anger. Vocal tone includes pitch, loudness, rhythm, rate, and clarity of speech. The standards for what is comfortable vary from one culture to another.

Object Language

Object language refers to the communicative use of material things, including clothing, cosmetics, furniture and architecture. A work area adorned with expensive objects communicate high status.

Territory

Employees' work areas are, in a sense, their territory. The way people arrange themselves and others within their territory also conveys messages. In a meeting or training session, arranging chairs in rows signals that participants will be lectured to and encourages passive behaviour. Arranging chairs in a circle signals that active participation is encouraged. When interviewing or meeting with someone in his or her office, a manager sends different messages depending on whether the manager remains behind the desk or joins the other person in comfortable chairs on the same side of the desk.

Physical Appearance

Aspects of personal appearance such as clothing, hairstyle, jewellery and makeup communicate people's values and social group. In the workplace, the norms for appropriate physical appearance depend on the industry, job, and organizational culture. People who fail to live up to these norms typically create a bad impression. Their physical appearance is interpreted as meaning they either do not understand their role or do not care about fulfilling it.

It is important for the receiver to be alert to these nonverbal aspects of communication. You should look for nonverbal cues as well as listen to the literal meaning of a sender's words. You should particularly be aware of contradictions between the messages. Nonverbal communication is important for managers because of its impact on the meaning of the message. However, a manager must consider the total message and all media of communication. A message can only be given meaning in context, and cues are easy to misinterpret. The figure below presents common nonverbal behaviour exhibited by managers and how employees may interpret them. Nonverbal cues can give others the wrong signal.

NONVERBAL COMMUNICATION	SIGNAL RECEIVED	REACTION FROM RECEIVER
Manager looks away when talking to the employee	Divided attention	My supervisor is too busy to listen to my problem or simply does not care.
Manager fails to acknowledge greeting from fellow employee.	Unfriendliness.	This person is unapproachable.
Manager glares ominously (i.e., gives the evil eye).	Anger.	Reciprocal anger, fear, or avoidance, depending on who is sending the signal in the organization.
Manager rolls the eyes.	Not taking person seriously	This person thinks he or she is smarter or better than I am.
Manager sighs deeply.	Disgust or displeasure.	My opinions do not count. I must be stupid or boring to this person.
Manager uses heavy breathing (sometimes accompanied by hand waving)	Anger or heavy stress.	Avoid this person at all costs.
Manager does not maintain eye contact when communicating.	Suspicion or uncertainty.	What does this person have to hide?
Manager crosses arms and leans away.	Apathy or closed-mindedness.	This person already has made up his or her mind; my opinions are not important.
Manager peers over glasses.	Scepticism or distrust.	He or she does not believe what I am saying.
Manager continues to read a report when employee is speaking.	Lack of interest.	My opinions are not important enough to get the supervisor's undivided attention.

Common Nonverbal Cues from Manager to Employee

5.11 BARRIERS TO EFFECTIVE COMMUNICATION

Barriers to communication are factors that block or significantly distort successful communication. Effective managerial communication skills helps overcome some, but not all, barriers to communication in organizations. The more prominent barriers to effective communication which every manager should be aware of is given below:

Filtering: Filtering refers to a sender manipulating information so it will be seen more favourably by the receiver. The major determinant of filtering is the number of levels in an organization's structure. The more vertical levels in the organization's hierarchy, the more opportunities for filtering. Sometimes the information is filtered by the sender himself.

If the sender is hiding some meaning and disclosing in such a fashion as appealing to the receiver, then he is "filtering" the message deliberately. A manager in the process of altering communication in his favour is attempting to filter the information.

Selective Perception: Selective perception means seeing what one wants to see. The receiver, in the communication process, generally resorts to selective perception i.e., he selectively perceives the message based on the organizational requirements, the needs and characteristics, background of the employees etc. Perceptual distortion is one of the distressing barriers to the effective communication. People interpret what they see and call it a reality. In our regular activities, we tend to see those things that please us and to reject or ignore unpleasant things. Selective perception allows us to keep out dissonance (the existence of conflicting elements in our perceptual set) at a tolerable level. If we encounter something that does not fit out current image of reality, we structure the situation to minimize our dissonance. Thus, we manage to overlook many stimuli from the environment that do not fit into out current perception of the world. This process has significant implications for managerial activities. For example, the employment interviewer who expects a female job applicant to put her family ahead of her career is likely to see that in female applicants, regardless of whether the applicants feel that way or not.

Emotions: How the receiver feels at the time of receipt of information influences effectively how he interprets the information. For example, if the receiver feels that the communicator is in a jovial mood, he interprets that the information being sent by the communicator to be good and interesting. Extreme emotions and jubilation or depression are quite likely to hinder the effectiveness of communication. A person's ability to encode a message can become impaired when the person is feeling strong emotions. For example, when you are angry, it is harder to consider the other person's viewpoint and to choose words carefully. The angrier you are, the harder this task becomes. Extreme emotions – such as jubilation or depression - are most likely to hinder effective communication. In such instances, we are most prone to disregard our rational and objective thinking processes and substitute emotional judgments.

Language: Communicated message must be understandable to the receiver. Words mean different things to different people. Language reflects not only the personality of the individual but also the culture of society in which the individual is living. In organizations, people from different regions, different backgrounds, and speak different languages. People will have different academic backgrounds, different intellectual facilities, and hence the jargon they use varies. Often, communication gap arises because the language the sender is using may be incomprehensible, vague and indigestible. Language is a central element in communication. It may pose a barrier if its use obscures meaning and distorts intent.

Words mean different things to different people. Age, education and cultural background are three of the more obvious variables that influence the language a person uses and the definitions he or she gives to words. Therefore, use simple, direct, declarative language.

Speak in brief sentences and use terms or words you have heard from you audience. As much as possible, speak in the language of the listener. Do not use jargon or technical language except with those who clearly understand it.

Stereotyping: Stereotyping is the application of selective perception. When we have preconceived ideas about other people and refuse to discriminate between individual behaviours, we are applying selective perception to our relationship with other people. Stereotyping is a barrier to communications because those who stereotype others use selective perception in their communication and tend to hear only those things that confirm their stereotyped images. Consequently, stereotypes become more deeply ingrained as we find more "evidence" to confirm our original opinion.

Stereotyping has a convenience function in our interpersonal relations. Since people are all different, ideally we should react and interact with each person differently. To do this, however, requires considerable psychological effort. It is much easier to categorize (stereotype) people so that we can interact with them as members of a particular category.

Since the number of categories is small l, we end up treating many people the same even though they are quite different. Our communications, then, may be directed at an individual as a member of a category at the sacrifice of the more effective communication on a personal level.

Status Difference

The organizational hierarchy pose another barrier to communication within organization, especially when the communication is between employee and manager. This is so because the employee is dependent on the manager as the primary link to the organization and hence more likely to distort upward communication than either horizontal or downward communication. Effective supervisory skills make the supervisor more approachable and help reduce the risk of problems related to status differences. In addition, when employees feel secure, they are more likely to be straightforward in upward communication.

Use of Conflicting Signals

A sender is using conflicting signals when he or she sends inconsistent messages. A vertical message might conflict with a nonverbal one. For example, if a manager says to his employees, "If you have a problem, just come to me. My door is always open", but he looks annoyed whenever an employee knocks on his door". Then we say the manager is sending conflicting messages. When signals conflict, the receivers of the message have to decide which, if any, to believe.

Reluctance to Communicate

For a variety of reasons, managers are sometimes reluctant to transmit messages. The reasons could be:-

- They may doubt their ability to do so.
- They may dislike or be weary of writing or talking to others.
- They may hesitate to deliver bad news because they do not want to face a negative reaction.

When someone gives in to these feelings, they become a barrier to effective communications.

Projection

Projection has two meanings

(a) Projecting one's own motives into others behaviour. For example, managers who are motivated by money may assume their subordinates are also motivated by it. If the subordinate's prime motive is something other than money, serious problems may arise.

(b) The use of defense mechanism to avoid placing blame on oneself. As a defense mechanism, the projection phenomenon operates to protect the ego from unpleasant communications. Frequently, individuals who have a particular fault will see the same fault in others, making their own fault seem not so serious.

The "Halo Effect"

The term "halo effect" refers to the process of forming opinions based on one element from a group of elements and generalizing that perception to all other elements. For example, in an organization, a good attendance record may cause positive judgements about productivity, attitude, or quality of work. In performance evaluation system, the halo effect refers to the practice of singling out one trait of an employee (either good or bad) and using this as a basis for judgement of the total employee (e.g., seeing the welldressed manager as the "good" manager).

Keys to Effective Supervisory Communication

Managers can and should improve communication in organizations. Interpersonal communication between managers and their employees is a critical foundation for effective performance in organizations. In his research work F. M Jablin has identified five communication skills that distinguish "good" from "bad" supervisors.

Expressive Speakers

Better supervisors express their thoughts, ideas and feelings. Supervisors who speak out let the people they work with know where they stand, what they believe and how they feel.

Empathetic Listeners

The better supervisors are willing, empathetic listeners. Empathetic listeners are able to hear the feelings and emotional dimensions of the messages people send them, as well as the content of the ideas and issues. Better supervisors are approachable and willing to listen to suggestions and complaints.

Persuasive Leaders

Better supervisors are persuasive leaders. They are distinguished by their use of persuasive communication when influencing others. Specifically, they encourage others to achieve results instead of telling others what to do. They are not highly directive or manipulative in their influence attempts.

Sensitive to Feelings

Better supervisors are also sensitive to the feelings, self-image and psychological defences of their employees. Care is taken to avoid giving critical feedback or reprimanding in public. They work to enhance that self-esteem as appropriate to the person's real talents, abilities and achievements.

Informative Managers

Finally, better supervisors keep those who work for them well informed. They give advance notice of organizational changes and explain the rationale for organizational policies.

5.13 HOW COMMUNICATION LEADS GLOBALLY?

Improved communication might be considered a supportive reason for opening up new markets overseas, because the reason for opening up new markets overseas, because the effective ability to communicate with subordinates and customers has given managers confidence in their ability to control foreign operations if they should undertake them.

- Good, relatively inexpensive international communication enables international firms to transmit computer-oriented tasks worldwide to a cheap but skilled labour force abroad.
- Shorter travelling time has also been responsible for numerous business opportunities because foreign businessmen have come to the home country to look for new products to import or to buy new technology.

UNIT EXERCISE

Short Answers

Q1. What is meant by communication.

Q2. What is the role of inter-personal communication?

Q3. Explain the concept of formal communication.

Q4. What are communication networks?

Q5. Is grapevine always bad?

Long Answers

Q1. What is meant by communication? What is the role of inter-personal communication?

Q2. Differentiate between formal and informal networks of communication.

Q3. What do you understand by 'Communication'? Explain the communication process.

Q4. Explain how communication is the essence of management and how formal channels of communication provide for vertical, horizontal and lateral flows.

Q5. What is informal communication? How can grapevine be used by the management for efficient management?

Chapter 6

Motivation

6.0 INTRODUCTION

Motivation is the process of channelling a person's inner drives so that he wants to accomplish the goals of the organization. Motivation concern itself with the will to work. It seeks to know the incentives for work and tries to find out the ways and means whereby their realization can be helped and encouraged. Managers, by definition, are required to work with and through people, so they must gain at least some understanding of the forces that will motivate the people they are to manage. People are complex and they are uniquely different. What motivates one person may not motivate another. Most successful managers have learned to understand the concept of human motivation and are able to use that understanding to achieve higher standards of subordinate work performance.

6.1 DEFINITION OF MOTIVATION

"Motivation" is a Latin word, meaning "to move". Human motives are internalised goals within individuals. Motivation may be defined as those forces that cause people to behave in certain ways. Motivation encompasses all those pressures and influences that trigger, channel, and sustain human behaviour. Most successful managers have learned to understand the concept of human motivation and are able to use that understanding to achieve higher standards of subordinate work performance.

Motivation has been defined by Michael J Juicus as "the act f stimulating someone or oneself to get a desired course of action".

In the words of **Lewis Allen**, "Motivation is the work a manager performs to inspire, encourage and impel people to take required action".

According to **Dubin**, Motivation is, "The complex of forces starting and keeping a person at work in an organization. To put it generally, motivation starts and maintains an activity along a prescribed line. Motivation is something that moves the person to action, and continuous him in the course of action already initiated".

According to **William G Scott**, "Motivation means a process of stimulating people to action to accomplish desired goals".

According to **Koontz and O'Donnell**, "Motivation is a general term applying to the entire class of drives, needs, wishes and similar forces".

In the words of **Brech,** "Motivation is a general inspiration process which gets the members of the team to pull their weight effectively, to give their loyalty to the group, to carry out properly the tasks they have accepted and generally to play an effective part in the job that the group has undertaken".

In the words of **Dalton E McFarland**, "Motivation refers to the way in which urges, drives, desires, aspirations, striving or needs direct, control or explain the behaviour of human beings".

In the words of **Tolman**, "The term motivation has been called an intervening variable. Intervening variables are internal and psychological process which are not directly observable and which, in turn, account for behaviour".

The **Encyclopaedia** of Management observes: "Motivation refers to the degree of readiness of an organism to pursue some designated goal, and implies the determination of the nature and locus of the forces, including the degree of readiness".

In the words of **C. B. Mamoria** - Motivation is - "a willingness to expend energy to achieve a goal or reward. It is a force that activates dormant energies and sets in motion the action of the people. It is the function that kindles a burning passion for action among the human beings of an organization".

Motivation is a process by which a need or desire is aroused and a psychological force within our mind sets us in motion to fulfil our needs and desire. An unsatisfied need becomes the motive for a person to spend his energy in order to achieve a goal. In a business organization the 4 P's praise, prestige promotion and pay are the best positive motivators.

6.2 NATURE AND CHARACTERISTICS OF MOTIVATION

Psychologists generally agree that all behaviour is motivated, and that people have reasons for doing the things they do or for behaving in the manner that they do. Motivating is the work a manager performs to inspire, encourage and impel people to take required action.

The process of motivation is characterized by the following:

1. **Motivation is an Internal Feeling:** Motivation is a psychological phenomenon which generates in the mind of an individual the feeling that he lacks certain things and needs those things. Motivation is a force within an individual that drives him to behave in a certain way.
2. **Motivation is Related to Needs:** Needs are deficiencies which are created whenever there is a physiological or psychological imbalance. In order to motivate a person, we have to understand his needs that call for satisfaction.
3. **Motivation Produces Goal-Directed Behaviour:** Goals are anything which will alleviate a need and reduce a drive. An individual's behavior is directed towards a goal.
4. **Motivation can be either Positive or Negative:** Positive or incentive motivation is generally based on reward. According to Flippo - "positive motivation is a process of attempting to influence others to do your will through the possibility of gain or reward". Negative or fear motivation is based on force and fear. Fear causes persons to act in a certain way because they are afraid of the consequences if they don't.

6.3 IMPORTANCE AND BENEFITS OF MOTIVATION

A manager's primary task is to motivate others to perform the tasks of the organization. Therefore, the manager must find the keys to get subordinates to come to work regularly and on time, to work hard, and to make positive contributions towards the effective and efficient achievement of organizational objectives. Motivation is an effective instrument in the hands of a manager for inspiring the work force and creating confidence in it. By motivating the work force, management creates "will to work" which is necessary for the achievement of organizational goals. The various benefits of motivation are:

(i) Motivation is one of the important elements in the directing process. By motivating the workers, a manager directs or guides the workers' actions in the desired direction for accomplishing the goals of the organization.

(ii) Workers will tend to be as efficient as possible by improving upon their skills and knowledge so that they are able to contribute to the progress of the organization thereby increasing productivity.

(iii) For performing any tasks, two things are necessary. They are: (a) ability to work and (b) willingness to work. Without willingness to work, ability to work is of no use. The willingness to work can be created only by motivation.

(iv) Organizational effectiveness becomes, to some degree, a question of management's ability to motivate its employees, to direct at least a reasonable effort towards the goals of the organization.

(v) Motivation contributes to good industrial relations in the organization. When the workers are motivated, contented and disciplined, the frictions between the workers and the management will be reduced.

(vi) Motivation is the best remedy for resistance to changes. When changes are introduced in an organization, generally, there will be resistance from the workers. But if the workers of an organization are motivated, they will accept, introduce and implement the changes whole heartily and help to keep the organization on the right track of progress.

(vii) Motivation facilitates the maximum utilization of all factors of production, human, physical and financial resources and thereby contributes to higher production.

(viii) Motivation promotes a sense of belonging among the workers. The workers feel that the enterprise belongs to them and the interest of the enterprise is their interests.

(ix) Many organizations are now beginning to pay increasing attention to developing their employees as future resources upon which they can draw as they grow and develop.

6.4 TYPES OF MOTIVATION

If a manager wants to get work done by his employees, he may either hold out a promise of a reward (positive motivation) or he may install fear (negative motivation). Both these types are widely used by managements.

1. Positive or Incentive Motivation: This type of motivation is generally based on reward. A positive motivation involves the possibility of increased motive satisfaction. According to Flippo - "Positive motivation is a process of attempting to influence others to do your will through the possibility of gain or reward". Incentive motivation is the "pull" mechanism. The receipt of awards, due recognition and praise for work-well done definitely lead to good team spirit, co-operation and a feeling of happiness.

Positive motivation include:

(a) Praise and credit for work done

(b) Wages and Salaries

(c) Appreciation

(d) A sincere interest in subordinates as individuals

(e) Delegation of authority and responsibility

2. **Negative or Fear Motivation:** This type of motivation is based on force and fear. Fear causes persons to act in a certain way because they fear the consequences. Negative motivation involves the possibility of decreased motive satisfaction. It is a "push" mechanism.

The imposition of punishment frequently results in frustration among those punished, leading to the development of maladaptive behaviour. It also creates a hostile state of mind and an unfavourable attitude to the job. However, there is no management which has not used the negative motivation at some time or the other.

6.5 THEORIES OF MOTIVATION

Motivation to work is very complex. There are many internal and environmental variables that affect the motivation to work. Behavioural scientists started to search new facts and techniques for motivation. These theories are termed as theories of motivation. The most important theories are explained below.

1. McGregor's Theory X and Theory Y

Different styles of management have a different bearing on the motivation of workers in the organization. The style adopted by a manager in managing his subordinates is basically dependent upon his assumption about human behaviour. Theory X is negative, traditional and autocratic style while Theory Y is positive, participatory and democratic. Thus, these labels describe contrasting set of assumptions about human nature.

Douglas McGregor has classified the basic assumption regarding human nature into two parts and has designated them as 'theory X' and 'theory Y'.

Theory X: This is the traditional theory of human behaviour, which makes the following assumptions about human nature:

1. Management is responsible for organizing the elements of productive enterprises - money, material, equipment, and people - in the interest of economic ends.
2. With reference to people it is a process of directing their efforts, motivating them, controlling their actions, modifying their behaviour in order to be in conformity with the needs of the organization.
3. Without this active intervention by management, people would be passive – even resistant to organizational needs. Hence they must be persuaded, rewarded, punished and properly directed.

4. The average human being has an inherent dislike of work and will avoid it if he can.
5. He lacks ambition, dislikes responsibility and prefers to be led.
6. He is inherently self-centred, indifferent to organizational needs.
7. He is by nature resistant to change.
8. He is gullible, not very bright.

Theory Y: The assumption of theory Y, according to McGregor are as follows:-

1. Work is as natural as play or rest, provided the conditions are favourable; the average human being does not inherently dislike work.
2. External control and the thrust of punishment are not the only means for bringing about efforts towards organizational objectives. Man can exercise self-control and self-direction in the service of objectives to which he is committed
3. Commitment to objectives is a result of the rewards associated with their achievement. People select goals for themselves if they see the possibilities of some kind of reward that may be material or even psychological.
4. The average human being, under proper conditions does not shirk responsibility, but learn not only to accept responsibility but also to seek it.
5. He has capacity to exercise a relatively high degree of imagination, ingenuity and creativity in the solution of organizational problems in widely, not narrowly distributed in the population.
6. Under conditions of modern industrial life the intellectual potentialities of people are only partially utilized. As a matter of fact, men, have unlimited potential.

Comparison of Theory X and Theory Y

THEORY X	THEORY Y
1. Theory X assumes human beings inherently dislike work and are distasteful towards work.	1.Theory Y assumes that work is as natural as play or rest
2. Theory X emphasizes that people do not have ambitions and they shrink responsibility	2. Theory Y assumes just the reverse. Given proper conditions, people have ambitions and accept responsibility
3. Theory X assumes that people in general have little capacity for creativity	3. According to Theory Y the creativity is widely distributed in the population
4. According to Theory X, people lack self motivation and require be externally controlling and closely supervising in order to get maximum output.	4. While in Theory Y people are selfdirected and creative and prefer Selfcontrol
5. Theory X emphasise upon centralization of authority in decision-making process	5. Theory Y emphasizes decentralisation and greater participation in decisionmaking process

2. Maslow's Need-Hierarchy Theory of Motivation

According to Abraham Maslow, a U.S psychologist, man is a wanting animal. He has a variety of wants or needs. All motivated behaviour of man is directed towards the satisfaction of his needs. The theory postulated that people are motivated by multiple needs, which could be arranged in a hierarchy. Maslow offers a general theory of motivation called the 'need hierarchy theory'.

The features of his theory are as follows:-

1. People have a wide range of needs which motivate them to strive for fulfilment.
2. Human needs can be definitely categorized into five types:
    a. Physical needs,
    b. Safety or security needs,
    c. Affiliation or social needs,
    d. Esteem needs and
    e. Self-actualisation needs.
3. These needs can be arranged into a hierarchy. Physical needs are at the base whereas self-actualisation needs are at the apex.
4. People gratify their physical needs first, when the need is satisfied, they feel the urge for the next higher level need.
5. Relative satisfaction of lower level need is necessary to activate the next higher level need.
6. A satisfied need does not motivate human behaviour. It only triggers or activates the urge for the next higher level of needs.

Deficit and Progression Principles: In order to comprehend the full meaning of Maslow's theory, it is necessary to understand the deficit and progression principles.

Deficit Principle: According to Maslow, once a need is fairly well satisfied, it is no longer a stronger motivator of behaviour. People are motivated to satisfy only those needs that are perceived to be deficient.

Progression Principle: Maslow contends that the five categories of needs exist in a hierarchy. A need at a given level is not activated until the need directly below it is fairly well gratified. Thus, the person is expected to progress step-by-step up the need hierarchy. The need-hierarchy theory must not be viewed as a rigid structure to be applied universally in all situations. The hierarchy represents a typical pattern that operates most of the time.

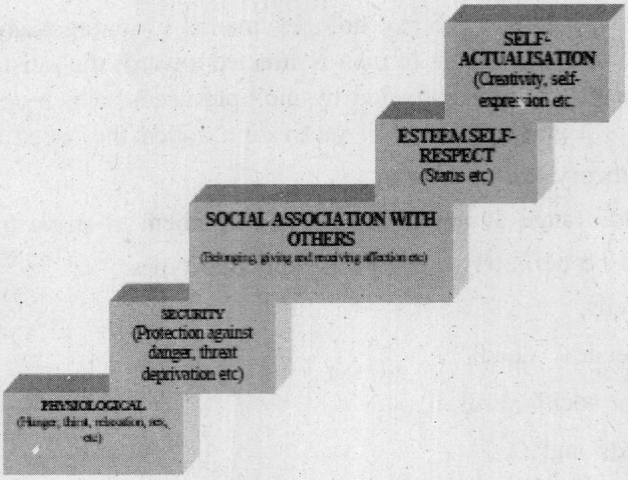

Figure 5.1: Maslow's Hierarchy of needs.

3. Hertzberg's Theory of Motivation

Hertzberg developed a theory of motivation on the premise that human nature has two separate elements - The motivators and maintenance factors. According to this theory of motivation the items that determine job content are considered motivational factors e.g.:- Achievement, recognition, responsibility, advancement and the work itself. The elements that influence the job context are the hygiene or maintenance factors e.g.:- company policy, salary, inter personal relations, working conditions etc. They must be adequate and if they are absent or inadequate, they will create dissatisfaction.

(a) ***Hygiene Factors:*** Hygiene factors represent the need to avoid pain in the environment. They are not an intrinsic part of a job, but they are related to the conditions under which a job is performed. They are associated with negative feelings. They must be viewed as preventive measures that remove sources of dissatisfaction from environment. Hertzberg believed that hygiene factors created a zero level of motivation and if maintained at proper level prevents negative type of motivation from occurring. Thus, hygiene factors, when absent, increase dissatisfaction with the job. When present, help in preventing dissatisfaction but do not increase satisfaction or motivation.

(b) ***Motivators:*** Motivators are associated with positive feelings of employees about the job. They make people satisfied with their job. Motivators are necessary to keep job satisfaction and job performance high. On the other hand, if they are not present they do not prove highly satisfying. Motivational factors or satisfiers are directly related to job content itself, the individual's performance of it, its responsibilities and the growth and recognition obtained from it. Motivators are intrinsic to the job. Thus, when motivators are absent, prevent both satisfaction and motivation. When, motivators are present, they lead to satisfaction and motivation. To apply the two-factor theory to the workplace, Hertzberg suggests a two-step process

(i) The supervisor should attempt to eliminate the hygiene factors that are found to be more basic than factors that lead to satisfaction.

(ii) Once the dissatisfies have been somewhat neutralized, the supervisor may be able to motivate workers through the introduction of motivational factors.

4. Victor Vroom's Expectancy Theory

Expectancy Theory was developed by Victor H Vroom. It is based on the notion that human behaviour depends on people's expectations concerning their ability to perform tasks and to receive desired rewards. The expectancy theory argues that the strength of a tendency to act in a certain way depends in the strength of an expectation that the act will be followed by a given outcome and on the attractiveness of the outcome to the individual. It includes three variables which Vroom refers to as -

(i) ***Valance:*** Valence means the strength of an individual's preference for a particular outcome. A valence of zero occurs when the individual is indifferent towards the outcome. The valance is negative when the individual prefers not attaining the outcome to attaining it.

(ii) ***Instrumentality:*** Instrumentality refers to the relationship between performance and reward. It refers to a degree to which a first level outcome (e.g.:-superior performance) will lead to a desired second level outcome (e.g.:- promotion). If people perceive that their performance is adequately rewarded the perceived instrumentality will be positive. On the other hand, if they perceive that performance does not make any difference to their rewards, the instrumentality will be low.

(iii) ***Expectancy:*** People have expectancies about the likelihood that an action or effort on their part will lead to the intended performance. Workers will be motivated by the belief that their performance will ultimately lead to payoffs for them. Expectancy is the probability that a particular action will lead to a particular first level outcome. In sum, Vroom emphasizes the importance of individual perceptions and assessments of organizational behaviour. The key to "expectancy" theory is the "understanding of an individual's goals" - and the linkage between "effort" and "performance" between "performance" and "rewards" and between "rewards" and "individual-goal satisfaction". It is a contingency model, which recognizes that there is no universal method of motivating people. Because we understand what needs an employee seeks to satisfy does not ensure that the employee himself perceives high job performance as necessarily leading to the satisfaction of these needs.

5. McClelland's Need for Achievement Theory

David C McClelland, a Harvard Psychologist, has proposed that there are three major relevant motives most needs in work-place situations. According to him, the motives are:-

a. The need for achievement i.e., strives to succeed.

b. The need for affiliation i.e., warm relationship with others the need for power i.e., controls other people.

According to McClelland, every motive is acquired except striving for pleasure and avoiding pain. He proposed that people acquire these needs for achievement, power and affiliation through experiences over the time. On the job, people are motivated by these needs, and the manager can learn to recognize these needs in workers and use them to motivate behaviour.

McClelland used the Thematic Apperception Test (TAT) to study human needs. The TAT process involves asking respondents to look at pictures and write stories about what they see in the pictures. The stories are then analysed to find certain themes that represent various human needs. From his research, McClelland found that, achievement motive is a "desire to perform in terms of a standard of excellence or to be successful in competitive situations". They (employees) seek situations where:

1. They can attain personal responsibility for finding solutions to problems.
2. They can receive immediate feedback information on how they are progressive towards a goal.
3. They can set moderately challenging goals.
4. They find accomplishing a task intrinsically satisfying. "High achievers" differentiate themselves from others by their desire to do things better.

Evaluation: Achievement motivated people is the backbone of any organization. As such considerable time and attention must be devoted to constructing ways of developing the achievement motive at the managerial level. Organizational climate must be conducive to high achievement. Managers must try to raise the achievement need level of subordinates by creating the proper work environment, increasing responsibility and autonomy and rewarding excellence in performance.

6.6 REQUIREMENTS OF A SOUND MOTIVATION SYSTEM

It is very difficult for an average manager to sort through all the different motivational theories and models and know when and how to maximize their application in widely differing situations. There should be a sound system of motivation to make the workers put forth their best efforts. A sound system of motivation should have the following essential features.

1. A sound motivation system should satisfy the needs and objectives of both organization and employees.
2. Motivational system should change with the changes in the situation.
3. Jobs should be designed in such a way as to provide challenge and variety.
4. Managers should recruit the active co-operation of subordinates in improving the organization's output. Subordinates should be made to realize that they are stakeholders in the organization.

5. The motivational system should satisfy the different needs of employees. It should be directly related to the efforts of the employers.
6. The motivational system should be simple so that it is easily understood by the workers.

6.7 METHODS OF MOTIVATING PEOPLE

Several factors influence human behaviour. There are numerous drives and needs which can act as good motivators moving people to work and getting things done through them as per the plan. People respond to physiological needs, social needs and egoistic needs. Human needs and desires are the door ways through which the manager channelises his motivation efforts. There are three types of motivational programmes to improve a person's behaviour towards his job. These are:-

1. Pay incentive plans,
2. Job enrichment and
3. Management by objectives.

6.8 FACTORS DETERMINING RESPONSE TO MOTIVATION

There are four important factors governing employee response to the measures of motivation:

i The intensity or urge of the Drive.

ii **Past Experience:** can he rely upon the promises given by the boss.

iii **Amount of Reward:** The quantity and quality of the reward can influence the amount of extra effort put forth by the employee.

iv **Time Relationship of Response to Reward:** Long range promises are less effective than immediate fulfilment.

6.9 UNIT EXERCISE

Short Answers

1. Explain the concept of motivation.
2. 'Motivation is the core of management.' Comment.
3. Explain the Theory X and Theory Y.
4. What is the major criticism of Two-Factor Theory of motivation.

Long Answers

1. Enumerate the assumptions of McGregor's Theory X and Theory Y. Which one is applicable in India?
2. Explain what is meant by hierarchical nature of the needs? Is this hierarchy rigid? Discuss with suitable examples.

3. Explain Herzberg's Two Factor Theory and differentiate it from Maslow's Theory of Need Hierarchy.
4. Which theory—Maslow's Need-Hierarchy Theory or Herzberg's Two-Factor Theory—does, in your opinion, better explain the behavior of people at work in India? Give reasons for your answers.

CHAPTER 7

Authority

7.0 INTRODUCTION

MAX WEBER defines authority, as the willing and unconditional compliance of people, resting upon their belief that it is legitimate for superior to impose his will on them and illegitimate for them to refuse to obey. It can be defined as legitimate right to give orders and get orders obeyed.

7.1 CHARACTERISTICS OF AUTHORITY

1. There is existence of RIGHT in authority
2. The RIGHT of giving order is legitimate
3. Authority gives a right to decision making.
4. A person with authority influences the behaviour of others that might otherwise not take place.
5. Exercising authority is subjective.

7.2 SOURCES OF AUTHORITY

There are 3 theories, namely, the Formal Authority Theory, the Acceptance Theory, and the Competence Theory.

Let us discuss each of them-

1. Formal Authority Theory

Authority does not vest in a managerial position. It is delegated from the top management. For e.g., a supervisor in production department gets authority from the production manager, a CEO gets from the Board of Directors or owners. In the Indian situation of public limited companies, owners have some limitations of authority. Similarly , a manager has limited authority delegated by his superior.

2. Acceptance Theory

The essence of this theory is that people differ in the degree of effort they contribute to achieve the objectives of the organisation. The degree of effective authority possessed by the manager is measured by the willingness of subordinates to accept it- There are numerous problems in this theory. A manager will not know whether the subordinate will accept the order. For e.g., For a manger to be successful, he needs both leadership and authority.

3. Competence Theory

There is a feeling that authority is generated by personal competencies. URWICK identifies formal authority as being conferred by organisation, technical authority as being implicit in special knowledge or skill and personal authority as being conferred by seniority or popularity.

7.3 LIMITATIONS OF AUTHORITY

In an organisation, the quantum of authority decreases at successively lower levels. K is maximum at the highest level, and minimum at the lowest level. The authority is not absolute. It is subject to various social, legal, political, and economic factors. Similarly, the use of authority by a superior over his subordinate is restricted by various factors.

Limits of authority at various level in an organisation

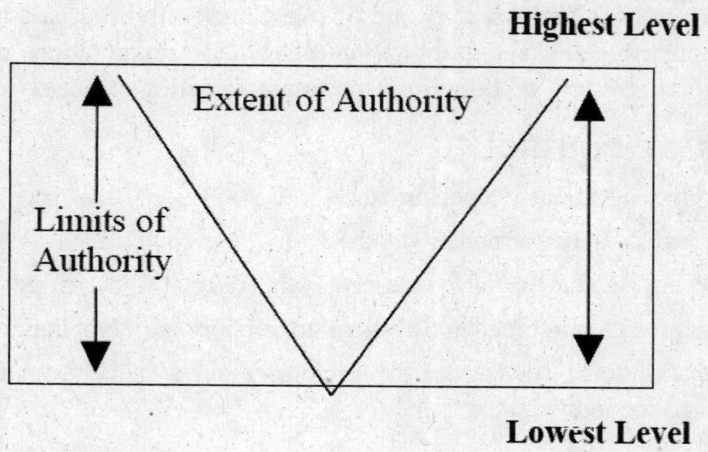

7.4 DIFFERENCES BETWEEN POWER AND AUTHORITY

Both power and authority, no doubt, has the objective of influencing the behaviour of others, but they are not synonymous . Power is q question of one's capability to exert influence in getting the desired result. Power has no legal sanctity, while authority does. Both have different mount of legitimacy. Authority is institution and legitimate, while power is personal and carries little legitimacy. Authority is delegated by higher management, while power is earned and gained by leaders on the basis of their leadership and personality, activities, and in situations.

7.5 HOW TO CONTROL O.B.?

Organisations are primarily people oriented. Through people, organisations achieve their established and predetermined goals. Organisations regulate the behaviour of their people through the process of control. There is a distinction between CONTROL and CONTROLS. The latter is not simply the plural of the former.

CONTROL is normative in approach, whereas CONTROLS deals with measurement, information, analysis and operation. CONTROL sets the direction, deals with the expectations of behaviour and performance.

CONTROLS are a means to achieve CONTROL at the end. CONTROL is the process of bringing congruence of the gap between the desired and actual state of things in the organisation. It can be taken at any stage - individual level, group level or organisational level.

WHY CONTROL?

While it is true that in natural social units like a family or community, there is in-built control mechanism, and, therefore, members fulfil their obligations by carrying on the activities of the units. In organisations, just because there is a structure of roles, responsibilities, and relationships they do not automatically contribute to organisational objectives. The organisations must devise ways and means to achieve conformity of behaviour to certain specified standards.

PRE REQUISITES OF CONTROL

1. Control should bring about set performance.
2. Therefore, establish a performance standard
3. Communicate the standard to all concerned both orally and in writing.
4. Establish reward and reinforcement systems to support the compliance of behaviour.
5. Study the organisational needs, and try to bring about a fit between the two needs of organisation and the individual.

MEANS OF CONTROL

According to A.ETZIONI, who has authored the book - MODERN ORGANISATIONS, 1964, an organization can apply 3 types of sanctions for controlling behaviour. Sanctions are a kind of rewards and penalties, which can be applied on individuals or groups to induce people to conform to norms. The 3 types of sanctions are as follows.

1. PHYSICAL SANCTIONS

This is a kind of coercive power, which includes inflicting pain, restricting movement etc. This is generally applied at lower levels of employees because they are not largely self motivated. Such people will have to be coerced to move towards corporate goals. For e.g., dismissals, suspensions, demotion etc.

2. MATERIAL SANCTIONS

These are just the opposite of physical sanctions. These are based on the control and allocation of material resources and rewards. People perceive benefits when material sanctions are applied, and, therefore, conform to the expected behaviour. These type of sanctions are common in most of the organisations. Carrot-and-stick policy in organisations, role of money, and other material awards and rewards at the lower level of employees become more important.

3. SYMBOLIC SANCTIONS

These sanctions are not a threat to the employees. There is no claim on material rewards too. But, symbolic sanctions are quite important for those who receive them. These are applied at higher levels of employees who get psychological satisfaction. Such symbols may be normative like prestige and esteem, love and acceptance etc.

REMEMBER the use of various sanctions is determined by the possession of power and authority, which are influencing factors in controlling behaviour. Modem organisations do not like to employ sanctions for controlling behaviour. They employ proper leadership, communication, and organizational climate.

UNIT EXERCISE

Short Answers

1. What is authority? What are the characteristics of authority?
2. Explain the various sources of authority?
3. Discuss the Formal Authority Theory and The Acceptance Theory.
4. Explain the Competence Theory in detail.
5. Define control? What are the prerequisites of control.

Long Answers

1. Define Power. Why is Power so important in organizations? What are the various bases of Power?
2. How is it that some people in an organization acquire and exercise greater power than others? Explain the nature and significance of power relations in a large industrial organization.
3. "Modern organizations are a fertile place for politics to thrive." Comment on this statement.

Chapter 8

Organisational Power and Politics

8.0 INTRODUCTION

Power is the ability to influence other people and events. Power is the ability to get things done the way one wants them to be done. More essentially, power is an exchange process i.e. a person who commands and the subordinates follow him or comply his request comply. Power is a function of ties of normal dependence in social relationships. Power is the ability of one to control the actions of others. In the organisational context, power is the ability of one person (or department) to influence the behaviour of others in the organisation to bring about desired outcomes from power holders.

8.1 OBJECTIVE

Power, though personal and lacks legitimacy, is a crucial factor in influencing the behaviour in organisational situation. Thus, power is one of the essential components of practically every organisation. Politics is universal phenomenon in organised society. Political behaviour is not limited to those who hold public positions. We can expect political behaviour in every organisation.

8.2 MEANING AND DEFINITIONS

"Power is the ability to influence flow of the available resources towards certain goals as opposed to other goals. Power is assumed to be exercised only when these goals are at least partially in conflict with each other."

—Nord

"Power refers to a capacity and A has to influence the behaviour of B, so that B does something he or she would not otherwise do."

—Robbins

"Power is the probability that one action within the relationship will be in a position to carry out his own will despite resistance."

—Max Weber

The essence of power is control over the behaviour of others. Power is also a reflection of influence that one person may have over others. If we are able to convince another person to agree to our views or change his opinion on a given issue, we have exercised influence over the other person and thus power has been used.

From this point of view, power has the following characteristics.

1. Power is one of the means to influence others for getting results. It implies that influence can be exercised by other means too, like use of authority, leadership, and communication.
2. Influence process occurs in a particular way when it is attempted by the use of power.
3. Power is used not only in getting certain results achieved but it also includes negative decisions, or the action of non-decisions. Thus, power is not only one's influence over the decision making, but also one's capability of limiting the scope of actual decision making.

4. Power is extra organisational in nature and any one in the organisation may have this type of influence through the use of power provided one is capable of doing so.

8.3 BASES/SOURCES OF POWER

French and Raven have identified following five sources of power exist at all levels of organisation.

1. Expert power
2. Reward power
3. Referent power
4. Legitimate power
5. Coercive power

1. **Expert Power** : It is based on the perception or belief that the influencer has some relevant expertise or special knowledge that others do not have. For example, a doctor has expert power on his patients. It is a type of personal power.
2. **Reward Power :** It is based on the influencer having the ability to reward the influence for carrying out orders. The extent of reward power depends upon the extent to which one has control over rewards that are valued by another.
3. **Referent Power :** It is based on the influences desire to identify with or imitate the behaviour of the influencer. It develops out of others administration for a person and their desire to model their attitudes and behaviour after that person. For example, a manager will have referent power over the subordinates if they are motivated to simulate his work habits.
4. **Legitimate Power :** It is based on the formal rights one receives as a result of holding a position in an organisation. It may also be called positional power because of authority inherent in the position. It exists when an influence acknowledges that the influencer is lawfully entitled to exert influence. It is also implied that the influence has an obligation to accept this power.
5. **Coercive Power :** It is based on the influencer's ability to punish the influencee for not carrying out orders or for not meeting requirements. Fear of punishment may make the subordinates execute the instructions of the boss.

Politics- Pfiffner and Sherwood have commented that "the 'who gets what' (politics) is endemic to every organisation, regardless of size, function, or character of ownership. Furthermore, it is to be found at every level of the hierarchy, and it intensifies as the stakes become more important and the area of decision possibilities greater." One survey of 400 managers provides the insight into their view towards organisational politics. To a larger extent, managers agreed that:

1. Politics is common in most organisations.
2. Managers must be good at politics to succeed.

3. Politics becomes more important at higher levels.
4. Politics can detract from organisational efficiency.

Thus, it is necessary for managers to understand the dynamics of politics so that they can take suitable course of actions to minimise its dysfunctional consequences.

8.4 DISTINCTION BETWEEN AUTHORITY AND POWER

The terms 'authority' and 'power' are generally used interchangeably in practice, but there is a clear-cut distinction between the two as discussed below:

(i) **Nature.** Authority is the right to command; power is the ability to exercise influence. Authority usually resides in the position in the organization, but power is exercised by the person- Authority includes the right to command which has been institutionalized. Thus, authority is always positional and legitimate and is conferred on the position. But power is not institutional, rather it is personal. It is acquired by people in various ways and exercised upon others. It is acquired through political means or by having certain personal attributes.

(ii) **Association with Position.** Authority of a person is associated with the position in the formal organization. It increases as one goes up the organization hierarchy. But it need not necessarily be accompanied by more power. In actual practice, power centres may be located at the lower levels in the organization. Thus, one cannot get any idea of power centres in an organization by merely looking at its organization chart.

(iii) **Relationship.** The structure of an organization merely shows authority-responsibility relationships. In practice, these relationships are modified by power politics in the organization. Some individuals may have more power and less authority or more authority and less power. It is the operating mechanism of the organization which is relevant for studying organizational-behaviour.

(iv) **Flow.** Authority is a downward flowing concept whereas power flows in all directions. Authority can be delegated to the lower levels in the organization. The lower we go down the hierarchy, the lesser is the authority. But it is not so in case of power which has been defined as the ability or capacity to influence the behaviour of others. Power can flow in any direction. If a worker succeeds to influence the behaviour of a departmental manager, it is implied that the worker has exercised power over the departmental manager.

(v) **Pervasiveness.** Authority rests with important positions in the organization whereas power is all-pervasive. For instance, an informal leader may be more powerful than a departmental head.

(vi) **Responsibility.** The extent of authority is limited to the amount of responsibility. Authority and responsibility are coextensive and balance each other. But in case of power, there is no such balancing factor. Persons having greater power may have only limited responsibility.

(vii) **Formal/Informal.** Authority is inherent in the official positions in the organization and so it is always formal. But power can be both formal and informal. Sometimes, informal power of a person exercises greater influence in the organization that his formal authority which is also called legitimate power.

8.5 POWER AND LEADERSHIP

Leaders use power as a means of realizing group goals. But there is a difference between the two terms. Firstly, powers does not require goal compatibility, it requires merely dependence. Leadership, on the other hand, requires some congruence between the goals of the leader and the led. The second difference related to the direction of influence. Leadership focuses on the downward influence on one's subordinates. It minimizes the importance of lateral and upward influence patterns. Power does not do so. It can move in any direction.

Power has been compared with electricity in a motor by Hicks and Gullett. They state, 'consider an electric motor, for comparison. The motor, like an organisation, can be explained partially by a description of its (1) external appearance and operation and (2) gears, inner mechanisms, and relationships; however, the essence of the motor cannot be understood without an appreciation of a third factor; how electricity as the power source makes the motor run, which may cause gears to turn, which operate mechanisms, and so forth.

Power is also the basis of responsibility. Responsibility is the obligation to carry on any function or discharge of duty. In formal organisations, responsibility is fixed on the basis of allocation of activities through the process of organising. However, the real cause of accepting responsibility is somewhat more deep-rooted. Psychologists suggest that responsibility is a function of personality, which in turn is largely shaped by significant person in the early childhood. For example, the parent may impress the child to bear the responsibility and when the child is grow up, he assumes it because of this value. The parent, while impressing the child to bear responsibility, is exercising some power, the moral power in the family. Thus, the basic root of the responsibility is found in the power, and not merely in the normal allocation of duties.

Some generalisations about the use of power and effectiveness of various bases of power are given below

1. There is no evidence of power unless it is exercised. The purpose of power is influence over others for getting certain things done.
2. Power is stronger than influence. It is the ability to bring about potential acts by commanding or exerting influence. But influence is a psychological force. In exerting influence, one person tries to influence the behaviour of another.
3. The effect of power is reduced when it is exercised outside its perceived limits.
4. The stronger the power base, the greater is the power. The strongest-power base is legitimacy (or formal authority) and the weakest is coercion.
5. A person difficult to be replaced has more power than others. If a low ranking employee has more knowledge than

Faces of Power

Two faces of power have been identified by David McClelland, viz., negative and positive. The negative face is usually expressed in terms of dominance-submission; "I win, you lose". To have power implies having power over another person who is less well off for lack of it. Leadership based on the negative face of power regards people as little more than pawns to be used or sacrificed as the need arises. This is self-defeating since people who feel they are pawns tend either to resist leadership or to become passive. In either case, their value to the manager is severely limited.

The positive face of power is best characterized by a concern for group goals-for helping to formulate and achieve such goals. It involves exerting influence on behalf of rather than over others. Managers who exercise their power positively encourage group members to develop the strength and competence they need to succeed as people and as members of the organization.

McClelland and David H. Burnham found that successful managers have a greater need to influence others for the benefit of the organization than for self-aggrandisement. Managers who use their power with self-control will be more effective than those who wield power to satisfy a need to dominate others or those who neglect to use their power out of a strong need to be liked. When a manager continually eases rules and changes procedures to accommodate subordinates, they will suspect that he is not flexible but weak and indecisive. McClelland concluded that good managers exercise power with restraint on behalf of others. Such managers encourage team spirit, support subordinates, and reward their achievement, thereby raising morale.

Acquisition of Greater Position Power in an Organization

A manager has a two-dimensional power base. The first is the positional power by virtue of the status in the organization and the personal power because of personal characteristics and knowledge. Building up of both the bases is essential for the acquisition of power in the organization. However, the position power can be increased by the following factors:

(1) **Centrality.** It refers to the activities that are most central to the work flow of the organization. If the information niters through a manager thus giving him some say in the work of many subunits, then the manager has acquired more positional power. For example, the finance manager is authorised in approving expenses and making payments of all departments in the firm. It gives the finance manager an extra power base to affect the behaviour of other departments.

(2) **Scarcity.** When critical resources are scarce and there is a struggle for acquiring these resources, then the winner of the struggle acquires power. When the organization is not able to supply sufficient resources, say, capital, space, support staff, etc., there will be conflicts among different units for maximum share of these resources. The powerful unit will be able to have a greater share of the resources. According to a study conducted in a large University, Seiznick and Pfeffer found that the power of academic departments was associated with their ability to obtain funds from research grants and other outside

sources and this was more critical to their power than was the number of undergraduates taught by the department.

(3) **Uncertainty.** Uncertainty about future events can play havoc with the plans of different departments. Some of the sources of uncertainty include reduction in supply of resources, fall in demand of company's products, changes in government policies. The executives who can profit from such uncertainty and are able to cope with uncertainty will tend to acquire power. According to Kanter "The most power goes to those people in those functions that provide greater control over what the organization finds currently problematic: sales and marketing people when markets are competitive; production experts when materials are scarce and demand is high; personnel or labour relations specialists when labour is important; lawyers, lobbyists and external relations specialists when government regulations impinge; finance and accounting executives when business is bad and money tight. There is a turning to those elements of the system that seem to have the power to create more certainty in the face of dependency, and to generate a more advantageous position for the organization"

(4) **Substitutability.** The greater the value of a person to an organization, me greater the power he holds. There are some people whose contributions to the organization make them more indispensable than others. This indispensability is the result of such speciality and expertise that cannot be substituted easily by others. However, a change in the marketability of such speciality may change the power bases as well.

8.6 TYPES OF POWER

Given below is the description of various types of powers.

Coercive Power. Coercive power rests upon the application or the threat of application of physical sanctions. The physical sanctions may be in any form depending upon the situation. Thus, it can be in the form of infliction of pain, deformity or death, generation of frustration through, restriction of movement; or controlling the satisfaction of basic needs such as those for food, sex, comfort, or the like. In organisational situation, it may be in the form of action for or threat for dismissal, suspension, demotion or other method of embarrassment for the people.

Reward Power. Reward power is based on one's control and allocation of material resources and rewards. In the organisational situations, this power is based on the control of salaries, wages, commissions, fringe benefits, and amenities. Reward power may be form of normative power also. Normative power is based on the allocation and manipulation of symbolic rewards which may be important for the people. The symbolic rewards may be in the form of prestige, affection, esteem, etc. Thus, anybody who can allocate or deny these holds the normative power. It can be exercised in limited interpersonal context or in wide context.

Legitimate Power. Legitimate Power. Is based on agreement and commonly held valued allowing one person to have power over another person. Such legitimacy may be either formal, as in the case with the organisation, or may be informal,. As is the case with social units. For example, in our culture, age, has certain premium and aged people have certain binding force over others even without having any other characteristics. In an organisational setting. This legitimacy is in the form of authority which is delegated to the positions of organisational members. Though a person may derive authority form other sources in the organisations, the superior subordinate relationship is enough to comply subordinates behaviour as directed particularly in bureaucratic organisations.

Referent Power. Referent power is based on identification. Identification is the process of learning where in a person copies the behaviour of other person whom he takes as ideal. This may occur in the context of power also. Thus, referent power is based on identification with the person who may have some form of power. The target of the influence feels attracted towards the person having power because of his personality characteristics and tries to behave accordingly. Then this becomes the basis of power exercise. Such identification process may take place without organisational context as most of the people take somebody as ideal and behave accordingly up to a certain stage.

Expert Power. Expert power is based on the famous proverb 'knowledge is power'. Expert power is that influence which one wields as a result of one's experience, special skill, or knowledge. This power occurs when the expert threatens to withhold his knowledge or skill. The implication of expert power is important in the sense that this is related with the individual's personal characteristics. Since more organisation are gradually falling under the category of high technology, they will have to utilize the services of these individuals. Consequently, organisational choice of replacing these people will be limited. Since any person who is not easily replaceable has more power as compared to those who are easily replaceable, these people will have greater power over others.

8.7 POWER DISTRIBUTION IN ORGANISATION

In an organisation, having hierarchical structure, varying amounts of power shall be bestowed upon certain roles within the system. The higher the level of a person the greater is the amount of his power. The matter is, however, not so simple because of the presence of the multiple bases of power. Lammers deals with this issue when he states 'manager and managed in organisations at the same time come to influence each other more effectively and thereby generate joint power as the outcome of a better command by the organisation over its technologies, economic and human resources in the service objectives. Thus, amount of power in an organisation as well as in single interpersonal situation is variable and the amount of power changes over time.

Tannenbaum has noted two classes of conditions under which expansion of power takes place. He observes that expansion of power may occur under either of two classes of conditions. The first is that of an external expansion of power into the organisation's environment. The second concerns a number of internal conditions that subsume; (i) structural conditions expediting interaction and influence among members; (ii) motivational conditions implying increased interest by members in exercising control and a greater amenability by members to being controlled. These conditions may sometimes be related. The amount of power is not something that varies dramatically from situation to situation; generally the change in the amount of power is gradual. Moreover, at any point of time, the amount of power in an organisation is fixed – a zero-sum game. If one person or group gains in power, another loses. Power pacts are carried out within a fixed amount of framework and it is the framework that changes over time. Discussion of both these factors may clarify the power distribution.

8.8 EXTERNAL FACTORS IN POWER DISTRIBUTION

Besides the internal organisational factors, external factors also play an important role in the power system of the organisation. Factors such as associations of similar organisations, relationship with suppliers and users of organisation's products, regulatory agencies, and other indirectly involved parties affect the amount and distribution of power in the organisation. This is so because the organisation is an open system and the relevant factors in the external environment affect the power distribution in the organisation. Thompson and McEwen have emphasized the role of environment to the power adjustments in the organisation. They have hypothesised that one way of analyzing the degree of power exercised by outside influences is to identify the time of entry of these forces into the decision-making structure. The earlier the entry, the greater the power. They have established four models of entry along a continuum : (i) competition, (ii) bargaining, (iii) co-operation, and (iv) coalition.

8.9 CONCEPT OF ORGANISATIONAL POLITICS

Politics is very common in modern organizations. In the words of Pfiffner and Sherwood, "Politics is endemic to every organization, regardless of size, function or character or ownership. Furthermore, it is to be found in every level of the hierarchy; and it intensifies as the stakes become more important and the area of decision possibilities greater" Organizational members resort to politics to gain more power, to have command over resources, to have more say in decision-making, to fulfil personal goals, etc.

What is Organizational Politics?

Politics relates to the way a person is able to get power over others and the way in which he uses power over others. In other words, it is the process whereby power is acquired and exercised upon others to influence their behaviour or to get things done. Thus, it is a method of operating in order to influence the behaviour of others.

According to Tushman, "Politics refers to the structure and process of the use of authority and power to affect definition, of goals, direction and the other major parameters of the organization. Decisions arc not made in a rational way but rather through compromise, accommodation and bargaining".

In the words of Farrell and Peterson, "Politics in an organization refers to those activities that are not required as part of one's formal role in the organization, but that influence or attempt to influence the distribution of advantages and disadvantages within the organization. Two key points emerge from the above definitions:

(i) Political behaviour is outside one's specified job requirements, and (ii) it generates efforts to influence the goals, criteria, or processes used for decision-making that will result in the distribution of advantages and disadvantages within the organization.[2]" Thus, political behaviour includes such activities as withholding key information from decision-makers, whistle blowing, spreading rumors, leaking confidential information about organizational activities, entering into coalitions, exchanging favours for mutual benefit, lobbying on behalf of or against a particular individual or decision, "horse trading", ingenious compromises, trade-offs and so on.

Farrel and Petersen talk of the **legitimate-illegitimate dimension of political behaviour** though a vast majority of political behaviour are of legitimate variety. Legitimate political behaviour refers to normal everyday politics-complaining to the supervisor, bypassing the chain of command, forming coalitions, obstructing organizational policies or decisions through inaction or excessive adherence to rules, and developing contacts outside the organization through one's professional activities. On the other hand, illegitimate political behaviour is of extreme type that violates the implied "rules of the game." Those who pursue such activities are often described as individuals who "play hard-ball." illegitimate activities include sabotage, whistle blowing, a group of employees simultaneously calling in sick, etc.

Features of Organizational Politics

The broad features of organizational politics are as under:

(i) Politics involves the use of some kind of power or pressure over other persons or groups. Rewards and punishments are commonly used.

(ii) Political behaviour is self-serving in nature. Attempts are made to use organizational resources for personal benefits or to give some benefits to others.

(iii) Political behaviour is outside one's specified job requirements. It involves ways of getting things accomplished that are not formally recognized practices or procedures.

(iv) Political decisions may not be rational from the point of view of the organization. They are usually taken to acquire more power.

Universality of Political Behaviour

Politics is inevitable in modern organizations. Political behaviour is seen in all types of organizations including industrial and commercial, social, educational, religious, government institutions, etc. Organizational members and groups use various tactics such as bargaining competition, cooptation, coalition, etc. to gain more power to have greater influence on the decision-making and other processes.

Causes of Political Behaviour

Politics has been a classic human activity since the beginning of civilization, so it is not unique to modern organizations. In fact, modern organizations are a fertile place for politics to thrive. Individuals resort to politics in organizations because of the following reasons :

1. **Lust for Power.** People play politics within the organization to gain power for control and decision-making. They aim at increasing the area of their influence. Conflict between line and staff elements is a typical example in this regard. Nobody wants to lose power in the power struggle because power can be used in the ways liked by the holders of power. If a person is able to gain more power, his area of influence over other organizational members would increase.
2. **Competition for Control over resources.** Organizations are composed of coalitions. A coalition is a group of persons formed to achieve some common interest. Coalitions are formed when individuals feel that they can't gain more power if they operate individually. The formation of different coalitions gives rise to political struggle in the organization. These coalitions compete with one another for command over organizational resources. A strong coalition is able to manoeuvre the things in its favour and acquire more power than others.
3. **Protection of Self-interests.** Various coalitions seek to protect their interests and positions of influence by moderating environment pressures and their effects. They will not like that any other coalition takes away the privileges they are enjoying.
4. **Discretionary Authority.** There are some positions in the organization which have discretionary powers to be used in case of emergency. The use of power depends upon the sole judgement of the position-holder. That is why, people indulge in politics to grab such positions or to be very close to such a position holder.
5. **Unequal Distribution of Authority.** Sometimes, there is unequal distribution of authority at a particular level in the organization or there is a big difference between the authority of two levels. This may have dehumanizing effects and lead to start of political activities in the organization.
6. **Saturation in Career.** Promotion in one's career is based on competence. But when a person cannot rise above a certain level because of lack of competence for the higher job, he may resort to political behaviour to move up in the organization hierarchy. In other words, each employee tries to achieve and remain at his level of incompetence. This is what the 'Peter principle' states. This type of behaviour is a universal phenomenon in modern organizations.
7. **Need for Inter-Department Coordination.** Relationships between major organization groups typically are not well defined. When joint issues arise, managers have to meet and work out solutions on an ad hoc basis. These on-going coordination activities are often political in nature. The ability of one group to achieve its goal often involves the cooperation of other departments. Interdepartmental coordination lacks rules and precedents to guide

it. Uncertainty and conflict are common, especially when the issue is departmental territory and responsibility. Political activities are resorted to by different departments to meet such challenges.

8.10 ORGANIZATIONAL CULTURE

Social (national) culture creates the wide-ranging context in which organizations operate. It provides the complex social system of laws, values, and customs in which organizational behavior occurs. Employee behavior (B), according to social psychologist Kurt Lewin, is a function of the interaction between personal characteristics (P) and the environment (E) around the person, or B = f (P, E). Part of that environment is the social culture in which the individual lives and works, which provides broad clues as to how a person with a given background will behave. The previous discussion indicated how employee actions are sharply affected by the roles assigned to them and the status level accorded to them.

Inside the organization lies another powerful force for determining individual and group behavior. Organizational culture is the set of assumptions, beliefs, values, and norms that are shared by an organization's members. This culture may have been consciously created by its key members, or it may have simply evolved across time. It represents a key element of the work environment in which employees perform their jobs. This idea of organizational culture is somewhat intangible, for we cannot see it or touch it, but it is present and pervasive. Like the air in a room, it surrounds and affects everything that happens in a organization. Because it is a dynamic sys-tems concept, culture is also affected by almost everything that occurs within an organization.

Organizational cultures are important to a firm's success for several reasons. They give an organizational identity to employees—a defining vision of what the organi-zation represents. They are also an important source of stability and continuity to the organization, which provides a sense of security to its members. At the same time, knowledge of the organizational culture helps newer employees interpret what goes on inside the organization, by providing an important context for events that would otherwise seem confusing. More than anything else, perhaps, cultures help stimulate employee enthusiasm for their tasks. Cultures attract attention, convey a vision, and typically honor high-producing and creative individuals as heroes. By recognizing and rewarding these people, organizational cultures are identifying them as role models to emulate.

Characteristics of Cultures

Organizations, like fingerprints and snowflakes, are unique. Each has its own history, patterns of communication, systems and procedures, mission statements and visions, sto-ries and myths which, in their totality, constitute its distinctive culture. Cultures are rel-atively stable in nature, usually changing only slowly over time. Exceptions to this con-dition may occur when a major crisis threatens a firm or when two organizations merge with each other (requiring a careful blending of the two so as to avoid culture clash). Most organizational cultures have historically been implicit rather than explicit. More recently, though, organizations have begun talking about their intended cultures, and many top leaders see one of their major roles as speaking out about the kind of envi-ronment they would like to create within their firms. A final defining characteristic of most cultures is that they are seen as symbolic representations of underlying beliefs and values. Seldom do we read a description of a firm's culture. More frequently, employees make inferences about it from hearing sto-ries about the way things are done from reading slogans that portray corporate ideals, from observing key artifacts, or from watching ceremonies in which certain types of employees are honored.

Over time, an organization's culture becomes perpetuated by its tendency to attract and retain people who fit its values and beliefs. Just as people may choose to move to a certain region because of geographic characteristics such n as temperature, humid-ity, and rainfall, employees also will gravitate toward the organizational culture they prefer as a work environment. This results in a good fit of employer and employee. Several other dimensions of culture are important to note. For one, there is no best culture for all firms; culture clearly depends on the organization's goals, indus-try, nature of competition, and other factors in its environment. Cultures will be more easily recognized when their elements are generally integrated and consistent with each other; in other words, they fit together like pieces of a puzzle. Also, most mem-bers must at least accept, if not embrace, the assumptions and values of the culture.

Historically, employees seldom talked explicitly about the culture in which they worked; more recently, culture has become an increasingly acceptable conversation topic among employees. Most cultures evolve directly from top management, who can have a powerful influence on their employees by what they say. However, man-agement's actions are even more important to watchful employees, who can quickly detect when managers give only lip service but not true support to certain ideals, such as customer service and quality products. A culture may exist across an entire organization, or it may be made up of various subcultures—the environment within a single division, branch, plant, or department. Finally, cultures have varying strengths—they can be characterized as relatively strong or weak, depending largely on the degree of their impact on employee behavior and how widely the underlying beliefs and values are held.

The effect of organizational culture on employee behavior is difficult to establish. Some research indicates that there must be, and is, a positive relationship between certain organizational cultures and performance. Agreement within an organization on a culture should result in a larger degree of cooperation, acceptance of decision mak-ing and control, communication, and commitment to the employer. Such a result is especially likely when a firm consciously seeks to create a performance-enhancing culture that removes barriers to success. Just as yeast is a critical ingredient in baking bread, a culture of productivity is an essential element in organizational success. How-ever, if the wrong ingredient is accented, the results can be costly.

Measuring Organizational Culture

Systematic measurement and comparison of cultures is difficult at best. Most early attempts by researchers relied on examination of stories, symbols, rituals, and cere-monies to obtain clues and construct a composite portrait. Others have used inter-views and open-ended questionnaires in an attempt to assess employee values and beliefs. In other cases, examination of corporate philosophy statements has provided insight into the espoused culture (the beliefs and values that the organization states publicly). Another approach is to survey employees directly and seek their perceptions of the organization's culture. One of the more interesting methods is to become a member of the organization and engage in participant observation. This approach allows direct sensing from the perspective of a member .who is experiencing the culture.

Prudential Insurance Company of America used a standard pencil-and-paper instrument to identify part of its culture. Prudential measured current norms and found strong perceptions of conformity, caution, competition with other work groups, risk avoidance, and top-down decision making. Then the company assessed desired norms, and found maj r gaps. Employ-ees wanted a culture that stressed teamwork, collaboration, customer service, initiative, train-ing, and cooperation. This measurement process allowed Prudential to involve employees in changing to a new culture—one where managers are measured against their culture-change goals.

Any attempt to measure organizational culture can be only an imperfect assess-ment. Such measurements capture only a snapshot of the culture at a single point in time. In reality, many organizational cultures are in the process of changing and need to be monitored regularly and by a variety of methods to gain a truer picture.

It can be observed that everyone plays some kind of politics at some point of time in the organisation. We can find references that define politics as one or more of the following; self-serving behaviour, acquisition of power, protection of one's own domain, building of support through group formation, or influence manoeuvring. In all these cases, politics involves acquisition of power or be around power and engage in self-serving behaviour. Therefore, politics can be referred to as actions for seizing, holding, extracting, and executing of power by individuals and groups for achieving personal goals. Because of organisational politics, organisational decisions are affected in such a way that they contribute to personal goals rather than organisational goals.

On the basis of the review of various definitions of organisational politics. Drory and Romm have arrived at the following definition of organisational politics.

"Organisational politics refer to intentional behaviours that are designed to enhance or protect a person's influence and self-interest".

Based on the definition of politics, its main features can be described as follows:

1. Political behaviour involves some kind of power either directly or indirectly. Power can be exercised by those who are in formal positions and enjoy authority. It can also be influenced by other persons close to those who hold formal authority.
2. Politics involves behaviour that is self-serving, it suggests that either organisational resources are used for personal benefits or benefits to be given to one person are given to another. In both the cases, the decision in not rational from organisation's point of view.

3. Politics takes place when an individual recognises that achievement of his goals in influenced by the behaviour of others. In such a case, politicking involves the elimination of adversaries by the influential manoeuvres of a member of the organisation.
4. All self-serving behaviours which do not involve use of power or threat of use of power cannot be termed as politics. For example, an employee's asking for a rise in pay is not political behaviour, but the use of threat to unionise to obtain in pay rise amounts to political behaviour.

Concept of Organisational Effectiveness

Organisations are interacting entities in which the desires of the individual, the group and the organisation are in a continual state of adaptation. So, there is not one goal but multiple goals. Further, organisations are a part of a total society. They do not exist in isolation. Therefore, how they persue their goals has a great deal to do with individual and group well being. It may, therefore, be necessary to conceptualise organisational effectiveness in such a way that the term encompasses a multiple criteria.

The conception of organisational effectiveness assumes the follo'wing general criteria :

(a) Organisational productivity.

(b) Organisational flexibility in the form of successful adjustment to internal organisational changes and successful adaption to externally induced change.

(c) Absence of intra-organisational strain or tension and of conflict between organisational sub-groups.

Likert has identified three variables useful in discussing effectiveness over time. One type of variable is the causal factors that influence the course of development in an organisation. These are independent variables like leadership style, organisation structure, objectives, technology, etc. These causal factors interact with intervening variables like perceptions, attitudes, norms and values, motivational forces etc. which represent the current conditions of the internal state of the organisation. These intervening factors, in turn, lead to end results like production, costs, sales, employee turnover, etc. and represent dependent variables that reflect the achievements of the organisation. According to him, effectiveness is actually determined by whatever the manager and the organisation decide are their goals and objectives, but they should consider following factors :

1. Output variables
2. Intervening variables
3. Short range goals
4. Long range goals.

Steps In Studying Organisational Effectiveness

Ghorpade layd down following steps (Fig. 8.1) for the assessment of organisational effectiveness. These steps will help design a methodology and an approach to the problem.

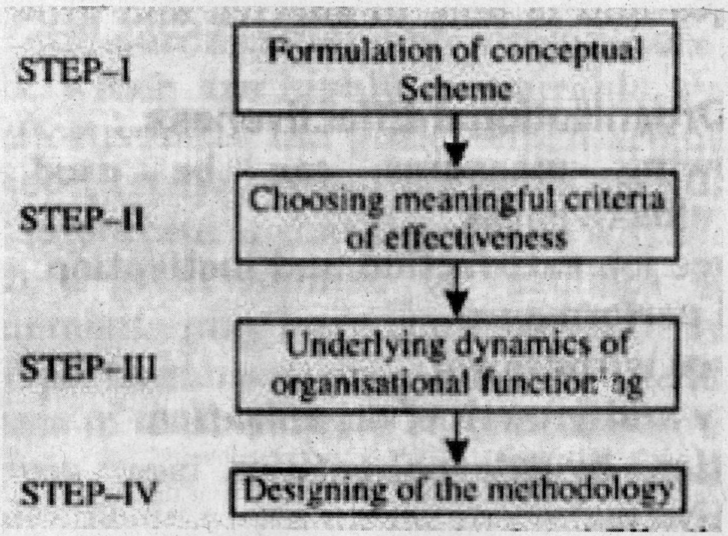

Fig. 8.1. Steps in Studying Organisational Effectiveness

(i) ***Formation of conceptual scheme:*** This means that a researcher should first find out what the composition of a organisation's internal structure is, what relationships this organisation has with other organisations, etc.

(ii) ***Choosing meaningful criteria of effectiveness:*** Effectiveness implies success in terms of given standards. One should decide consideration of goals — short terms or long terms, and one should also decide the frame of reference, *i.e.,* from whose angle the situation is being looked at. If it the owners, workers, customers, organisations or society at large from whose angle effectiveness is being assessed? It is necessary to find an answer to this question as the criteria of effectiveness would be different for a different frame of reference. Effectiveness is a multivariate concept and the choice of criteria depends ultimately on the values and needs of the parties involved in the evaluation process.

(iii) ***Underlying dynamics of organisational functioning:*** This implies an understanding of processes such as what are the parts of the system. The nature and their relationships among themselves and to the whole, which parts are functional or dysfunctional, etc.

(iv) ***Designing of a methodology:*** When decisions are taken regarding the three points, the researcher should be able to identify suitable data, tool, techniques and method.

A study of the assessment of organisational effectiveness, on the basis of these steps, is likely to bring out the organisational situation as it is, rather than present a fallacious, misleading or distorted picture. A study of effectiveness is full of hazards and a study conducted on the basis of the system's approach requires a great deal of effort, resources and time. However, there is *escape* from following a system level criteria if we wish to evaluate an organisation realistically from a long term point of view. Normally an organisation, which is able to adapt itself to internal and external changes and is able to survive and grow, is regarded as effective.

Measures of Organisational Effectiveness

The following measures can be used to determine organisational effectiveness.

1. Employee job satisfaction and motivation.
2. Overall performance.
3. Employee withdrawal.
4. Stability and growth of organisation.
5. Evaluations by external entities.
6. Productivity.
7. Flexibility or adaption.
8. Rate of return on investment.

Achieving Organisational Effectiveness

Every organisation makes efforts to increase the effectiveness. In this process, the organisation must diagnose the source, the nature and causes of low effectiveness. Alwin Brown had identified the following reasons for the failure to achieve organisational effectiveness :

(a) Failure of administrators to act when they need to
(b) Delay in taking action
(c) Taking the wrong action
(d) Lack of sufficient effort
(e) Excessive effort in relation to the need
(f) Excessive quality or effort in relation to the problem
(g) Wasted effort.

After diagnosing the causes of low effectiveness, the organisation can take necessary and corrective action over the controlled factors.

Problems In Measurement Of Organisational Effectiveness

The study to measure the organisational effectiveness is difficult because of the following reasons :

1. There is a difficulty to set in the standards for measuring organisational effectiveness. No one is able to say whether an organisation should be regarded as effective, as profits are high but there is high labour unrest and absenteeism etc.
2. If even goals are set, then it is difficult to set the measurable standards. Some standards are tangible while others are intangible. Hence, the goals, which are highly measurable, do not pose any problem in the effectiveness, but goals, which are not subject to do much measurement, create several problems of estimation.

3. The very important is that there is no way of estimating the degree to which a great number of variables other than the organisational elements may have contributed to the achievement of certain objectives. Organisations can hardly be classified as good or bad on the basis of their earning records alone.
4. The criteria used to measure effectiveness may not be sufficiently stable. Their meaning for organisational performance may change. In times of fast changing price levels, comparing profits for one year with those of another year may be of no use. Instability effectively precludes the possibility of a long lasting, generalisable set of performance indicators on which the manager, administrator or researcher can rely.

8.12 MAXIMISATION OR OPTIMISATION OF EFFECTIVENESS

Maximisation: Economic Man Approach

This approach evolved by classical economic theory. The economic man is completely rational and tries to maximize returns by his efforts. The decisions which he takes are based on the following conditions : (1) The decisions are completely rational in terms of means-ends relationships, that is, he always identifies clearly the ends to which he wants to reach and the means which are available for the purpose. (2) There is a complete and consistent system of preferences which allow a choice among alternatives. (3) There is awareness of complete information and alternatives out of which he has to choose. (4) There is no limit on computations that can be performed to determine the best alternatives.

The first basic problem in maximisation of organisational effectiveness relates to desirability of maximisation itself. Maximisation of effectiveness, even if possible, is destructive from the viewpoint of organisation because an organisation that fully actualizes its exploitative potential may risk its own survival since the exploited environment may become so depleted as to be unable to produce further resources. Furthermore, an organisation which ruthlessly exploits its environment is more likely to incite a strong organized opposition that may weaken or even destroy the organisation's bargaining position. Thus, a short-term gain may result into long term-losses. Thus, the highest level of effectiveness for an organisation is reached when the organisation maximizes its bargaining position and optimizes its resources procurement. Optimum is the point beyond which the organisation endangers itself because of the depletion of its resource producing environment, or the devaluation of resources, or because of the generation of the countervailing forces in the environment to weaken the organisations position.

The second problem in maximisation is more serious and often is related with the basic process of decision-making itself, that is, it is not possible to become wholly rational because of certain limitations on rationality, as discussed earlier. The limits of rationality suggest another alternative to maximisation, that is optimisation which is reflected by administrative man.

Optimisation: Administrative Man Approach

As contrast to economic man approach of perfect rationality, administrative man emphasizes optimisation in decision-making which satisfices him. Thus, he tries for satisfactory alternatives only. Simon who has given the concept of administrative man has described the following behaviour in decision-making process.

1. In choosing among alternatives, administrative man attempts to satisfy or look for the one which is satisfactory or good enough. Examples of satisficing criteria would be market share, adequate profit, and fair price.
2. He recognises that the world he perceives is a drastically simplified model of the world. He is content with this simplification because he believes the world is mostly empty.
3. Because he satisfices, rather than maximizes, he can make his choices without first determining all possible alternatives and without ascertaining that these are in fact all the alternatives.
4. Because he treats the world as rather empty, he is able to make decisions with relatively simple rules to thumb or tricks of the trade, or from force of habit. These techniques do not make impossible demands upon his capacity for thought.

8.13 ORGANISATIONAL EFFECTIVENESS VERSUS MANAGERIAL EFFECTIVENESS

While analyzing the problem of effectiveness, the difference between organisational and managerial effectiveness can be made. Such a distinction may be helpful in the sense that managerial effectiveness is a causal variable in organisational effectiveness. The managerial effectiveness has been mostly defined in terms of organisational goal-achieving behaviour. For example, Guion states that the success of an executive lies largely in meeting major organisation goals through the coordinated efforts of his organisation; in part, at least, these efforts depend upon the kind of influence the executive has upon those whose work behaviour touches... The executive's own behaviour contributes to the achievement of organisational goals only by its influence on the perceptions, attitudes, and motives of other people in the organisation and on their subsequent behaviour.

Managerial effectiveness, like organisational effectiveness, must be seen in terms of optimisation and not maximisation. The effective manager is an optimizer in utilizing all available and potential resources—material, human and financial—both within and without the organisation, toward its sustained, long-term functioning. Based on this, effective managerial job behaviour has been defined as 'any set of managerial actions believed to be optimal for identifying, assimilating, and utilizing both internal and external resources toward sustaining, over the long term, the functioning of the organisational unit for which a manager has some degree of responsibility.

8.14 FACTORS IN ORGANISATIONAL EFFECTIVENESS

1. **Causal Variables**. Causal variables are those factors that influence the course of development within an organisation and its results or accomplishment. Likert states that 'causal variables are independent variables which determine the course of developments within an organisation and the results achieved by the organisation. These causal variables include only those independent variables which can be altered or changed by the organisation and its management. Causal variables include the structure of the organisation and management's policies, decisions, business and leadership strategies, skills, and behaviour.
2. **Intervening Variables**. Intervening variables are those factors which are reflected as the internal state of organisation. Many of these variables are caused by causal variables. Likert states that 'the intervening variables reflect the internal state and health of the organisation, e.g., the loyalties, attitudes, motivations, performance goals, and perceptions of all members and their collective capacity for effective interaction, communication, and decision-making. The intervening variables may be divided into two broad categories : (i) the intervening attitudinal, motivational, and perceptual cluster, and (ii) the intervening behavioural cluster. Intervening variables are concerned with building and developing the organisation, and they tend to be long-term goals. This is one part of effectiveness that many managers overlook because it emphasizes long-term potential as well as short-term performance.
3. **End-result Variables.** End-result variables are those factors which are caused by causal and intervening variables and are often in terms of the factors in which managers are interested or measures their effectiveness. According to Likert, 'end-result variables are the dependent variables which reflect the achievements of the organisation, such as its productivity, costs, scrap loss, and earnings.

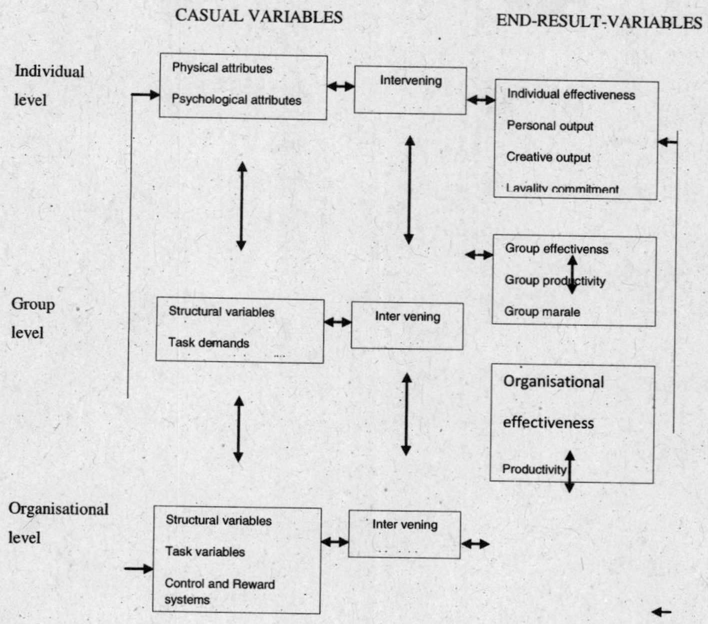

Figure- A complex model of organisational effectiveness

The different variables have been identified at three different levels and hence three levels of effectiveness. Many variables seem to be common, structural, task, and environmental, for example. These variables have been separated because they work in different ways at group and organisational levels. In this model, variables influencing effectiveness at the organisational level are influenced directly and indirectly by variables at the individual and at the group. The effective organisation is built of effective individuals who work effectively in groups. For example, the control and incentive systems instituted by the organisation depend on its individual members as well on the degree of autonomy granted to groups and divisions within the organisation.

UNIT EXERCISE

1. "Politics in modern organizations is not new." Comment.
2. State the dysfunctional aspects of organizational politics.
3. Define power. Why power so important in organizations? What are the various bases of Power?
4. What is meant by organizational politics? Why do organizational members resort to political behavior?
5. What are the features of organizational politics? What are the tactics which the groups employ to gain power in organization.

Chapter 9

Organisational Development

9.1 INTRODUCTION

Organisation development can be defined as a technique for bringing change in the entire aspect of the organisation, rather than focusing attention on individuals, so that change is easily absorbed.

The organisation development strategy addresses the question what organisation needs to learn to achieve a particular change, and assesses the training need required for the change. The people are trained accordingly with more emphasis on human relations. This is used for more general and lasting aim of developing the organisation's own training function rather than accomplishing an immediate discrete change.

Business organisations seek growth and enhancement. They operate in a Kaleidoscopic environment where political-economic, sociological and tech-nological changes are constantly weathering the landscape into a fascinating dance. To many organisations, this is a saraband and they die, unable to cope with change. When organisations succeed and grow, they tend to 'freeze' into their way of being. They take the environment that confers success on them for granted. When the changing PEST withdraws the conferred favors, the no longer relevant organisation withers. The long term 'relevancy' of organisation is the focal point for long-range planners relating to organisations. The word 'relevance' implies internal change or dynamism. It is the process of renewing oneself to remain relevant and capture happy days forever. It is, as a matter of fact, the process of organisational development.

Definition of Organisation Development

According to one author, "OD is not a framework of structures, formulae and prescriptions but a continuous experience that seeks to refine the organisation in terms of effectiveness, i.e., relevance and competitive edge."

According to Richard Beckhard, "OD is a planned effort, organisation-wide and managed from the top, to increase the organisation effectiveness and health through planned intervention in the organisation's processes using behavioural science knowledge. According to Frank and Brown, "OD is a method for facilitating change and development in people in technology and organisational processes and structures."

According to Warren G. Bennis, "Organisation Development can be defined a'Sa technique for bringing change in the entire aspect of the organisation, rather than focussing attention on individuals, so that change is easily absorbed."

In the words of Keith Davis, "Organisational development is an intervention strategy that uses group processes to focus on the whole culture of an organisation in order to bring about planned change. It seeks to change beliefs, attitudes, values, structures, and practices-in fact, the entire culture of the organisation-so that the organisation can better adapt to technology and line with that fast pace of change." Thus organisational development is just like a training to the employees to mould themselves in a planned way so that the necessary changes may be introduced in the organisation without much resistances of workers and it is possible only through the change in the whole culture, *i.e.*, beliefs, attitudes, values, structures, and practices of the organisation.

9.2 OBJECTIVE

There are two major factors which have caused the use of OD as a technique for planned change. These are as follows :

1. Training for change does not work properly only through reward structure on the job, unless there is a proper change in the environment of organisation in which people work. The old mores and structures of the organisation do not support training adequately, and trained people even fail to bring the desired change. This requires a change in the organisation environment so that it supports training. This is the basic objective of OD.
2. In the dynamic environment, the change is extremely rapid. This requires a highly receptive and effective organisation so that changes are implemented and absorbed to keep organisations survive and prosper. OD tries to make organisation receptive and effective. As Keith Davis has observed, "it (OD) tries to free up communication tightness by increasing the amount, trust, and candour of communication. It seeks to build problem-solving capacity by improving group dynamics and problem confrontation. In short, it reaches into all aspects of organisation culture in order to make it more humanly responsive."

9.3 CHARACTERISTICS OF OD

From the analysis of various definitions of OD, the following characteristics emerge :

1. **Long Range Effort**-OD is a long term approach meant to elevate the organisation to a higher level of functioning by improving the performance and satisfaction of organisation members. It does not solve temporary or isolated problems. It generally covers over-all change for a fairly long period, say, 5 to 10 years.
2. **Broad-based-**OD is very broad-based. It covers the change in the over all culture of organisation-beliefs, attitudes, values, structures and practices of the organisation.
3. **Focus on Whole Organisation**-Organisational development focuses on a whole organisation or a major unit of it so that the environment in the whole organisation tends to reinforce the employees to learn whatever the programme includes. It differs from the traditional training programme that emphasises on a small group or a certain job.
4. **System Oriented**-Organisational development is system oriented. It is concerned with the interactions of the various parts of the organisation which affect each other. It stresses on inter-group and interpersonal relationship.
5. **Action Research**-Organisation development is action research. It works with the actual working conditions existing on the job and has no consideration of artificial ones. It is such a key characteristic that organisational development is sometimes defined as the organisational improvements through action research.

6. **Problem Solving**-Organisation development is concerned with the prob-lem solving. It seeks to solve the problems through practical experiences gained on the work and not merely through theoritical discussion as in a class room. These problems mainly occur at the time when working on the job hence the problems are real and interesting to them. Thus, it develops an attitude of problem solving among workers on the job.
7. **Group Processes**-Organisational development uses the group processes rather than individual process. It makes sincere efforts to improve the group performance. There are group discussion, inter-group conflicts, confrontation and team building. Sensible efforts are made to develop and improve interpersonal relations, open co communication channels, build trust and encourage responsiveness to others.
8. **Feedback**-Organisation development supports feedback to participants so that they may be able to collect the solid original data on which decisions are based. For this purpose participants may be divided into several groups according to the functions. Each such group takes its own decision on the subjects referred to it, and then, the decision is forwarded to the other group for feedback. Each group comes to know the impression of other groups about it and then groups meet together to thrash out any misunderstanding developed among them. In this way, decisions of each group are checked by other groups and the final decision is reached.
9. **Experimental Learning**-Organisational development provides experi-mental learning just to help the participants learn new behaviour patterns through experience. People develop behavioural concepts through experience and no expert guidance's needed for this purpose.
10. **Contingency Oriented**-Organisational development is situational and contingency oriented. As because people learn to develop their behavioural concepts through experience, they can suggest various ways to solve a particular problem and to adapt any of them most suited in the present situation, considering all contigencies. Conversely, the traditional training programme suggests only one best way. So, organisational development is more flexible and programatic as compared to the historical training programme.
11. **Uses Change Agent**—The final characteristic of the organisational devel-opment is that is uses change agent or consultants and not the experts to guide and affect the change. Thus change-agents or consultants are process consultants and not expert consultants and their role is to guide groups towards more effective group processes rather than playing the role of experts and telling them what to do. The simply assist the group in problem solving processes and the groups solve the problems themselves.

In short, we can say that organisation development deals with the whole process and not the parts. It integrates four parts of the organisation, i.e. people, structure, technology and social system into an effective unit that improves the organisational effectiveness.

9.4 PROCESS OF ORGANISATION DEVELOPMENT

Organisational development is a continuous process. It takes at least one year to have a start and may continue for indefinite long period. It is a complicated process and hence needs top management support without which the process cannot be adopted or if adopted cannot be successfully implemented in the organisation. Organisation development has various approaches but a whole typical programme may include the following steps :

1. **Initial Consultation**—The first step in the organisational development process is to approach the organisational development consultant to determine the type of O.D. programme to be developed. The consultant may be a professional consultant from outside or he may internal service personnel expert in organisation development programmes. At this point, the consultant may have consultations with persons from various levels in the organisation in order to gain the knowledge of imports. For this purpose, he may interview such persons or he may adopt any other way to be acquainted with the necessary information.
2. **Data Collection**—The next step is data collection. The consultant meets various groups away from the workplace in order to determine the organisational climate and behavioural problems faced by the organisation. They gather informa-tion through surveys and develop information through interviews etc.
3. **Data Feedback and Confrontation-**Data**,** so collected are made known to work-groups concerned or key members of the organisation and are asked to review the data collected. They go through the data and locate the points of disagreement, discuss such points and take the decision and then suggest the priorities for change.
4. **Action Planning and Problem Solving**—Data are used by the group to suggest specific recommendations for change. They discuss the problems, faced by the organisation and sketch specific plans including who is responsible for problems and their solutions and what action should be taken and at what time.
5. **Team Building**-During the whole process, group meetings are convened to discuss the programme and the consultant in the whole process encourage the groups to examine how they work together as a group or as a team. The consultant helps them see the value of open communication and trust them. These are essential prerequisites for improved group functioning. Consultant also encour-age team building through organising meetings with managers and their imme-diate subordinates so that they can improve the functioning of the work group with the guidance of consultant.
6. **Inter-group Development**-With the development of natural team (a manager and his subordinates), the larger groups comprising several team may be developed. In this way, it will include the whole organisation.
7. **Appraisal and Follow up**-The consultant further helps the organisation in making an appraisal of the programme and find out the deficiencies if any. He can develop additional

programmes in areas where the original programme is felt ineffective and results are poor and that requires improvement. Thus the consultant advise follow up for better understanding.

Thus, the above social process and the steps discussed are not the same with every type of organisation. They may differ from organisation to organisation depending upon the culture of the society in which it is being applied. For example, where trade unions have political bent, the workers are on the board of directors. There is also more industry-government interaction. In such climate, organisational development is more concerned with power and political implications of the action plans.

9.5 ACTION RESEARCH MODEL OF OD

The OD process can be conveniently presented in the form of action research model. OD emphasizes the process of problem solving, and trains the participants to identify and solve problems that are important to them. For this purpose, various steps of OD-problem identification and diagnosis, planning for change, interventions for change, and evaluation of change-are undertaken on continuous and cyclical basis. This cyclical process of using research to guide action, which generates new data as the basis for new actions, is known as action research. French and Bell have defined action research as follows:

"Action research is the process of systematically collecting research data about an ongoing system relative to some objective, goal, or need of that system; feeding these data back into the system; taking actions by altering selected variables within the system based both on the data and on hypothesis; and evaluating the results of actions by collecting more data".

Various activities involved in action research are presented in Figure below

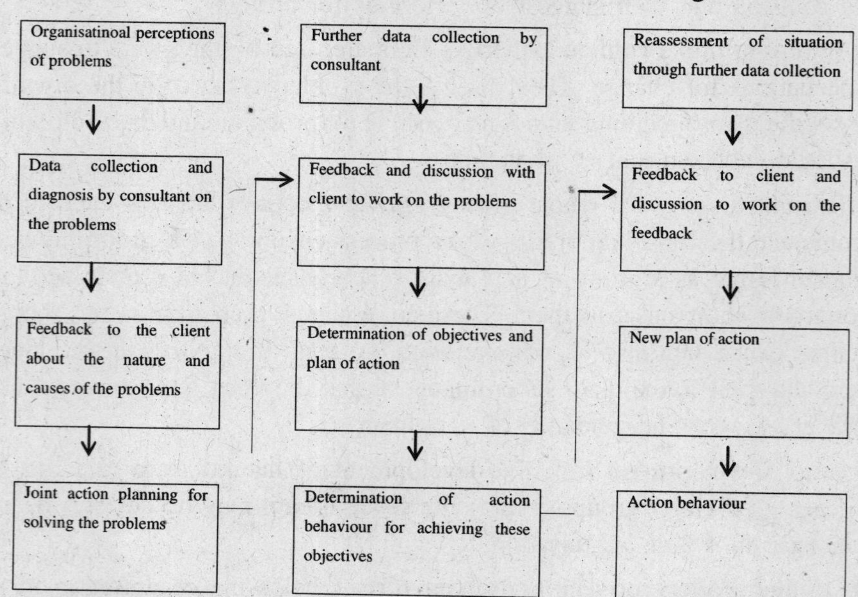

Figure- Action research model of OD

The action research model given in figure 2.1 is self-explanatory. The model involves data collection and diagnosis, providing feedback to client, and discussion and determination of action at various stages. Action research is the basis for designing strategies for OD. Specifically, it is important in the following context.

1. It involves all those who take action or who are affected by change in the organisation. Therefore, chances of willing acceptance of change are quite high.
2. It accustoms the members of a group to work together effectively and to develop way for emotional and philosophical adjustments to change.
3. It rationalizes the action by providing accurate knowledge of the context in which it occurs.

9.6 LIMITATIONS OF OD

As a method of inducing change, organisation development has certain limitations. These are as follows :

1. Organisation development can be no more powerful than the behavioural science concepts on which it rests. Behavioural science itself has various limitations, and these are applicable to OD also.
2. There are some persons, specially complacent ones, who are not prepared to apply diligence of effort for improvement and the methods of work involved in OD are sometimes not of sufficient strength to challenge the motivation of highly complacent people.
3. Task of the organisation and the characteristics of its membership also put limitations on the effectiveness of OD. Thus OD cannot be applied without giving due regard for the local circumstances existing within any given organisation. For example, Research and Development organisations are less responsive to change potential of OD.

9.7 OD AND MANAGEMENT DEVELOPMENT

Organisation development differs from management development. While the latter aims at developing the managers individually for the accomplishment of better performance in organisational setting, the former goes one step further and purports to change the entire organisational climate where the mangers work. Miner has drawn difference between two processes. According to him, there are four attributes of effective managers in large organisations. These are : (i) a positive attitude towards authority, (ii) competitiveness, (iii) assertiveness, and (iv) a sense of responsibility. He feels that management development reinforces the above four qualities and helps managers cultivate and develop the will to manage, whereas OD efforts within organisations may cause confusion and chaos for incoming human resources if the organisation is underplayed and the humanistic dimension alone emphasized. If OD efforts train people towards anti-authority value, more attention to peer-groups, less individual competitiveness, and greater display of feelings and emotions, then would the results be functional for managing organisation activity in a competitive world? Thus, according to him, OD tries to fit the organisation to the men, MD tries to fit the men to the organisation, with their existing objectives and structures. However, the real distinction between OD and MD lies in between two extremes. Thus, in OD efforts, too, organisation structure may change should the need arise and in MD efforts, the men may also have to adopt new ways of training and behaviour. In many situations, MD becomes a part of OD because OD seeks to improve the entire system so that the full potentiality of the managers is actualized and there is a constant improvement in their behaviour. Thus, to make an integration between changed systems and managers, training and development programmes for managers are required. From this point of view, both are complementary rather than conflicting.

9.8 STEPS IN OD

Lawrence and Lorsch have provided five steps in OD, which are explained below:

1. Diagnosis of the Problem

OD programme starts with the identification of the problem in the organization. Analysis of various symptoms-both overt and covert-may help in identifying the problem. Diagnosis of a problem will provide its causes and determine the nature of future action needed. A lot of bad decisions are taken because the decision maker does not have a good grasp of the problem. Therefore, adequate information should be gathered to identify the real problem. If proper care is not taken at this stage, what may appear at first sight to be the real problem may ultimately turn out to be a mere symptom. The manager should try to have an overall view of the situation to find the real problem.

Change is to be introduced with the help of change agents who act as catalysts or facilitators of change in organization. A change agent is a pace setter in the process of organization development. Change agents may be outsiders or insiders. External change agents are consultants appointed by the management to advise, oversee and initiate change. They must have the support of internal change agents who are managers working at different positions in the organization. The in-house change agents must be given adequate training so that they are effective in implementing the change.

4. Implementing the Change

Although it is quite simple to identify change after it has occurred, it is very difficult to influence the direction of change while it is under way. Planning and implementation of change are interdependent. The way in which a change is planned has an important impact on the way in which it is carried out; and conversely, the problems in implementing change have also an impact on the modification of change plan. OD practitioners have an important role in implementing change. They will interfere if the change is not taking place in the direction it is desired.

5. Evaluation

OD is a very long process. So there is a great need for careful monitoring to get precise feedback regarding what is going on after the OD programme starts. This will help in making suitable modifications whenever necessary. For evaluation of OD programme, the use of critique sessions, appraisal of change efforts and comparison of pre-and post-training behavioural patterns are quite effective.

9.9 OD INTERVENTIONS

OD interventions refer to various activities which consultant and client organisation perform for improving organisational functioning through enabling organisation members better mange their team and organisation cultures. French and Well have defined OD interventions as 'sets of structured activities in which selected organisational units (target groups or individuals) engage with a task or a sequence of tasks where the task goals are related directly or indirectly to organisational improvement. Interventions constitute the action thrust of organisation development; they make things happen and are what is happening.

2. Planning Strategy for Change

Many firms employ management consultants to suggest strategy for change. The management consultant or OD practitioner should attempt to transform diagnosis of the problem into a proper action plan involving the overall goals for change, determination of basic approach for attaining these goals and the sequence of detailed scheme for implementing the approach.

3. Preparation of Change Agents

Change is to be introduced with the help of change agents who act as catalysts or facilitators of change in organization. A change agent is a pace setter in the process of organization development. Change agents may be outsiders or insiders. External change agents are consultants appointed by the management to advise, oversee and initiate change. They must have the support of internal change agents who are managers working at different positions in the organization. The in-house change agents must be given adequate training so that they are effective in implementing the change.

9.10 OD INTERVENTIONS

OD interventions refer to various activities which consultant and client organisation perform for improving organisational functioning through enabling organisation members better mange their team and organisation cultures. French and Well have defined OD interventions as 'sets of structured activities in which selected organisational units (target groups or individuals) engage with a task or a sequence of tasks where the task goals are related directly or indirectly to organisational improvement. Interventions constitute the action thrust of organisation development; they make things happen and are what is happening.

Classification of OD Interventions

(1) **Behavioural Techniques.** These techniques are designed to affect the behaviour of individuals and groups. These include;

(i) Sensitivity training.

(ii) Management by objectives.

(iii) Grid training and development.

(2) **Non-Behavioural Techniques.** These techniques are much more structured than the behavioural techniques. These include:

(iv) Changes in organization structure.

(v) Work design.

(vi) Job enrichment.

(3) **Miscellaneous Techniques.** In addition to the above techniques, there are certain other techniques which are used in organization development, such as:

(vii) Survey feedback.

(viii) Process-consultation.

(ix) Team building.

1. Sensitivity Training

Sensitivity training is the most controversial laboratory training method. Many of its advocates have an almost religious zeal in their enhancement with the training group experience. Some of its critics match this fervour in their attacks on the technique. As a result of criticism and experience, a somewhat revised approach, often described as 'team development' training, has appeared. It was first used by National Training Laboratories at Bethel, U.S.A., the training groups themselves called 'T Group'. Since then its use has been extended to other organisations, and institutes.

Sensitivity training is a small-group interaction under stress in an unstructured encounter group which requires people to become sensitive to one another's feelings in order to develop reasonable group activity. T group has several characteristic features : (i) the T-group is generally small, from ten to twenty members; (ii) the group beings its activity with no formal agenda; (iii) the role of trainer is primarily to call attention from time to time to the ongoing process within the group; (iv) the procedure tends to develop introspection and self-examination, with emotional levels of involvement and behaviour and the possibility of colleagues and some breakdown of established insulation and self-defence on the part of individuals. The objectives of such training are increased openness with others, more concern for others, increased tolerance for individual differences, less ethnic prejudice, understanding of a group process, enhanced listening skills, and increased trust and support. Two studies, one by Argyris and another by Sikes, found support for the effectiveness of laboratory training in improving social sensitivity and effectiveness behavior in groups.

2. Process Consultation

Process consultation (P-C) represents a method for intervening in an ongoing system. The basic content of P-C is that the consultant works with individuals and groups to help them learn about human and social processes and learn to solve problems that stem from process events. Schein has defined P-C as activities on the part of the consultant which helps the client to perceive, understand, and act upon process events which occurs in the client's environment. P-C consists of many interventions and activities which affect the various organisational processes, such as, communications, roles and functions of group members, group problems-solving and decision-making, group norms, authority and leadership, and intergroup co-operation and conflicts. Such processes are attempted to be modified by P-C. Schein has suggested major activities which the consultant undertakes in consultation. These are: agenda-setting, feedback of observation or other data, coaching and counseling of individuals, and suggestion regarding structural modifications.

Process consultations model places emphasis on diagnosis and understanding of process events. Thus, aim is to bring change in the various processes as an on going process of OD. The role of consultant is non-directive as he helps the groups to solve their problems.

3. Team Development

There are many interventions for team development. The basic objective of using team development interventions is to increase effectiveness of various teams within the organisations. The team work requires a supportive climate. In applying this principle, the relationship between the superior and subordinate is crucial. This relationship should be one which is supportive and ego-building. The more often the superior's behaviour is ego-building on organisational performance. This relationship may work equally in the case of peer relationship in group-building.

The underlying aim of team development is to increase trust among the members because people work better together when there is open and honest sharing about the problems and difficulties that they have with one another. As such, at the initial level, the attempt should be to develop such an environment where such trust can be developed among the team members. Though organisational climate, in general, provides such a trusting conditions, management may take specific measures in this direction. Such measures, in order to be more effective, should proceed in the following procedure:

1. **Problem–Sensing.** There are a number of ways in which problems of a team can be identified. Often the team itself defines which aspects of teambuilding it wishes to work on. This problem can between be identified in terms of what is hindering group effectiveness. At this stage, generally most of the members cone forward with their arguments as to what the real problems are. The views may be quite different ranging from the organisational problem, groups problems to even personal problems. In problem identification, the emphasis should be on consensus. The consensus-seeking part of the process necessitates that each person becomes thoroughly aware and understand clearly the basic concepts of team-

development. Much of the problems may be solved through effective communication and training sessions.

2. **Examining Effects of Differences in Perception.** The perception of people on an issue differs because of their differing backgrounds, such as, their value systems, personality, and attitudes. The perception may be brought to conformity through the process of exercise on perception which involves a number of psychological exercises particularly on perceptual differences. The role of communication is important in this context because it will help in clarifying the actual problems to the members.
3. **Giving and Receiving Feedback.** The step of perceiving things and listening to each other may be relayed back to the members as there is a possibility that such processes may create tense situation in the group. Often, members report about the painful feelings that they have at the time of evaluation of their feelings. The discussion should continue until all members of the team have commented. The feedback should be given to the members about their feelings, about the issue, the way people talk about the issue, the staying with the topic or going off on tangents, who was talking more or who was talking less, who was trying to resolve the differences, etc. Such feedback generally provides members to evaluate the values but at the same time also provides opportunity to understand themselves. The concept of Johri window may also be applied. This suggests that even people are not fully aware of themselves.
4. **Developing Interacting Skills.** The basic objective of this process is to increase the ability among the people as to how they should interact with others and engage in constructive behaviour. Following are the examples of constructive and negative behaviours:

Constructive Behaviour

(i) **Building :** developing and expanding the ideas of others.

(ii) **Bringing in :** harmonizing, encouraging others to participate.

(iii) **Clarifying :** resting, ensuring, understanding, seeking relevant information.

(iv) **Innovating :** bringing in new relevant ideas, information, feelings, etc.

Negative Behaviour

(i) **Overtalk :** interrupting, talking together with speaker.

(ii) **Attacking :** deriding, belittling, criticizing person.

(iii) **Negating :** cooling, cynicism, undermining morale.

At the time of discussion of feedback, people take themselves assignments to increase specific constructive behaviours and decrease specific negative behaviours. If this process is adopted several times, there is a strong possibility that members may learn constructive behaviours and leave negative behaviour. This is quite helpful in developing teamwork.

5. **Personal contracting with team members.** Many problems in the organisation start with a conflict between two persons. While it is true that external forces can increase the level of conflict within the organisation, the kinds and intensity of the conflict are often determined by the individual pairs that make up the organisation. Thus, managers must take steps to reduce one-to-one conflict.
6. **Follow-up-action.** This is the final stage in team-building. At this stage, the total team is convened to review what has been learned and to identify what the next step should be. Follow-up action also helps in overcoming the drawback involved at the initial stages of team building. It involves deciding who will take care of each area of the team's responsibilities, and who will be responsible for team projects in a group that has not developed a satisfactory division of responsibility; clarifying and setting differences in perception concerning responsibility and authority in the team, with complex division of responsibility and authority among members.

These attempts bring co-operative and supportive feelings among people involved in the team functioning. When this exercise is undertaken at the initial stage, it contributes positively towards the feelings of the people. However, to encourage and sustain such feelings, management should take such actions at regular intervals so that members feel reinforced and sustain their positive behaviour. Such actions will go a along way in shaping the organisational climate quite conducive to members for their efficient working.

4. Grid Organisation Development

Grid organisation development, developed by Blake and Mouton, is a comprehensive and systematic OD programme. The programme aims at individuals, groups, and the organisation as a whole. It utilizes a considerable number of instruments, enabling individuals and groups to assess their own strength and weaknesses; focuses on skills, knowledge, and processes necessary for effectiveness at the individual, group, intergroup, and total organisation levels.

The basic content of grid organisation development in managerial grid as discussed in Chapter 14. The whole orientation is to develop 9,9 managerial style through the application of behavioural science knowledge. The grid organisation development consists of six phases.

(i) Managerial Grid. It covers various aspects of assessing managerial styles, problem-solving, communication skills, and teamwork. The individuals try to learn to become 9,9 managers by practice.

(ii) Teamwork Development. The focus in this stage is to develop teamwork by analyzing team culture, traditions, and alike. The skills relating to planning, objective-setting, and problem-solving are also developed.

(iii) Intergroup Development. At this phase, the focus is on intergroup behaviour and relations. The thrust is on moving groups from conflict to co-operation. Each group separately analyses the ideal intergroup relationship. Action steps to move towards the ideal are developed and assigned to individuals who may be engaged in building co-operative intergroup relationships.

(iv) Developing Ideal Strategic Corporate Model. At this stage, the focus shifts to the total organisation and to develop skills necessary for organisational excellence. The action is designed to identify the characteristics of the ideal organisation. The members of the organisation are trained for achieving this excellence.

(v) Implementing the Ideal Strategic Model. The implementation stage includes the building of the organisation on the model of ideal organisation on the basis of concepts developed under stage 4. Each group may be given assignment to evolve strategy for making ideal organisation with the help of the consultant. The strategy is then implemented.

(vi) Systematic Critique. In this stage, the various efforts from phase 1 to 5 are evaluated and critical analysis is made. The analysis will bring out the shortcomings that may be there. In this light, the various programmes may be redesigned.

In addition to these people focused interventions, there may be other types of interventions also. For example, structural and job interventions-job enlargement, job enrichment, management by objectives, rules, procedures, authority structure, etc. However, these aspects are also covered in comprehensive people-focused interventions.

9.11 CONFLICT MANAGEMENT

The management within an organisation should function in such a way so as to maximize the coordination of human resources and work system and to minimize conflict. There may be two approaches for managing organisational conflict : preventive measures and curative measures. In the preventive measures, management tries to create an environment where dysfunctional conflicts do not take place. Conflict is not primarily a result of individual neurotic traits but arises under given conditions even when people involved are well adjusted. Since situational variables induce conflict, it is possible to modify situations so as to avoid conflict. However, there may not be any specific standard of situation in which conflict will not grow, there might be certain positive programmes and actions that might reasonably lead to avoidance of conflict in the organisation. The development of effective leadership, participative decision-making, effective two-way communication with proper emphasis on upward communication, improvement in interpersonal relationship, provision for facilities and opportunities to develop informal groups may be some of the ways to which management should pay special attention. The curative measures include the resolution of conflicts when they take place and become dysfunctional in the organisation. Such preventive and curative attempts may be made in the following ways.

Establishing Common Goals

Most of the conflicts assume that incompatible goals are a necessary antecedent for the development of conflict. It means that the existence of superordinate goals – common goals – will reduce the occurrence of dysfunctional conflicts. This is true particularly in the case of conflict among groups and between individuals and organisation. Schein observes that 'the fundamental problem of intergroup competition is the conflict of goals and the breakdown of interaction between the groups. This breakdown in turn permits and stimulates perceptual distortion and mutual negative stereotyping. The basic strategy of reducing conflict, therefore, is to find goals upon which groups can agree and to reestablish valid communication between the groups. The tactics to employ in implementing this strategy can include locating a common enemy, locating a superordinate goal. The mutual dependence of groups can be brought through the superordinate goals because these are the goals which are of high value to groups. Superordinate goals are those that take precedence over other goals that may separate the conflicting parties.

Sherif has conducted a series of experiments in intergroup conflict and common goals. He concludes the finding as such : 'what our limited experiments have shown is that the possibilities for achieving harmony are greatly enhanced when groups are brought together to work toward common ends. Then favourable information about a disliked group is seen in a new light, and leaders are in a position to take bolder steps toward co-operation. In short, hostility gives way when groups pull together to achieve overriding goals which are real and compelling to all concerned.

Goal differences can also be reduced through the adoption of appropriate incentive systems. Many organisational reward systems often result in 'win-lose' mentality in organisation because the reward systems focus attention on the individual rather than on the group or organisation as a whole. It has been observed that goal differentiation can also be reduced through the use of incentive systems designed to reward activities that benefit the larger system, as opposed to those that are primarily in the interest of subunits.

Changing Structural Arrangement

In some cases, the change in organisation structure or some part of it can reduce dysfunctional conflicts. While there are some basic guidelines in this respect, Katz et el have given some more suggestions in this respect. They observe that conflicts can be reduced by decentralisation, restructuring to remove obvious differentials in status symbols between hierarchical interest groups, development of cycles of work, with opportunity to employees to complete tasks and sharing in organisational rewards. Such structural variables, more specifically, can be used in the following ways.

1. **Reduction in Interdependence.** The basic reason in the intergroup conflict is interdependence among them. As such less such interdependence, less will the amount of conflict among them. Thompson distinguished three types of interdependence : pooled, sequential, and reciprocal. In the pooled interdependence, the various divisions of the organisation are relatively self-contained and independent. In sequential interdependence, there is high degree of interdependence between two or more departments which might be using the product of others in a particular sequence. The units are most interdependent when the interdependence is reciprocal, that is, the output of various units becomes input

for others. According to conflict model, the degree of conflict is high in the case of latter two relationships, that is, more the interdependence, more the chances for conflict. In organisations, such interdependence cannot altogether be avoided, however, instead of separating units organisationally, they can be separated physically. Physically separating the conflicting groups has the distinct advantage of preventing more damage from being done and of preventing the creation of further rationale for fighting. However, this tactic may require continuous surveillance to keep the parties separate, especially if tempers are hot and energy levels high. The physical separation, however, is not a permanent measure for managing conflict.

2. **Reduction in Shared Resources.** When two are more units are required to share resources, particularly scarce ones, the potential for conflict increases. The management of conflict suggests reducing such sharing. One technique for reducing such sharing in the increase in such resources so that each unit is independent in using them. However, since resources are scarce, it is not always possible to do so. As such, measures may be adopted for their optimum allocation.
3. **Exchange of Personnel.** Personnel of the conflicting groups may be exchanged for a specified period as a way to reducing and managing conflict. An exchange of people is very similar to role reversal, which is aimed at greater understanding between people by forcing each to present and defend the others position. In a research study, it was found that the exchange of people programme was effective at reducing conflict and speeding agreement. It was successful even though it was mandatory, involved the less influential members of the organisations, and was of relatively short duration.
4. **Creation of Special Integrators.** To resolve conflict, organisation may create provisions for the appointment of special integrators who may manage the interdependence of various groups so that unresolved matters can be solved through them. Lawrence and Lorsch have found that in certain situations, particularly when there are much differentiation between departments in terms of time span, goals, and values, the use of special integrator departments or individuals facilitates the management and resolution of interdepartmental conflicts. For example, they found that integrators were more effective when they were viewed as about intermediate in position between the conflicting departments, where they were viewed as high in influence, and where they perceived that their rewards were tied to the total performance of the two groups they were integrating.
5. Reference to Superior's Authority. Conflicts may be resolved through the hierarchy. If resolution cannot be attained by two organisational members, they may take the issue to a common superior who resolves the conflict by making a decision. Such a decision is usually accepted by organisational members because of the recognised superior authority of high-ranking individual. Such a decision may not necessarily bring agreement but it will usually be accepted.

9.12 CONFLICT-RESOLUTION ACTIONS

The various measures, discussed above, undoubtedly help in reducing the occurrence of conflict in the organisation but they cannot guarantee the complete absence of conflicts. As such, whenever conflicts arise, these have to be resolved by some specifications, known as conflict-resolution actions. There may be many such actions. For example, March and Simon say that an organisation may react to conflict by problem-solving, persuasion, bargaining, and politics. Ruble and Thomas have identified five types of actions : competing, avoiding, accommodating, compromising, and collaborating. Lawrence and Lorsch have identified three types of behaviour in conflict resolution : confrontation, smoothing, and forcing. Some major actions in conflict resolution take place in the following ways :

1. **Problem-solving.** The problem-solving technique is considered to be the most positive technique available for conflict resolution because it emphasizes the attaining of the common interests of both conflicting parties. In mutual problem-solving process, the conflicting parties must come together with the responsibilities of solving the mutual problem that faces rather than merely finding a way to accommodate their different perspectives. Questions of who is right or wrong are generally avoided, but sharing and communicating are required in order to find areas of common interest. This process causes the doubts and misunderstandings that underlie the conflict to become more obvious to the parties so that they may more effectively deal with them. Problem-solving technique can be applied effectively where conflict is based on misunderstanding of the parties concerned. However, this technique is not effective when conflicts stem from value systems that differ and that are the one of the major sources of conflicts.
2. **Avoidance.** Another method of overcoming conflict is its avoidance, that is, parties to the conflict may either withdraw from the conflict or conceal the incompatibility. Withdrawal may be observed when one party leaves the field of conflict so that other party may win by being in sole possession of the goal in dispute. Alternatively, the goal may be redefined through mutual withdrawal from the field and the redefinition of other and non-overlapping goal priorities. Concealing the incompatibility is another form of conflict resolution when it is not possible for any party to withdraw from the conflict. In such a case, the conflict may be eliminated by withholding the information that the parties are in conflict because of goal incompatibilities. However, these are the methods for avoiding conflicts rather than solving the actual conflicts.
3. **Smoothing.** Smoothing can be defined as the process of playing down differences that exist between individuals or groups while emphasizing common interests. Differences are suppressed and similarities are accentuated in smoothing process. Finding and emphasising similarities between conflicting parties, while suppressing differences, can eventually lead the parties to realize that they are not far apart as was first believed. With shared viewpoints on an issue, the ability to work together towards a commonly held goal must be facilitated. This again, however, is not a long-term solution for the conflicts.

Compromise. Compromise is a well-accepted technique for resolving conflict, yielding neither a definite loser nor a distinct winner. Included here are external or third-party interventions, plus internal compromise between conflicting parties through both total-group and representative negotiation and voting. Such a compromise may be achieved either through the intervention of third party, the process is commonly known as mediation, or without the intervention of the external parties, the method is known as bargaining. In both such cases, the conflicting parties arrive at some compromise which is mostly mutual give-and-take situation. Compromise may be effectively used when the goal object may be divided up in some way among the competing parties. In cases where this is not possible, one group may yield to the other something of value in exchange for a concession of value. Both parties then give something up. In a compromise situation, the outcome depends primarily on the relative strength of the parties. In situations in which one of the parties is much stronger than the other, little actual compromising may occur, and one side dictates to the other. This is quite effective method of conflict resolution between management and workers.

Confrontation. The various actions enumerated above may not bring resolution of conflict between parties if they take very rigid stand. In such a case, the parties are left to confrontation to settle the conflict themselves. This strategy may result into win-lose situation. The parties concerned may settle their score by applying their strength against each other. Confrontation may be used for organisation development and increasing organisational effectiveness. Lawrence and Lorsch have observed that high performing organisations use confrontation techniques far more frequently than do the lower producing organisations. However, confrontation may not be treated as ideal technique for most of the organisations specially if they are not equipped with taking the advantages of confrontation. It can be desirable only if the organisation is working on competitive spirit basis. Since this is the part of organisational climate and if organisational climate may not be developed on this basis, it is not desirable to go for confrontation.

The parties involved in conflict must analyse certain aspects before going for confrontation. The first basic question is : What are the issues of conflict? What are the costs for achieving a particular thing? Often conflict is based not on actual issues but on misperception which may aggravate the situation leading to conflictual behaviour. In such a case, self-introspection provides the real understanding of conflict phenomenon. The second aspect which must be analysed is the cost involved. In such a case, self-introspection provides the real understanding of conflict phenomenon. The second aspect which must be analysed is the cost involved. Thing is obtained by paying cost for it. Often the cost involved is much more than the achievement in confrontation. Therefore it cannot always be relied upon. What type of conflict resolution actions would be taken depends on a variety of factors like nature of the conflict, nature of the parties involved in the conflict, and behavioural strategies adopted in conflict resolution. In this context, Wall and Callister have presented some interesting conclusions.

1. Males tend to use the forcing approach as their dominant styles; females use forcing less and often rely on a range of other tactics.

2. Managers tend to use forcing approach; employees prefer avoiding, smoothing, or compromising.
3. American managers tend to be competitive; Japanese managers prefer a cooperative approach.
4. Each party tries to mimic the style of the other-forcing induces forcing: accommodating induces accommodating, and so on.
5. People tend to use different resolution styles for different issues; confrontation is used in performance appraisals, compromise is used in issues involving habits and mannerisms.

Another issue which is important in conflict resolution is the outcome of conflict resolution. This is important in the sense that a new conflict between the parties may depend on the conflict aftermath. Conflict resolution outcome is presented in Figure given below.

Party A's outcomes		Party B' outcome: Win	Party B' outcome: Lose
	Win	Win-win	Win-lose
	Lose	Lose-win	Lose-lose

Figure- Outcomes of conflict resolution

Out of the four possible outcomes of conflict resolution, win-win situation is ideal as both the parties feel satisfied. In lose-lose outcome, both the parties feel cheated. In other two alternatives, only one party wins at the cost of the other, and the conflict becomes a zero-sum game. Such a situation may generate more conflicts in future. The various approaches of conflict management suggest that management can take a variety of actions depending on the situations, parties to conflicts, issues in conflicts, and the organisational resources available. In many cases, a change in organisation structure, process, or the value systems of people is required. This requires the detailed understanding of organisational change and development which will be discussed in the next part.

UNIT EXERCISE

Short Answers

Q1. What do you mean by organizational change?

Q2. Explain any two techniques of overcoming resistance to change.

Q3. Explain the significance of Organization Development.

Q4. Write a note on OD interventions.

Q5. Define conflict.

Q6. Enumerate the stages in conflict.

Long Answers

Q1. Why are organizational changes often resisted by individuals and groups within the organization? How can such resistance be prevented or overcome?

Q2. "Every business needs a strategy to take care of change both expected and unexpected." Comment.

Q3. 'Several economic, social and psychological factors contribute to resistance to change whether such change relates to technology, work relationship, working conditions or other allied matters." In the light of the statement, discuss the reasons for resistance to change.

Q4. Discuss the nature of Organization Development (OD). What are the assumptions underlying O.D.?

Q5. Explain the concept of conflict and discuss the various stages in conflict in an organization.

CHAPTER 10

Organisational Climate

10.0 INTRODUCTION

Organisational climate is a set of characteristics that describe an organisation and that distinguishes one organisation from another, and are relatively enduring over a period of time and influence the behaviour of people in the organisations. It is the summary perception which people have about the organisation. Thus, it is the global expression of what organisation is.

Organisation climate is thus, THE MANIFESTATION OF ATTITUDES OF ORGANISATIONAL MEMBERS TOWARD THE ORGANISATION ITSELF. An organisation tends to attract and keep people who fit its climate, so that its pattern is perpetuated atleast to some extent. Organisation climate is a very important factor to be considered in studying and analysing organisations because it has a profound influence on the outlook, well being and attitudes of organisational members and thus on their total performance.

It affects the behaviour of the people in 3 ways as under:-

1. Defining the stimuli that confront the individual.
2. Placing constraints upon the individual's freedom of choice
3. Providing source of reward and punishment.

Organisational climate thus provides a useful platform for understanding each characteristics of organisations, such as stability, creativity, and innovation, communication and effectiveness etc. Organisational climate should be viewed from total system's point of view. There may exist different climates within different departments in the organisation and the se sub climates will be integrated to form the organisation climate.

10.1 FACTORS AFFECTING ORGANISATIONAL CLIMATE

In every organisation, there exist certain elements which exercise influences on the existing climate. These are:-

1. Organisation structure.
2. Organisation context.
3. Physical environment
4. Process
5. System values and norms

Let us study each of the above in some detail: -

1. Organisation Structure

Structure is a framework that establishes formal relationships and delineate authority and functional responsibility. The actual arrangement of hierarchy affects the climate. Highly decentralised structure results in sound climate when the management feels the necessity of high degree of inputs to the total output. In a sharp contrast, if the management feels the necessity of maintaining greater degree of consistency in operations regarding decision making, it will follow decentralised nature and structure. Thus structure affects climate.

2. Organisational Context

If the company is wedded to such a policy, then it is effectively utilising the resources - both human and nonhuman. In that case, one can say that the climate is good. The manpower philosophy is generally expressed by rules, regulations and policies etc. The point is that the reactions of the employees and the degree to which they welcome and accept the managerial philosophy is very critical to the development of sound and favourable organisational climate. The climate is said to be highly favourable wen the existing management techniques are such that the employee's goals are perfectly matched to the ideals of organisation.

3. Physical Environment

It includes the external conditions of environment, the size and location of the building in which am employee works, the size of place, the size of city - all these affect the organisational climate. Office decor, size and space a person has in doing the work are important factors to be borne in mind as they affect climate. High level of noise brings a bad feeling and leads to frustration, nervousness. And aggression and will have a negative effect on the organisational climate. An employee performing his job in a relatively clean, quiet, and safe environment will have a favourable perception of organisational climate.

4. Process

There are so many elements of the process which an organisation follows to achieve its objectives. The elements include communication, decision making, innovation and leadership. In all these processes the relationship between superior and subordinate is visible and therefore the superior cannot afford to ignore this visible interface.

A leader has to be aware of the possible influence of his actions on the climate when deciding about the most appropriate control and supervision technique for a given situation. When a leader mismatches his style to the situation it might abort any hope of attaining organisational objectives.

5.System values and norms

Every organisation has a formal value system where certain kinds of behaviours are rewarded and encouraged and certain kinds of behaviour forces an individual to formal sanctions. The formal value system is communicated to employees through rules, regulations and policies. From the organisational point of view, both formal and informal groups are very powerful in exercising influence on climate.

10.2 WHAT CONSTITUTES A FAVOURABLE CLIMATE?

Climate can range along a continuum from favourable to neutral to unfavourable. Both employees and employers want a more favourable climate, because of its benefits, such as better performance and job satisfaction.

The typical elements which contribute to make a climate favourable are given below: -

1. Quality of leadership.
2. Amount of trust.
3. Communication, both upward and downward.
4. Feeling of useful work.
5. Responsibility
6. Fair rewards
7. Reasonable job pressures
8. Opportunity
9. Reasonable controls, structure and bureaucracy
10. Employee involvement, and participation.

Employee feels that the climate is favourable when they are doing some thing useful that provides a sense of personal worth. They frequently want challenging work that provides intrinsic satisfaction. Many employees also want responsibility. They want to be listened to and treated as if they have value as individuals. They want to feel that the organisation really cares about their needs and problems.

10.3 MEANING OF ORGANISATIONAL CHANGE

There is nothing permanent except change. It has become an inescapable fact of life; a fundamental aspect of historical evolution. Change is inevitable in a progressive culture. Change in fact, is accelerating in our society. Revolutions are taking place in political, scientific, technological and institutional areas. Organizations cannot completely buffer themselves from this environmental instability. Change is induced by the internal and external forces. Meeting this challenge of change is the primary responsibility of management. An organization lacking adaptability to change has no future. Adaptability to change is a necessary quality of good management. Modern managers have the responsibility to device the management practices to meet the new challenges and make use of the opportunities for the growth of the organization.

10.4 MANAGING CHANGE IN THE ORGANISATIONAL CONTEXT

The topic of managing change is one that comes closest to describe the totality of a manager's job. Practically everything a manager does is in some way concerned with implementing change.

- Hiring a new employee - Changing the work group
- Purchasing a new piece of equipment - Changing work methods
- Rearranging work station - Changing work flows

All require knowledge of how to manage change effectively. Organizational change refers to a modification or transformation of the organization's structure, processes or goods. Flexibility requires that organizations be open to change in all areas, including the structure of the organization itself. In a flexible organization, employees can't think of their roles in terms of a job description. They often have to change the tasks they perform and learn new skills. The most flexible organizations have a culture that values change and managers who know how to implement changes effectively.

10.5 FORCES FOR CHANGE IN ORGANIZATION

More and more organizations today face a dynamic and changing environment that, in turn requires these organizations to adapt. Change has become the norm in most organizations. Plant closing, business failures, mergers and acquisitions, and downsizing have become common experiences for most organizations. Adaptiveness, flexibility and responsiveness are terms used to describe the organizations that will succeed in meeting the competitive challenges that businesses face. In the past, organizations could succeed by claiming excellence in one area – quality, reliability or cost. But this is not the case today. The current environment demands excellence in all areas.

The figure below summarizes six specific forces that are acting as stimulants for change.

Force	Examples
Nature of the workforce	• More cultural diversity • Increase in professionals • Many new entrants with inadequate skills
Technology	• More computers and automation • TQM programs • Reengineering programs
Economic shocks	• Security market crashes • Interest rate fluctuations • Foreign currency fluctuations
Competition	• Global competitors • Mergers and consolidations • Growth of specialty retailers
Social trends	• Increase in college attendance • Delayed marriages by young people • Increase in divorce rate
World politics	• Collapse of Soviet Union • Iraq's invasion of Kuwait • Overthrow of Haitian dictator

Figure 10.5: Forces for Change

Why is Organizational Change so Important?

From outside and inside the organization a variety of forces press for change. "We live in the midst of constant change" has become a well-worn but relevant cliché. Pressures for change are created from both inside and outside the organization. Organization must forge ahead on these forces to survive. Some of these are external, arising from outside the company, whereas others are internal arising from sources within the organization.

1. ***External Forces:*** When the organization's general or task environment changes, the organization's success often rides on its ability and willingness to change as well. Modern manager is change-conscious and operating in the constantly changing environment. Many external changes bombard the modern organizations and make change inevitable. The general environment has social, economic, legal and political and technological dimensions. Any of these can introduce the need for change. In recent years, far-reaching forces for change have included developments in information technology, the globalization of competition, and demands that organizations take greater responsibility for their impact on the environment. These forces are discussed below:

(a) ***Technological Change:*** Rapid technological innovation is a major force for change in organizations, and those who fail to keep pace can quickly fall behind. It is perhaps the greatest factor that organizations reckon with. According to C. Handy "the rate of technological changes is greater today than any time in the past and technological changes are responsible for changing the nature of jobs performed at all levels in the organization". For example, the substitution of computer control for direct supervision is resulting in wider spans of control for managers and flatter organizations.

Technological innovations bring about profound change because they are not just changes in the way work is performed. Instead, the innovation process promotes associated changes in work relationships and organizational structures. Sophisticated information technology is also making organizations more responsive. The team approach adopted by many organizations, leads to flatter structures, decentralized decision making and more open communication between leaders and team members.

(b) ***Globalization:*** The global economy means competitors are likely to come from across the ocean. The power players in the global market are the multinational and trans-national organizations. This has led companies to think globally. There are no mental distinctions between domestic and foreign operations. Globalization, for an organization, means rethinking the most efficient ways to use resources, disseminate and gather information and develop people. It requires not only structural changes but also changes in the minds of employees. Successful organizations will be the ones that can change in response to the competition. They will be fast on their feet, capable of developing new products rapidly and getting them to market quickly.

(c) ***Social and Political Changes:*** A firm's fate is also influenced by such environmental pressures as social and political changes. Many new legal provisions in the corporate sector get introduced every time that affects the organizations.

(d) ***Workforce Diversity:*** Related to globalization is the challenge of workforce diversity. Workforce diversity is a powerful force for change in organization. The demographic trends contributing to workforce diversity are :

- The workforce will see increased participation form females, as the majority of new workers will be female.
- The workforce will be more culturally diverse than ever (part of this is attributable to globalization).
- The workforce is aging. There will be fewer young workers and more Organisational Change middle aged working.

(e) ***Managing Ethical Behaviour:*** Employees face ethical dilemmas in their daily work lives. The need to manage ethical behaviour has brought about several changes in organizations. Most centre on the idea that an organization must create a culture that encourages ethical behaviour. Society expects organizations to maintain ethical behaviour both internally and in relationships with other organizations. Ethical behaviour is expected in relationships with customers, environment and society. These expectations may be informal or they may come in the form of increased legal requirements.

These challenges are forces that place pressures to change on organizations. Organizations cannot afford to be rigid and inflexible in the wake of environmental pressures, they must be rather dynamic and viable so that they survive.

2. ***Internal Forces:*** Besides reacting to or anticipating changes on the outside, an organization may change because someone on the inside thinks a new way of doing things will be beneficial or even necessary. Pressures for change that originate inside the organization are generally recognizable in the form of signals indicating that something needs to be altered. These internal forces are discussed below:

(a) ***Changes in Managerial Personnel:*** One of the most frequent reasons for major changes in an organization is the change of executives at the top. No two managers have the same styles, skills or managerial philosophies. Managerial behaviour is always selective so that a newly appointed manager might favour different organizational design, objectives procedures and policies than a predecessor. Changes in the managerial personnel are thus a constant pressure for change.

(b) ***Declining Effectiveness:*** Declining effectiveness is a pressure to change. A company that experiences losses is undoubtedly motivated to do something about it. Some companies react by instituting layoffs and massive cost cutting programmes, whereas others view the loss as symptomatic of an underlying problem, and seek out the cause of the problem.

(c) ***Changes in Work Climate:*** Changes in the work climate at an organization can also stimulate change. A workforce that seems lethargic, unmotivated, and dissatisfied is a symptom that must be addressed. This symptom is common in organizations that have experienced layoffs. Workers who have escaped a layoff may find it hard to continue to be productive. They may fear that they will be laid off as well and may feel insecure in their jobs.

(d) ***Deficiencies in the Existing System:*** Another internal pressure for organizational change is the loopholes in the system. These loopholes may be unmanageable spans of control, lack of coordination between departments, lack of uniformity in politics, non-cooperation between line and staff etc.

(e) ***Crisis:*** A crisis may also stimulate change in an organization. Strikes or walkouts may lead management to change the wage structure. The resignation of a key decision maker is one crisis that causes the company to rethink the composition of its management team and its role in the organization.

(f) ***Employees, Expectations:*** Changes in employees expectations can also trigger change in organizations. These forces may be:-

- Employees' desire to share in decision-making.
- Employees' demand for effective organizational mechanism.
- Higher employees' expectation for satisfying jobs and work environment.
- Employees' desire for higher wage payment.

All these forces necessitate change in organizations. Besides these forces, a company that hires a group of young newcomers may be met with a set of expectations very different from those expressed by older workers.

Although organizational changes are important, managers should try to institute changes only when they make strategic sense. A major change or two every year can be overwhelming to employees and create confusion about priorities. A logical conclusion is that managers should evaluate internal forces for change with as much care as they evaluate external forces.

10.6 FORMS OF CHANGE

Change has become the norm in most organizations. Adaptiveness, flexibility and responsiveness are terms used to describe the organizations that will succeed in two basic forms of change in organizations that will succeed in meeting the competitive challenges that businesses face. There are two basic forms of change in organizations:

Planned Change and Unplanned Change

(a) ***Planned Change:*** Planned change is a change resulting from a deliberate decision to alter the organization. It is an intentional, goal-oriented activity. The goals of planned change are:

- First it seeks to improve the ability of the organization to adapt to changes in its environment.
- Second, it seeks to change the behaviour of its employees.

(b) ***Unplanned Change:*** Not all change is planned. Unplanned change is imposed on the organization and is often unforeseen. Responsiveness to unplanned change requires tremendous flexibility and adaptability on the part of organizations. Examples of unplanned changes are changes in government regulations and changes in the economy.

10.7 THE ROLE OF CHANGE AGENTS

Change in organizations is inevitable, but change is a process that can be managed. The individual or group who undertakes the task of introducing and managing a change in an organization is known as a change agent. Change agents can be of two types:

(a) ***Internal Change Agents:*** Change agents can be internal such as managers or employees who are appointed to oversee the change process. Internal change agents have certain advantages in managing the change process.

They are:

- They know the organization's past history, its political system, and its culture.
- Internal change agents are likely to be very careful about managing change because they must live with the results of their change efforts.

There are also disadvantages of using internal change agents.

They are:

- They may be associated with certain factions within the organization and may easily be accused of favouritism.
- Internal change agents may be too close to the situation to have an objective view of what needs to be done.

(b) ***External Change Agents:*** Change agents can also be external, such as outside consultants. They bring an outsider's objective view to the organization.

External Change Agents have Certain Advantages

- They may be preferred by employees because of their impartiality.
- They have more power in directing changes if employees perceive the change agents as being trustworthy, possessing important expertise, having a track record that establishes credibility.

There are also disadvantages of using external change agents. They are:

- External change agents face certain problems, including their limited knowledge of the organization's history.
- They may be viewed with suspicion by organization members.

10.8 RESISTANCE TO CHANGE

As the manager contemplates and initiates change in the organization one phenomenon that is quite likely to emerge anytime in the change process is the resistance to change. People often resist change in a rational response based on self-interest. Resistance to change doesn't necessarily surface in standardized ways. Resistance can be overt, implicit, immediate, or deferred. It is easiest for management to deal with resistance when it is overt and immediate. The greater challenge is managing resistance that is implicit or deferred.

The sources of resistance to change can be categorized into two sources: individual and organizational.

1. ***Individual Resistance:*** One aspect of mankind that has remained more or less constant is his innate resistance to change. Individuals resist change because they attach great preference to maintain *status quo*. Individual sources of resistance to change reside in basic human characteristics such as perceptions, personalities and needs. The following are the reasons:-

(a) *Economic Reasons:* The economic reasons to fear change usually focus on one or more of the following:

- Fear of technological unemployment.
- Fear of reduced work hours and consequently less pay.
- Fear of demotion and thus reduced wages.
- Fear of speed-up and reduced incentive wages.

Changes in job tasks or established work routines can also arouse economic fears if people are concerned they won't be able to perform the new tasks or routines to their previous standards, especially when pay is closely tied to productivity.

(b) *Fear of the Unknown:* Change often bring with it substantial uncertainty. Employees facing a technological change, such as the introduction of a new computer system, may resist the change simply because it introduces ambiguity into what was once a comfortable situation for them. This is especially a problem when there has been a lack of communication about the change.

(c) *Fear of Loss:* When a change is impending, some employees may fear losing their jobs, particularly when an advanced technology is introduced. Employees may also fear losing their status because of a change. Another common fear is that changes may diminish the positive qualities the individual enjoys in the job. For example, computerizing the customer service positions, threaten the autonomy that sales representatives previously enjoyed.

(d) *Security:* People with a high need for security are likely to resist change because it threatens their feeling of safety.

(e) *Status quo:* Perhaps the biggest and most sound reason for the resistance to change is the *status quo*. As human beings, we are creatures of habit. Change may pose disturbance to the existing comforts of *status quo*. When confronted with change, this tendency to respond in our accustomed ways becomes a source of resistance. Change means they will have to find new ways of managing them and their environment – the ways that might not be successful as those currently used.

(f) *Peer Pressure:* Individual employees may be prepared to accept change but refuse to accept it for the sake of the group. Whenever change is unwilling to the peers, they force the individuals who want to accept change to resist change.

(g) *Disruption of Interpersonal Relationships:* Employees may resist change that threatens to limit meaningful interpersonal relationships on the job.

(h) *Social Displacement:* Introduction of change often results in disturbance of the existing social relationships. Change may also result in breaking up of work groups. Thus when social relationships develop, people try to maintain them and fight social displacement by resisting change.

2. ***Organizational Resistance:*** Organizations, by their very nature are conservative. They actively resist change. Some of the organizational resistances are explained below:

(a) *Resource Constraints:* Resources are major constraints for many organizations, The necessary financial, material and human resources may not be available to the organization to make the needed changes. Further, those groups in organization that control sizable resources often see change as a threat. They tend to be content with the way things are.

(b) *Structural Inertia:* Some organizational structures have in-built mechanism for resistance to change. For example, in a bureaucratic structure where jobs are narrowly defined, lines of authority are clearly spelled out change would be difficult. This is so because formalization provides job descriptions, rules, and procedures for employees to follow. The people who are hired into an organization are chose for fit; they are then shaped and directed to behave in certain ways. When an organization is confronted with change, this structural inertia acts as a counterbalance to sustain stability.

(c) *Sunk Costs:* Some organizations invest a huge amount of capital in fixed assets. If an organization wishes to introduce change then difficulty arises because of these sunk costs.

(d) *Politics:* Organizational change may also shift the existing balance of power in organization. Individuals or groups who hold power under the current arrangement may be threatened with losing these political advantages in the advent of change.

(e) *Threat to established power relationships:* Any redistribution of decision making authority can threaten long established power relationships within the organization. Managers may therefore resist change that introduces participative decision making because they feel threatened.

(f) *Threat to expertise:* Change in organizational pattern may threaten the expertise of specialized groups. Therefore specialist usually resists change.

(g) *Group Inertia:* Even if individuals want to change their behaviour, group norms may act as a constraint. For example, if union norms dictate resistance any unilateral change made by management, an individual member of the union who may otherwise be willing to accept the changes may resist it.

10.9 MANAGING RESISTANCE TO CHANGE

Although resistance to change is a common phenomenon in organizations, it must be noted that not all changes are resisted. In fact, if we look at any organization closely we would probably find that far more changes are accepted than resisted. The traditional view of resistance to change treated it as something to be overcome, and many organizational attempts to reduce the resistance have only served to intensify it. The contemporary view holds that resistance is simply a form of feedback and that this feedback can be sued very productively to manage the change process.

One key to managing resistance is to plan for it and to be ready with a variety of strategies for using the resistance as feedback and helping employees negotiate the transition. Some tactics have been suggested for sue in dealing with resistance to change.

(a) ***Education and Communication:*** Communication about impending change is essential if employees are to adjust effectively. The details of the change should be provided, but equally important is the rationale behind the change. Employees want to know why change is needed. If there is no good reason for it, why should they favour the change? Providing accurate and timely information about the change can help prevent unfounded fears and potentially damaging rumours from developing. It is also beneficial to inform people about the potential consequences of the change. Educating employees on new work procedures is often helpful.

(b) ***Participation:*** It is difficult for individuals to resist a change decision in which they participated. Prior to making a change, those opposed can be brought into the decision process. When employees are allowed to participate, they are more committed to the change.

(c) ***Empathy and Support:*** Another strategy for managing resistance is providing empathy and support to employees who have trouble dealing with the change. Active listening is an excellent tool for identifying the reasons behind resistance and for uncovering fears. An expression of concerns about the change can provide important feedback that managers can use to improve the change process.

(d) ***Negotiation:*** Another way to deal with potential resistance to change is to exchange something of value for a lessening of the resistance. Where some persons in a group clearly lose out in a change, and where groups have considerable power to resist, negotiation and agreements are helpful. It becomes relatively easy to avoid major resistance through negotiation. Negotiation as a tactic may be necessary when resistance comes from a powerful source.

(e) ***Manipulation and cooperation:*** Manipulation refers to covert influence attempts. Twisting and distorting facts to make them appear more attractive, withholding undesirable information and creating false rumours to get employees to accept a change are all examples of manipulation. It involves giving individuals a desirable role in design or implementation of change.

(f) ***Coercion:*** Coercion is the application of direct threats or force on the resisters. They essentially force people to accept a change by explicitly or implicitly threatening them with the loss of their jobs, promotion possibilities and transferring them. Coercion is mostly applied where speed is essential in implementing change and the change initiator possesses considerable power.

UNIT EXERCISE

Short Answers

1. Explain the meaning of organizational climate.
2. Explain the various factors affecting organization climate.
3. What are the various elements that constitute a favorable climate.
4. What is the importance of change in the organization.

Long Answers

1. Why are organizational changes often resisted by individuals and groups within the organization? How can such resistance be prevented or overcome?
2. What do you understand by organizational climate? Explain the factors affecting climate of work organizations.
3. Explain the features of organizational climate. What factors influence the climate of an organization.

CHAPTER 11

Group Dynamics and Behavior

11.1 NATURE OF GROUP DYNAMICS

Meaning of Group Dynamics

Social needs are among the most powerful and compelling on-the-job motivating forces. In order to fulfill their social needs, workers form small groups on the job itself. It was shown by Hawthorne experiments that people behave as members of a group and their membership of group helps shape their work-behavior and attitudes towards the organization. Management can use groups successfully for the accomplishment of organizational objectives. According to Likert, an organization will function best when its personnel function not as individuals but as members of highly effective work-groups with high performance goals.

The social process by which people interact face-to-face in *small groups* is *called groups dynamics.* Group dynamics is concerned with the interaction of individuals in a face-to-face relationship. It focuses on teamwork wherein small groups are constantly in contact with each other and share common ideas to accomplish the given tasks. The group develops its goals clearly and furnishes suggestions to its members for the accomplishment of goals. Every group chooses its leader (who may be called informal leader as he is not recognised in the formal organizational structure) who may effectively coordinate the group efforts towards the accomplishment of its objectives.

Concept and Features of Groups

A group consists of two or more persons who interact with each other, consciously for the achievement of certain common objectives. The members of the group are inter-dependent and are aware that they are part of a group. They influence and are influenced by each other. In the words of David H. Smith, "A group is a set of two of more individuals who are jointly characterized by a network of relevant communications, a shared sense of collective identity and' one or more shared dispositions with associated normative strength. In other words, a group is a collection of two or more people who have a common goal and interact with each other to accomplish the goal, are aware of one another and perceive themselves to be a part of the group.

In order to be called a group, an aggregation of persons must satisfy the following conditions:

(i) People must interact with one another.

(ii) People must be psychologically aware of one another.

(iii) People should perceive themselves to be a group.

Thus, mere interaction among the people is not sufficient to be called a group. They should be aware of one another and perceive the existence of a group. If we apply these tests, many aggregations of people will not qualify as groups. Some illustrations are: people sitting in a cinema hall and people waiting for a bus at a bus stop. However, a family is treated as a group as it satisfies all the above tests to a large extent.

A group should be distinguished from a mere aggregation of persons. By group we mean two or more persons who are interacting with regard to a common explicit goal. Every job in the organization is interdependent and every task requires the cooperation of more than one individual. Groups facilitate this cooperation. Though persons in a bus probably have a common intent to go home, they remain a mere aggregation unless they also interact to accomplish the common goal in some way, such as pushing the bus out of a mud-hole. In the latter case, they interact, create a leader and behave differently than as individuals.

Groups are useful for the organization as they provide norms of behaviour for its members. Groups provide personal relationships at the work place as members talk to one another about job or personal pr6blems. They provide understanding, companionship, supportive relations and friendship. Everyone needs the company of people at work to go to lunch and on tea breaks with them and to share experiences with them. Groups provide an identity for the person at the workplace to achieve a feeling of 6elongingness from which he can derive esteem, recognition and status. Work groups also provide security to the individual member from pressure by management and other groups. Whenever there is a problem, the group reacts collectively and it resists any change which is imposed upon the members without their consent. Management can use group dynamics to bring adaptability among the organization members and to introduce change successfully.

11.2 TYPES OF GROUPS

Two types of groups coexist in every organization. These are: (i) formal groups, and (ii) informal groups.

Formal Groups

Such groups are a part of the organization structure. They are created deliberately by the management to perform the assigned duties. The examples are *work group, task force, committee* and *quality team.* These groups are characterized by clear-cut authority-responsibility relationships. The pattern of communication is also well defined. Rules are laid down to regulate the behavior of group members. The formal groups are integral parts of the official organization.

Informal Groups

Informal groups arise spontaneously in the organization because of social interaction between the people. They are created by individuals rather than by management. They are natural groupings of people at work in response to the need for social interaction. They are based on common interest, language, taste, caste, religion, background, etc. Thus, informal groups are alliances that are not officially planned. These groups are natural entities in the work environment. In every organization, a large number of informal groups are formed and they are collectively referred to as the informal organization.

The informal organization represents unofficial groups which have focus on person rather than position. Every group develops norms to regulate the behavior of its members. There is no fixed pattern of communication between the members. That is why informal groups are more flexible than the formal groups. Since they concentrate on personal contacts between the members, they represent the human side of enterprise as compared to technical side represented by the formal groups.

Command and Task Groups

Formal groups may be sub-classified into command and task groups. The command group is composed of subordinates who report directly to a common boss. Thus, a supervisor and the operative employees reporting to him form a command group.

The boundaries of a task group are not confined to its immediate superior. It can cross command relationships. A task group or team says for the introduction of a new product or service, is usually formed to complete an assignment that involves a number of departments.

Interest and Friendship Groups

Informal alliances may take the shape of interest and friendship groups. An interest group consists of people having a specific objective and not aligned to common command or task groups. For instance, employees who group together to pressurize the management for subsidized transport constitute an interest group. But a friendship group includes close friends or relatives. These relations even extend outside the organization. The group members know each other very well and have good relations.

Formal Organization

A formal organization is deliberately designed to achieve some particular objectives. *It refers to the structure of well-definec jobs, each bearing a definite measure of authority, responsibility and accountability.* The structure is consciously designed to enable the organizational members to work together for accomplishing common objectives. The individual must adjust to the formal organization. It tells him to do certain things in a specified manner, to obey orders from designated individuals and to cooperate with others. Co-ordination also proceeds according to prescribed pattern in the formal organization structure.

The basic characteristics of formal organization are as follows;

(i) Organization structure is laid down by the top management to achieve organizational goals.

(ii) Organization structure is based on division of labour and specialization to achieve efficiency in the operations.

(iii) Organization structure concentrates on the jobs to be performed and not the individuals who are to perform these jobs.

(iv) The organization does not take into consideration the sentiments of organizational members.

(v) The authority and esponsibility relationships created by the organization structure are to be honoured by everyone. The position in the organization hierarchy determines the relative status of the incunbent.

Informal Organization

Informal organization refers to, the relationship between people in' the organization based on personal attitudes, emotions, prejudices, likes, dislikes, etc. These relations are not developed according to procedures and regulations laid down in the formal organization structure; generally, large formal groups give rise to small informal or social groups. These groups may be based on common taste, language, culture or some other factor. These groups are not preplanned, but they develop automatically within the organization according to its environment.

In the words of Joseph A. Litterer, "The informal organization refers to people in group associations at work, but these associations are not specified in the blueprint of the formal organization. The informal organization means natural groupings of people in the work situation'. Whenever people work together, they evolve informal groups bound together by common social, technological, work or goal interests. Such groups constitute an informal organization. To quote Keith Davis, *"Beneath the cloak of formal relationships in every institution, there exists a more complex system of social relationships called the informal organization'.* The social relations are complex because there are many causes of their origin and they can't be planned. Moreover, the informal groups may not be stable. It is because of these reasons that it is very difficult to depict informal relations on the organization chart.

Generally, a number of small informal or social groups evolve within a large organization. These groups may be based on common taste, language, culture or some other factor. These groups are not pre-planned. They develop automatically within the organization according to the environment in the organization. The salient features of informal organization are as follows:

(i) Informal relations are unplanned. They arise spontaneously.

(ii) Formation of informal organization is a natural process.

(iii) Informal organization reflects human relationships.

(iv) Informal organizations are based on common taste, problem, language, religion, culture, etc.

(v) The membership of informal organizations is voluntary. At the same time, a person may be a member 'of a number of informal groups. Thus, there can be overlapping in these groups.

Is Informal Organization Really Necessary?

Modern behavioural scientists view organization as consisting of both types of relationships, *i.e.,* formal and informal. It is true that while laying down an organizational plan, management can only develop formal structure of relationships, but organization is not only a formal chart or structure of relationship. Formal organization, ·no doubt, is an important part of the organization. But informal organization is also not less important. If handled properly, it will help in performing the activities of the organization very efficiently and effectively. The role of informal groups has been discussed later in the chapter. In short, informal relations are complementary' to formal relations and procedures laid down in the organization. Both formal and informal organizations are necessary

for any group action just as two blades are essential to make a pair of scissors workable. The management should give due importance to the informal organization as it arises spontaneously along with the formal organization and fills in some of the vital gaps in the formal organization. It may be noted that formal organization is unable to meet all the needs (*e.g.*, affiliation, affection, esteem, etc.) of its members. Management can fulfill these needs of the workers by encouraging healthy interaction among informal groups and their members. Also, informal organization provides a cushion to absorb the shock of tensions and frustrations among the members as a result of organizational pinpricks.

Informal organization can operate to fill in gaps in a manager's abilities. For instance, if a manager is weak in planning, one of his subordinates may informally help him in such a situation. Management may also make use of informal group leaders by taking them into confidence to mediate as bridges of understanding between the management and the employees. Shartle has rightly said, "Informal structure is one index of the dynamics of getting work done and it appears that, for efficiency, it will necessarily deviate from the formal structure." Therefore, management should adopt a positive attitude' towards informal organization. It should use it along with formal structure to make a workable system for achieving the organizational objectives.

Sayles' Classification of Group

On the basis of pressure tactics adopted by small groups, Sayles 6 identified four kinds of groups in organizations which are discussed below:

(i) *Apathetic groups.* These groups are composed of relatively low paid and low skilled assembly line workers who lack unity and power and hardly use any pressure tactics. Such a group has no acceptable leader and· is indifferent to the formal organization.

(ii) Erratic groups. These groups are composed of semi-skilled workers who work together in performing jobs that require interaction. They display considerable unity. In their relations with management, they are erratic or lack consistency in behaviour. Sometimes, they show antagonism towards management while on other occasions they. may be cooperative. It is very difficult to predict the behaviour of such groups.

(ill) *Strategic groups.* The members of such groups are able to prepare a strategy for putting pressures on other groups and management. The members are engaged in jobs (better than the 'earlier two categories) requiring use of special skills and judgement. Their jobs are considered as key jobs in the plant. Such groups are found to be highly united and taking active part in union activity.

(iv) Conservative groups. These groups are composed of professionals and highly skilled employees in the plant. They are found at higher levels of the organization and display considerable self-confidence. They work on their own and the nature of their jobs is such that they can shut down the plant if they so desire. Such groups have been found to be very strong and most stable among informal groups. They exercise restrained pressure for' highly specified objectives.

Clique

A clique consists of those people who have frequent interactions and observe certain norms and standards. Its purpose is to gain and control power. The number of members of a clique is restricted to five or six organizational members. Some members of a clique may also form another group which may even consist of some persons who are not members of the organization. Thus, this group known as sub-clique is partially external to the organization.

Dalton has identified three types of cliques as follows:

(i) *Vertical clique.* It consists of people working in the same department drawing membership regardless of ranks. For example, superior may be a member in a group consisting mainly of subordinates. Such groups cutting across hierarchical lines develop because of the earlier acquaintance of people or because the superior is dependent upon his subordinates for some formal purposes.

(ii) *Horizontal clique.* It consists of people of more or less same rank and working in the same unit. This is the commonest kind of informal group. The members have certain common interest for whose achievements they follow certain norms and standards.

(iii) *Mixed* or *random clique.* Such a group draws members from different ranks, departments and physical locations who come together for a common purpose. The members may be residing in the same locality and travelling by the common bus, or they may be members of the common club).

11.3 THEORIES, OF GROUP FORMATION

There are four theories which explain why the groups are formed. These include:

(1) Propinquity Theory

Quite often, individuals affiliate with one another because of spatial or *geographical proximity.* In an organization, employees who work in the same area *of* the plant or office would more probably form into groups than those who are not physically located together. The propinquity theory explains a basic factor, i.e. proximity of people at the workplace, which leads to formation of groups. This phenomenon is observed in daily practice by all of us.

However, it is not essential that groups must come up because of proximity of people at the workplace. There may be several other reasons for the formation of groups. Thus, the propinquity theory is not analytical; it does not consider the complexities of group behaviour.

(2) Homans' Theory

According to George C. Homans, "The more activities persons share, the more numerous will be their interactions and the stronger will be their shared activities and sentiments; and the more sentiments persons have for one another, the more will be their shared activities and interactions. The Homans theory has contributed a great deal to the understanding of group formation. It is based on three concepts, namely, *activities, interactions* and *sentiments* which are directly related to each other. The members of a group share activities and interact with one another not just because of physical proximity, but also to accomplish group goals. The key element is interaction because of which they develop common sentiments for one another.

(3) Balance Theory

The theory as proposed by Theodore Newcomb states that "persons are attracted to one another on the basis- of similar attitudes towards commonly relevant objects and goals. Once a relationship is formed, it strives to maintain a symmetrical balance between the attraction and the common attitudes. If an imbalance occurs, attempts are made to restore the balance.' If the balance cannot be restored, the relationship, dissolves. Both propinquity and interaction play a role in the balance theory. Thus, the balance theory is additive in nature in the sense that it introduces the factor of 'balance' to the propinquity and interaction factors. There must be a balance in the relationship between the group members for the group to be formed and for its survival.

(4) Exchange Theory

This theory is based on *reward-cost outcomes of interactions between people.* To be attracted towards a group, a person thinks in terms of what he will get in exchange of interaction with the group members. Thus, there is an exchange relationship in terms of rewards and costs of associating with the group. A minimum positive level (rewards greater than costs) of an outcome must exist in order for attraction or affiliation to take place. Rewards from interactions gratify needs while costs incur anxiety, frustrations, embarrassment, or fatigue. Propinquity, interaction and common attitudes all have roles in the exchange theory.

Besides the theoretical explanations for group formation discussed above, there are some very practical reasons for joining and/or forming a group. For instance, employees in an organization may form a group for eco-nomic security or social reasons. Economically, Workers may form a group to work on a project that is paid for on a group-incentive plan or form a union to demand higher wages. For security, joining a group provides the individual with a united front in combating indiscriminate, unilateral treatment. The adage that there is strength in numbers applies here. The most important prac-tical reason why individuals join or form group is, however, that groups tend to satisfy the very intense social needs of most people. Worker's generally have a very strong .desire for affiliation. This need is met by belonging to a group.

11.4 REASONS FOR FORMATION OF GROUPS

1. *Companionship.* The need for relationship with other people is one of the strongest and most constant of human drives. One can express his feelings only through companionship. Many research studies have indicated that the employees who have no opportunity for close social contacts find their work unsatisfying and this lack of satisfaction often ref1ectsitself in low productivity and high rate of absenteeism and turnover. Elton Mayo observed that the employees in a textile plant who worked at isolated jobs were highly dissatisfied and consistently failed to meet production

standards and staggered rest period helped a little. But when the company permitted these workers to take rest period as a group, production and satisfaction both increased.

2. *Sense of Identification.* Workers get more identified in small groups, and so small groups tend to enjoy high morale. Employees working in large departments where everybody does the same type of job find it hard to form stable social groupings and so they have low morale.

3. *Source of Information.* Informal group is a source of information to its members. Informal communication is very fast. A piece of information available to a member will reach nearly all the members of the group in a short span of time. The group may develop a special code or language for speedy communication. Psychological barriers to communication are also overcome by the group.

4. *Job Satisfaction.* The group's solution to a problem may be different from what management expects and it may even be more efficient. Red tap ism is eliminated, shortcuts are evolved and informal channels of communication are established to cut across department boundaries. By the same token, work groups may also facilitate job satisfaction. Many jobs which appear superficially dull and routine are made interesting by the group and spontaneity .is encouraged and protected by the group. Certain jobs can be done by isolated workers, but working as a group often results in higher motivation of the individuals.

5. *Protection of Members.* Groups help to protect their members from outside pressures. Groups often resist management's demands for additional output, increased working hours, and higher quality. But dynamic organiza-tions have a tendency to introduce changes in work methods and routines at a faster rate than the individuals can adjust to them. The speed at which these changes are introduced can be materially altered by a determined work group. Without a sense of group allegiance, individual workers may behave in ways which incite their fellow workers. Group members often agree on the level of output that each will put forth so that no member may outperform the others.

6. *Outlet for Frustration.* An individual may be faced with several problems relating to his family life and work life: At times, he feels tremendous stress in life and gets frustrated. If he shares his feelings and anxieties with someone, his tension is released to a great extent. The social relations provide' an .important outlet for frustration. An informal group, as a matter of fact, serves as a safety valve which helps release tension and frustration and checks the mental breakdown of the individual. Organizations that lack this outlet sometimes rely on the expensive system of employee counselling in which outsiders hear employees' problems and advise them accordingly.

7. *Perpetuation of Cultural Values.* Sometimes, groups are formed by individuals belonging to a common cultural background. Such people can preserve their cultural identity and also feel a sense of security by associating with those pursuing the same cultural values and social norms. Maintenance of cultural values will also provide them psychological satisfaction.

8. *Generation of New Ideas.* Informal groups are a breeding ground for new ideas as they provide a supportive environment in which the members can engage themselves in creative thinking.

Quality circles in Japan are an important example in this regard. Under quality circles, workers meet periodically and discuss problems relating-to quality and come out with new ideas to solve the problems.

11.5 IMPORTANCE OF GROUPS TO THE ORGANIZATION

Informal groups are important not only from the point of view of their members they have a great utility from organization's point of view also. They help the organization in better administration by performing the following functions:

1. *Filling in Gaps in Manager's Abilities.* Informal organization may act to fill in gaps in a manager's abilities. For example, if a manager is weak in planning, one of his subordinates may help him informally in such a situation.

2. *Solving Work Problems.* Informal organization helps in solving the Work problems of members. It allows them sharing job knowledge and taking decisions which affect a number of jobs.

3. *Better Coordination.* Informal groups evolve short-cuts and eliminate red tapism. They facilitate smooth flow of information and quick decision-making. All these ensure better coordination among various individuals and departments.

4. *Channel of Communication.* Informal groups act to fill up the communication gaps which arise in the organization. Informal communication cuts across the hierarchical and *departmental* boundaries and transmits information with greater speed. Management can use informal *channels* to share information with the workers and get their reaction to management's proposals. Informal communication can be of great use to the organization, if it is *handled* by the management properly.

5. *Restraint on Managers.* Informal groups do not allow the managers to cross these limits. They restrict them from acquiring unlimited power and from using their power *unjudiciously.*

6. *Better Relations.* A manager can build better relations with his subordinates through informal contacts. He can consult the informal leaders and seek their cooperation in getting the things done from the workers.

7. *Norms of Behaviour.* Informal groups develop certain norms of behaviour which differentiate between good and bad conduct and between legitimate and illegitimate activities. These bring discipline and order among the employees.

8. *Satisfied Workforce.* Cohesive informal groups provide satisfaction to the workers. As a result, *labour* turnover and absenteeism are reduced and organization's productivity is increased.

9. *Developing Future Executives.* Informal groups recognize talented workers as their leaders. Such leaders can be picked by the management to fill vacancies of the junior executive level in the future.

11.6 PROBLEMS CREATED BY SMALL GROUPS

Informal groups have dysfunctional aspect too. They may create the following problems for the organization:

1. Negative Attitude of Informal Leaders. The informal leader may turn out to be a troubleshooter for the organization. In order to increase his influence, he may work against the policies of management and manipulate the behaviour of his followers. Thus, he can be a source of conflict between the management and the workers. He may induce the followers to work against the interests of the organization. If such a leader is promoted to the rank of an executive, he may turn out to be a work shirker and an arrogant and autocratic boss.

2. Conformity. The informal group exerts strong pressure on its members for conformity. The members may become so loyal to their group that following the group norms becomes a part of their life. This implies that members become subject to willful control of the group leader who may lead the group towards selfish ends. This will lead to dilution of the effect of organizational policies and practices on the group members.

3. Resistance to Change. Informal groups generally have a tendency to resist change. Change requires group members to make new adjustments and acquire new skills. But groups want to maintain *status quo.* Sometimes, groups rea2t violently to the proposed changes being brought by the management.- This creates obstructions in implementing new ideas for organization's survival and growth in the changing environment.

4. Rumour. Informal communication may give rise to rumours. This is not desirable from organization's point of view. Rumour originates for a number of reasons. One cause is plain maliciousness, but it is probably not the most important. A more frequent cause is employee's anxiety and insecurity because of poor communication in the organization. Rumour also serves as a means of wish fulfilment for some employees or applying pressure upon management.

5. Role Conflict. Every member of the informal group is also a member of the formal organization. Sometimes, there may be role conflict because what, the informal group requires of a member is just the opposite of what is expected of him by the formal organisation. In such a situation, group members may conform to their social norms. And if an individual member wants to follow the formal instructions of his boss, he may be snubbed by the informal leader and compelled to conform to informal group norms. Thus, organizational interests are likely to suffer in case of conflicts between formal and informal roles.'

11.7 DETERMINANTS OF GROUP BEHAVIOUR

Group behaviour in an organization is quite complex. As shown in Fig. 4, group behaviour is influenced by a number of factors which can be classified as follows:

(1) External Factors.

(2) Group Members' Resources.

(3) Group Structure.

(4) Group Processes.

(5) Group Tasks.

Group and External Factors

There are generally several groups is an organization. Each group is a sub-system of the organization. It interacts with other sub-systems and the organization system. The organization system influences the groups through corporate strategy, organization structure, rules and regulations, organizational resources, staffing policies, appraisal and reward system, organizational culture, physical work environment such as layout, lighting, interior decoration, seating arrangement, temperature, etc.

Group Members' Resources

Group performance depends, to considerable extent, on the member resources which comprise (i) abilities of members, and (ii) personality characteristics.

(i) Abilities. The performance of a group may be influenced by the task relevant and intellectual abilities of each of its members. Research evidence indicates that individuals who hold crucial abilities for attaining the group's task tend to be more involved in group activity, generally contribute more, are more likely to emerge as the group leaders, and are more satisfied if their talents are effectively utilized by the group. Further, intellectual ability and task relevant ability have both been found to be related to overall group performance.

(ii) Personality Characteristics. The personality traits of group members can shape group attitudes and behaviour. The attributes that have a positive connotation tend to be positively related to group productivity, morale and cohesiveness. These include traits such as sociability, self-reliance, and independence. In contrast, negatively evaluated traits such as authoritarianism, dominance and manipulation tend to have adverse effect on group performance in the long run.

11.8 CONCEPT AND FUNCTIONS OF ORGANIZATION STRUCTURE

What is Organization Structure?

An organization structure depicts the authority and responsibility relationships between the various positions in the organization by showing who reports to whom. It is a set of planned relationships between groups of related functions and between physical factors and personnel required for the achievement of organizational goals.

Organization involves establishing an appropriate structure for the goal-seeking activities. The structure of an organization is generally shown on an organization chart or a job-task pyramid. It shows the authority and responsibility relationships between various positions in the organization. It is significant to note that the organization structure is directly related to the attainment of the organization objectives. For instance, if an undertaking is in production line, the dominant element in its organization chart would be manufacturing and assembling. A good organization structure should not be static but dynamic. It should be subject to change from time to time in the light of the changes in the business environment. While designing the organizational structure due attention should also be given to the principles of sound organization.

Functions and Significance of Organization Structure

Organization structure contributes in the following ways to the efficient functioning of organizations:

1. *Clear-cut Authority Relationships.* Organization structure allocates authority and responsibility. It specifies who is to direct whom and who is accountable for what results. The structure helps each organization member to know what his role is and how it relates to other roles.

2. *Pattern of Communication.* Organization structure provides the patterns of communication and co-ordination. By grouping activities and people, structure facilitates communication between people centred on their job activities. People who have joint problems to solve often need to share information.

3. *Location of Decision Centres.* Organization structure determines the location of decision-making in the organization. A departmental store for instance, may follow a structure that leaves pricing, sales promotion and other matters largely up to individual departments to ensure that varied departmental conditions are considered. In contrast, an oil refinery may concentrate on production, scheduling and maintenance decisions at top levels to ensure that interdependencies along the flow of work are considered.

4. *Proper Balancing.* Organization structure helps in proper balance and emphasis of activities. Those more critical to the enterprise's success might be placed higher in the organization. Research in a pharmaceutical company, for instance, might be singled out for reporting to the general manager or the managing director of the company. Activities of comparable importance might be given roughly equal levels in the structure to give them equal emphasis.

5. *Stimulating Creativity.* Sound organization structure stimulates creative thinking and initiative among organizational members by providing well defined patterns of authority. Everybody knows the area where he specialises and where his efforts will be appreciated.

6. *Encouraging Growth.* An organization structure provides the framework within which an enterprise functions. If it is flexible, it will help in meeting challenges and creating opportunities for growth. A sound organization structure facilitates growth of enterprise by increasing its capacity to handle increased level of activity.

7. *Making Use of Technological Improvements.* A sound organization structure which is adaptable to changes can make the best possible use of latest technology. It will modify the existing pattern of authority-responsibility relationships in the wake of technological improvements.

In short, existence of a good organization structure is essential for sound management. Properly designed organization can help improve teamwork and productivity by providing a framework within which the people can work together most effectively. While building the organization structure, it is essential to relate the people to design. The organization structure which has technical excellence may be quite useless for practical purposes because it is not suited to the needs of the people. Thus, an organization structure should be developed to the needs of the people in the organization.

Developing the Organization Structure

There are two types of structural variables, namely, basic structure and operating mechanism. Designing of basic structure involves such central issues as how the work of the organizations will be divided and assigned among positions, groups, departments, divisions, etc. and how the coordination necessary to achieve organizational objectives will be brought about. But operating mechanism, on the other hand, includes such factors as information system control procedures, rules and regulations, system of reward and punishment, etc.

The development of organization structure deals with two facets, namely, the functions which are to be performed, and the form of structure.

The first facet requires the determination of activities, the organization needs and division of these activities keeping in mind degree of specialisation it can afford. The second facet, *i.e.*, form of structure, requires a detailed study and application of many organizational principles and practices.

Organization structure establishes formal relationships among various positions in the enterprise. The formal relations may be classified into the following categories:

(i) Relations between the senior and the subordinates and *vice versa;*

(ii) Relations between the specialist positions and the line positions;

(iii) Staff relations; and

(iv) Lateral relations.

The formal relations in an organization arise from the patterns of responsibilities that are created by the management. They are static in nature, but afford the framework for dynamic action. As soon as management action starts, the formal relations are absorbed or overlayed by the personal attitudes and behaviour patterns of the individual in the organization. The latter are generally described as 'informal relations'. Such relations must also be kept in mind while developing the organization structure. If the formal relations are rigid and lay down long procedures, the individuals will develop certain 'short-cuts' to perform their responsibilities in a better way. '

Open System and Closed System

Organization theorists look at organization designs or structures by classifying them into two broad categories, *viz., closed systems* and *open systems.*

Closed System Approach. The basic feature of the closed system view is that organization is isolated from the environment. It aims at developing a structure of organization which is capable of maintaining maximum efficiency, by striving for optimal contribution of all the factors of production-technology, materials, power, capital and human resources-for the accomplishment of, organizational goals. The classical organization theory is based on the close system viewpoint.

Open System Approach. The open system viewpoint acknowledges the influence of environmental factors on the organization's working. The managers subscribing to this approach are ready to adapt to environmental changes in order to ensure the survival and growth of the organization. The organization's ability to respond to changing environment to keep its working smooth is significant for the following two reasons:

(i) Since the change is often unpredictable, the organization should not attach much importance to rigid rules and regulations which may proves inadequate in dealing with uncertain and uncontrollable events.

(ii) Organizations should aim at providing opportunities for human fulfilment of ambitions and values. It would be in the fitness of things to so design the structure of the organization as to place importance on the individual and his work.

Classical Organization Design

The classical organization theorists were primarily concerned with the design of efficient organization. The structure was emphasized as the most important and endeavouring characteristic of the organization. They emphasized such concepts as objectivity, impersonality and structural form with well defined relationships and clearly established lines of authority and communication. The essential pillars of the classical school are the classical principles discussed below.

Principles of Organization

The management thinkers have laid down certain statements from time to time, from certain generally accepted understandings, which may be called the principles of organization. The principles can serve as guidelines for designing an efficient organization structure. Therefore, a thorough, understanding of the principles of organization is essential. The important principles of organization are discussed below:

1. *Consideration of Objectives.* An enterprise strives to accomplish certain objectives. Organization serves as a tool to attain objectives. The objectives must be stated in clear terms as they play an important role in determining the type of structure which should be developed. The principle of consideration of objectives states that only after the objectives have been stated, an organization structure should be developed to achieve them.

2. *Division of Work and Specialisation.* The entire work in the organization should be divided into various parts so that every individual is confined to the performance of single job, as far as possible, according to his ability and aptitudes. This is also called the principle of specialisation. More a person continues on a particular job, the better will be his performance.

3. *Definition of Jobs.* Every position in the organization should be clearly defined in relation to other positions in the organization. The duties and responsibilities assigned to every position and its relationship with other positions should be clearly defined so that there may not be any overlapping of functions.

4. *Separation of Line and Staff Functions.* Whenever possible, line, "'functions should be separated from staff activities. Line functions are those which accomplish the main objectives of the company. In many manufacturing companies, the manufacturing and marketing departments are considered to be accomplishing the main objectives of the business and so are called the line functions and other functions like personnel, plant maintenance, financing and legal are considered as staff functions.

5. *Scalar Chain.* There must be clear lines of authority running from the top to the bottom of the organization. Authority is the right to decide, direct and coordinate. The organization structure should facilitate delegation of authority. Clarity is achieved through delegation by steps or levels from the top position to the operating level. From the chief executive, a line of authority may proceed to departmental managers, to supervisors or foremen and finally to workers. This chain of command is also known as scalar principle of organization.

6. *Parity of Authority and Responsibility.* Responsibilities should always be coupled with corresponding authority. Each subordinate must have sufficient authority to discharge the responsibility entrusted to him. This principle suggests that if a plant manager in a multi-plant organization is held accountable for all activities in his plant, he should not be subject to orders from company headquarters specifying the quantity of raw materials he should buy or from whom he should purchase raw materials. If a supervisor is responsible for the quality of work of his department, he should not be asked to accept as a member of his workforce an employee who has been hired without consulting him.

7. *Unity of Command.* No one in the organization should report to more than one supervisor. Everyone in the organization should know whom he reports and who reports to him. Stated simply, everyone should have only one boss. Receiving directions from several supervisors may result in confusion, chaos, conflicts and lack of action. So each member of the organization should receive directions from and report to one superior only. This will avoid conflict of command and help in fixing responsibilities.

8. *Span of Supervision.* The span of supervision means the number of persons a manager or a supervisor can direct. If too less number of employees are reporting to a supervisor, his time will not be utilised properly. But, on the other hand, there is a limit to the number of subordinates that can be efficiently supervised by an executive. Both these points should be kept in mind while grouping and allocating the activities to various departments. It is difficult to give a definite number of persons a manager can direct. It will depend upon the nature of the work and a number of other factors.

9. *Balance of Various Factors.* There should be proper balance in the formal structure of the organization in regard to factors having conflicting claims, *e.g.* between centralization and decentralization, span of supervision, and lines of communication and authority allocated .to departments and personnel at various levels.

10. *Communication.* A good communication network is essential to achieve the objectives of all organization. No doubt the line of authority provides readymade channels of communication

downward and upward, still some blocks in communication occur in many organizations. The confidence of superior in his subordinates and two-way communication are the factors that unite an organization into an effectively operating system.

11.9 CREATION OF HIERARCHY OF AUTHORITY

According to classical approach, the starting point in managerial attempts to coordinate organization is the design of a system of authority. The idea is to establish a hierarchy (or job-task pyramid) that prescribes what positions are responsible for what activities and what reporting or subordinacy relationships are to exist. This hierarchy of authority is meant to channel the direction of employee activity and interaction. In turn, the activity and interaction, thus channelled, are supposed to constitute the coordinated effort that fulfils the organization's objectives. The classical theorists argued that everyone in the pyramid knows his place; he knows who reports to him and to whom he reports in turn.

For designing the hierarchy of authority, the following prescriptions have been offered by the classical writers:

(i) Chain of command;

(ii) Unity of command; and,

(iii) Span of management.

Chain of Command or Scalar Principle

The concept of chain of command refers to an interconnected and unbroken set of reporting relationships extending from the top of the "organization to the bottom". Each level in the structure from the bottom up is accountable to a superior. By holding every person accountable to some superior, the chain of command operates to test everyone's performance against the expectations of a superior. The effect is to induce interlevel coordination.

The principle of scalar chain provides for an unbroken flow of communication and control of subordinates by the superior. But this ideal is impractical. Sometimes, the chain of command is too long. Complete adherence to the chain of command would mean that interdepartmental problems could not be resolved unless each department manager proceeded up the chain of command until a common superior was reached. Fayol felt that the chain of command may often be a good idea, but it can be grossly inefficient or even silly in trivial matters. Speed and efficiency dictate that many interdepartmental problems can be resolved by department managers and other subordinates on the same level or various levels without recourse to superiors. If this did not occur commonly, organizations would be paralyzed. For instance, a small problem between two workers WR and WS may be resolved by them through direct talks. This arrangement is known as 'gang plank' which allows quick communication and proper understanding between the concerned persons

Unity of Command

According to the principle of unity of command, each subordinate is accountable to only one superior. To require a subordinate to satisfy two or ' more bosses may leave him with conflicting requirements and instructions. As a result, the subordinate may not carry out the instructions satisfactorily and may experience considerable tension in the process.

It is very difficult to observe the principle of unity of command in practice. In a typical organization, a worker might have to respond to Personnel Officer, Accounts Officer and Quality Controller in addition to his section Supervisor. In functional organisation, this principle is not adhered to. The matrix structure also violates unity of command by substituting a dual system of command. Thus, in practice, the principle of unity of command is more honoured in the breach than in the observance.

Span of Control

The term 'span of control' is also known as, 'span of supervision' and 'span of authority'. It represents the maximum number of subordinates any manager can directly supervise. The classical writers suggested that, "No executive should attempt to supervise directly the work of more than five, or at the most six, direct subordinates whose work interlocks'. But this prescription is not followed because of improvement of means of communication and several other factors.

Span of control is an important principle of organization. This principle is based on the theory of relationship propounded by V.A. Graicunas, a French management consultant. Graicunas analysed superior-subordinate relationships and developed mathematical formulae based on the geometric increase in complexities of managing as the number of subordinates increases.

Impact of Span of Supervision on Organization Structure

The number, of persons an executive supervises has an important influence on the nature of organization structure. If the span is small, the structure would be narrow and tall. More people will have to communicate to the top manager through intervening layers of executives.

Thus, there is centralisation of authority at the top level. The possibility of communication blockages and distortions would increase. If the span is large, it means that fewer levels are needed in the organization. The structure would tend to be flat and wide. Presumably the possibility of communication blockages would be minimized because more people report directly to the top executive.

For instance, if there are 256 persons in an organization and all are reporting to one executive, there win be one-level of management. If it is thought that only four subordinates should directly report to the chief executive, then the number of management levels will increase to two as four executives directly report to the top executive and each executive controls 64 persons. This structure is flat as the span of control is very large at the lowest level and there are only two layers of management. If it is thought that an executive can manage only 4 subordinates effectively, the number of managerial levels will increase to four. This will make the organization structure look like a tall pyramid.

Factors Determining Span of Supervision

The span of control varies from individual to individual, time to time and place to place. The factors which determine the span of control are discussed below:

1. *Ability of the Managers.* Individuals differ in various qualities like leadership, decision-making and communication. The span may be wider if the manager possesses these skills in greater degree as compared to others.

2. *Time available for Supervisors.* The span should be narrow at the higher levels because top managers have less time available for supervision. They have to devote the major portion of their time to planning, organizing, directing, and controlling. Each top manager will delegate the task of supervision to his subordinates who have to devote comparatively less time on the important functions of management.

3. *Nature of Work.* When the spans are narrowed, the levels in the organization increase. This involves delegation of authority and responsibility. If the work is of a routine and repetitive nature, it can easily be delegated to the subordinates.

4. *Capacity of Subordinates.* If the subordinates are skilled, efficient and knowledgeable, they will require less supervision. In such a case, the superior may go in for a wider span.

5. *Degree of Decentralisation.* Under decentralisation, the power to make decisions is delegated to the lower levels. The span of management will be narrow in such cases so as to exercise more and more control.

6. *Effectiveness of Communication.* An effective system of communication in the organization favours large number of levels because there will be no difficulty in transmission of information in spite of a large number of intervening layers.

7. *Control Mechanism.* The span of control also depends upon the control mechanism being followed. Control may be followed either through personal supervision or through reporting. The former favours narrow span and the latter favours a wide span.

To sum up, it can be said that an executive should be expected to supervise a reasonable number of subordinates. What is reasonable depends on a variety of factors like individual differences in executives, number and capacity of subordinates, the nature of work, availability of time, ease, of communication, internal checks and controls and degree of delegation in the organization. If the span of control is narrow, there will be more organizational levels, which in turn may impede communication. If the number of levels is reduced and the span of control is widened, the supervisory load may become too heavy. Sound management requires a proper balance between supervisory load and organization levels.

UNIT EXERCISE

Short Answers

1. What do you mean by a group?
2. Explain command and task group.
3. What are informal groups?
4. What is meant by group cohesiveness.
5. What should be the attitude of management towards small groups?

Long Answers

1. What is a group? Describe its features. Provide guidelines to practicing managers for effective utilization of informal groups.
2. Define group dynamics. Why informal groups come into existence? What factors influence group cohesiveness.
3. What is meant by Group Dynamics? What problems may be created by informal groups for the organization?
4. "High cohesiveness in a group leads to high productivity". Do you agree? Discuss.

Index